SOCIOLOGY
THROUGH THE EYES OF FAITH

OTHER BOOKS IN THIS SERIES:

Biology Through the Eyes of Faith

Business Through the Eyes of Faith

History Through the Eyes of Faith

Literature Through the Eyes of Faith

Psychology Through the Eyes of Faith

SOCIOLOGY
THROUGH
THE EYES OF FAITH

David A. Fraser
and
Tony Campolo

Christian College Coalition
For Enduring Values

HarperSanFrancisco
A Division of HarperCollins*Publishers*

The Christian College Coalition is an association of Christian liberal arts colleges and universities across North America. More than thirty Christian denominations, committed to a variety of theological traditions and perspectives, are represented by our member colleges. The views expressed in this volume are primarily those of the authors and are not intended to serve as a position statement of the Coalition membership.

FIRST EDITION

Library of Congress Cataloging-in-Publication Data

Fraser, David Allen
    Sociology through the eyes of faith / David A. Fraser and Tony Campolo. — 1st ed.
        p.   cm.
    "Christian College Coalition for enduring values."
    Includes bibliographical references.
    ISBN 0-06-061315-7 (alk. paper)
    1. Sociology, Christian. I. Campolo, Anthony. II. Christian College Coalition (U.S.) III. Title.
    BT738.F657 1992
    261.5—dc20

                                                        91-55337
                                                            CIP

92 93 94 95 96 MCN 10 9 8 7 6 5 4 3 2 1

This edition is printed on acid-free paper that meets the American National Standards Institute Z39.48 Standard.

This book is dedicated to:

James M. "Buck" Hatch,
exemplary teacher and integrator
of faith and learning

CONTENTS

Foreword   ix

Introduction   xi

        1. The Beast in the Courtyard   1

PART I.   The Confrontation Between Christian
Faith and Sociology
      2. To See Is Not to See   13
      3. Putting Religion in Its Place   27
      4. Putting Sociology in Its Place   45
      5. Hallucinations of Direct Encounters   62
      6. Guerrilla Warfare at the Boundaries   79

PART II. The Varieties of Sociological Experience
      7. Sociological Paradigms   103
      8. A Case Study in Socialization   122
      9. The Rise of the Modern World   138
     10. The Perennial Quests of Social Insight   154

PART III. Faith Seeking Social Understanding
     11. Learning to Speak with a Biblical Accent 171

12.	God and Culture	191
13.	Theological Paradigms	213
14.	The Elementary Forms of Thinking Christianly About Society	236
15.	What Christians Want in Society	255
16.	The Kingdoms of This World and the Kingdom of God	270
17.	Blending Sociology and Faith	290

Scripture Index | 309
Name Index | 310
Subject Index | 313

FOREWORD

Sociology, as this book argues, is modernity struggling to come to self-understanding. Beyond a doubt our modern social world is profoundly different from any other. What accounts for its emergence? What are its most fundamental traits? What sustains it in existence? What are the characteristic sorrows of those who live in this world; what, their characteristic joys? Is there any way to diminish the sorrows without eliminating the joys? These are sociology's questions. And as the authors remark, "Sociology both cries with those who lament the loss of the old and rejoices with those who celebrate the new. It is an ambivalent discipline which, given the paradoxes of modernity, has every right both to rejoice and to weep."

Whereas sociology is thus a perspective on modernity, this book is in turn a perspective on sociology. When one looks at sociology through the eyes of faith, what does one see? What is the aim of the sociologist? Is that aim important? What are the characteristic assumptions of sociologists? Are those assumptions correct? What are the achievements? What, the failures?

To fully describe the genius of this book we must use a second metaphor as well. Not only do the authors *look* at sociology through the *eyes* of faith and tell us what they have seen. They also *listen* to sociology with the *ears* of faith—listen to what sociology has to say to and about Christianity—and tell us what they have heard.

The book is thus more a conversation than a perspective. Two authors, both deeply embedded in the Christian faith, richly acquainted with its theological history, both skilled professional sociologists, obviously in love with their field, bring these two sides of themselves into a fascinating and illuminating conversation with each other. Questions that we had already been asking get discussed; most if not all Christians have questions about sociology and most if not all sociologists have questions about Christianity. But from the authors' deft use of examples new and probing questions emerge that most of us had never thought of. They don't all get answered; but the asking itself is illuminating.

Nicholas Wolterstorff
Yale University

INTRODUCTION

There is only one truth. It belongs exclusively neither to science nor to Christian faith. Nor do humans have a neat map with science in one corner of their intellectual world and religious faith at a different zip code. For better or worse, faith and science intertwine in actual practice.

As the authors of this book, we are writing from within a Christian worldview. Our conviction is that the relations between faith and sociology can be quite positive. We believe the Christian worldview provides motivations and resources that lead to energetic and careful work in sociological arenas.

The early history of sociology contains many surprises for those who think that sociology's roots are purely secular. Several of the earliest founders of empirical and theoretical sociological work were people motivated by their Christian faith. For the most part, their stories have not been told by later secular sociologists. There are many reasons for this. We will examine a few of them in this book. There is, however, widespread agreement that the Christian tradition was the soil from which modern Western science sprang and flourished.[1]

Many early scientists, particularly those who studied the physical world, were Christians. They studied the universe as God's rational and contingent creation, seeking in its mysteries parables of the wisdom and power of God. They believed that their studies would unravel truths about God and the creation. They felt that what they learned would help make a better world, more in line with what God wanted. Many contemporary scientists continue to practice science as an expression of their Christian faith.

Modern sociology emerged with the modern industrial world in Western Europe and North America. Part of its originating impulse came from Christians who wished to understand the social world. These early thinkers felt that the systematic study of society could help create a better world for people. They wanted society to conform to the norms of the Kingdom of God. They sought knowledge that would help humans achieve higher levels of justice and righteousness in society. Around them the old social world was melting down in the fiery heat of modernity. It needed rebuilding. They hoped for a better society, not just a society with better machines.

An alternative and (as time passed) stronger impulse in the West sought to create a purely secularized social science. Its roots were in Enlightenment skepticism rather than Christian thought. In the nineteenth century, God's obituary appeared several times as part of this effort. Some of the early secular sociologists portrayed religion as a vanishing species of human practice and knowledge. Several nineteenth-century pioneers of sociology expressed aggressive hostility toward religion. Not a few even took sociology to be a secular alternative to religion and claimed that traditional Christianity was a hindrance to progress.

Unfortunately, a secularized version of sociology triumphed in the early twentieth century.[2] Christian voices became fewer and less vocal as the decades flew by. Yet something new began to stir in the 1960s and 1970s. Christians began again to find a stronger voice within the discipline. They actively published sociology with clear Christian accents. During those two decades, professional associations of Christian academics formed in sociology (and in other disciplines as well). Strangely enough, Christian intellectual activity expanded at the very time that public and civic institutions were losing traditional religious symbols and practices—and perhaps because of this. Prayer and Bible reading in the public schools vanished as the courts pushed society into an increasingly secular mold. Partly in response, Christian thinkers became more concerned with thinking and living Christianly in a world that was growing more indifferent and hostile to Christian practices.

In principle, the problems of thinking from Christian assumptions about the full range of issues and mysteries in sociology are no different from those encountered in thinking Christianly in physics, biology, philosophy, or business. In practice, these problems have particular intensity and gravity. Part of the reason for this is that the social sciences and Christian faith contain overlapping cognitive models and moral ideas about human beings. Both attempt to speak about human nature, social institutions, cultural practices, and historical development. Both focus on the human network of connections. For both, modernity raises profound and difficult questions.

The world of modernity forms the context of sociology.[3] More than any other single motivation, modernization stimulated the development of all the social sciences. What frequently divides the practices of Christian faith from those of sociology are disagreements over the meaning, nature, and necessities of modernization and modernity.

The Great Chain of Being

Social thought has a long history. The science of sociology, however, is only as old as the modern world. Its intellectual and institutional connections came into being as traditional social connections snapped. With the coming of the modern age, a long-established order of life and society was suddenly overturned. Sociology sought to explain and make sense out of what was going on.

The old model of living things and society was known as the "Great Chain of Being."[4] This image became a prominent expression for European life only in the eighteenth century. Still, it is a good summary of the major organizing principle behind the connectedness of life from the Middle Ages onward. This metaphor (the Great Chain) places everything within a hierarchy. God is at the top. The chain reaches down to the lowest, most inert, insignificant bit of physical stuff at the bottom. Humanity stands above and distinct from nature, just as the living creatures of nature stand above and separate from the inanimate world. Yet the whole series is connected. Human beings link downwardly to the earth as earthly. So too are they linked upwardly to God as the bearers of God's image in the visible creation. Humans are creatures a little lower than angels; they are earthly but with a heavenly destiny.

A similar hierarchy structures the social order, with kings, potentates, nobles, and bishops sitting in seats of authority designed by God. Ordinary souls give obeisance to this order as a necessary reflection of God's Great Chain of Being. Whether in court, church, countryside, corporation, or convent, there is an order of priority and preference. All things, not just the heavens:

> Observe degree, priority, and place . . .
> The primogenitive and due of birth,
> Prerogative of age, crowns, sceptres, laurels,
> But by degree, stand in authentic place. . . .[5]

In this picture, the cosmos and the social world consist of an organically connected, hierarchically arranged, interlinked chain, with everything in its proper place. The whole universe is a stable and orderly world, run according to eternal, unchanging divine laws.

Suddenly this neatly structured worldview fell apart—along with the social world that gave it vitality. The changes of the eighteenth century were great tidal waves, engulfing this chain, corroding its links. For some, the end of the Great Chain of Being was a welcome event. For them, the ties of the chain were oppressive bonds creating servitude and despair. Breaking the chain meant progress and liberation from the ancient regime. For others, the links were necessary restraints on the beastly and sinful nature of humans ready to break out in chaos. For them, the breaking down of the old order was the end of all that was good and true. The breaking of such connections meant disrupting a world ordered as God meant it to be. Some even concluded that they were living in the last days immediately prior to Christ's return.

The snapping of the links of the Great Chain of Being and the loosening of old connections comprise the quintessential nature of the modern world. The dual industrial and French revolutions (the economic and political revolutions) intensified and symbolized these changes. The labor pangs that brought a new world into being gave birth also to the social sciences. At first, secular enthusiasts were exhilarated by a wave of utopian hopes for societies of peace, prosperity, and progress. Many early sociologists predicted the coming of a glorious society. Yet some also had moments of doubt. This latter group of sociologists lamented the old links lying broken everywhere. They viewed the breaking of old ties with gloomy fears. "Perhaps," their fears whispered, "modernity means the dissolution of community, the destruction of morality, and the degeneration of personality."

The Living Web of Interconnection

What replaced the Great Chain metaphor for understanding the world was the notion of a "web of interconnections." Its most developed location on the modern intellectual map lies in the field of ecology. This metaphor evokes the image of a many-stranded, closely woven fabric, being tugged and pulled from many directions. Such an image lends itself to an organic, living picture of the world. It is a more dynamic, multicausal model than the Great Chain of Being.

Until Newton, inanimate nature was seen as a securely continuous chain of reality. But the demonstration that a vacuum can exist undermined the conviction that nature makes no leaps, that all links in the Chain of Being are full. Newton's laws of attraction connected apple and planet, moon and tide by ties resembling the mechanisms of a machine more than the links in a living Chain of Being. To be sure, Newton's vision produced its own picture of a continuous, immobile, fixed world. It taught people to think in terms of unvarying laws and perfect mechanical models. But along with Galileo's telescope, it also taught people to challenge traditional ideas and to adopt a restless state of mind, one that is never content with current truths.

Animate nature took its fateful step away from the Great Chain with the modern invention of "biology" in 1802 by Gottfried Reinhold. This new word referred to a science of physical life; it saw life as a dynamic, progressive development of animate forms. Taxonomies that had previously classified and *arranged* life forms in a hierarchy from simplest to most complex became genealogies that *derived* the higher orders from the lower. The connections between life forms became the movements of evolution. The chain of life was seen in perpetual motion, its links altering and vanishing, constantly throwing up new forms.

Roaring ironwork forges, hissing steam engines, and the burning barricades of revolution ignited the fires that melted the old links of hierarchy and tradition in the social world. The industrial and French revolutions symbolize the dramatic changes in economic, social, and political connections. Modern, liberal democratic capitalism gradually displaced the older aristocratic, agrarian feudalism of European nations.

Links with God also changed dramatically. Christendom fragmented into dozens and then hundreds and thousands of denominations. Institutionally, the Church, once a giant in Western civilization, shrank into a small, specialized role and lost much of its authority. Intellectually, Enlightenment thought severed various links to God (and angels) or so transformed ideas of God as to create a non-Christian faith in support of a secularized civilization.

All of this meant the snapping of old ties. It is no wonder that people lamented a collapsing world. Their lament still rings in people's ears today. Nature is given over to the tyranny of a mechanistic science. Science's fragmented, analytic approach, now integrated into the profit motives of large corporations, portends ecological disaster. Progress and profit murder nature. The Enlightenment has brought environmental violence.

Human relations are equally denatured. The capitalist, industrial revolution transformed the old warmth of human connections into the cold logic of financial ones. All values were reduced to those of efficiency; all relationships became united by the nexus of cash. The democratic political revolution reduced all hierarchies to a single flat plain of equality. Pluralism came to mean not so much an enrichment as a thinning out of culture, a weakening of family and of community. Relativism triumphed. The state became more and more encompassing and remote. The new feudal lords are now as inaccessible in their bureaucratic hierarchies as the old nobility were behind the moats to their castles.

Yet by some law of the conservation of social energy, the construction of new linkages grew almost as fast as the disintegration of old. Once, the universe, life, society, even thought itself were considered stable, eternal forms of "being." Now all are changing, unstable, temporary forms of "becoming."[6] Everything (including social arrangements) seems forever to evolve into something different. Instead of the absolute, there is the relative; instead of immobility, movement; instead of fixities, flux. A sense of becoming is the heart of what is meant by the term *modernity*. Modernity means that connectedness no longer exists through a set of stable positions or places as it did in the Great Chain. Now it is a matter of process, growth, movement—a living web of changing interconnectedness.

"Becoming" is exhilarating and liberating. It sets people free from the restricting chains of the past, inviting them to sail on an open sea to new vistas and ports. "Becoming" is equally enervating and depressing, undermining every landmark, obscuring even the stars by which people formerly navigated life. To some, a constantly changing world is an adventure and a delight, a perpetual source of wonder and surprise. To others, it is a wearisome abyss, requiring constant adjustments. To them, it is a great perplexity with no stability or certainties.

Sociology Laughing and Weeping

Heraclitus (540–470 B.C.) took flux to be the ultimate reality. He is known as the weeping philosopher. Fire, he said, lies behind everything. Yet fire is born only through the death of something else. No wonder he wept. Yet he never saw a civilization change so rapidly as has the modern world. The great fire of modernity consumed an older, more stable world. Sociology is the study of that fire.

Sociology both cries with those who lament the loss of the old and rejoices with those who celebrate the new. It is an ambivalent discipline that, given the paradoxes of modernity, has every right both to rejoice and to weep. Christian sociology is also ambivalent. Contrary to some impressions, the Christian perspective on society is not one simply of lament, a type of conservative nostalgia for the good old days. No social order fulfills the best of its own cultural ideals, much less achieves the standards of the Kingdom of God. Christians lament the enormous cost that every social order exacts of its members and its neighbors. They lament the human costs that accompany modernity's power to produce a sharply divided globe of haves and have-nots while poisoning the planet. But they also lament the enormous costs of premodern social orders with their pervasive ignorance, technical weaknesses, and narrow life opportunities.

On the other hand, Christians also rejoice in the great goods that are liberally distributed in every human group. They celebrate the modern world and its innovations, which have secured real goods for a larger proportion of people than ever before. Dramatic increases in longevity, in disease control, in productivity, in living standards, in real freedoms and knowledge are reasons for Christian sociologists to cheer. Even as they do so, they refuse the utopianism of those who think that the highest fulfillment of modernity's promises can bring the Kingdom of God. Thus, they recognize that premodern societies often contain deeply satisfying networks of family and friends as well as richly meaningful cultures that modern civilizations seem incapable of producing. Whether, on balance, people are happier, culturally richer, and relationally more stable because they are modern is not clear.

In the Beginning . . . Without Modernity, Without Sociology

There was a time before modernity or sociology. But no more. What difference does it make that the past four hundred years have ripped up and relandscaped the whole of human life? Is life better now for human beings? Is the future more secure and promising, human character more virtuous, culture richer? In short, is the quality of life measurably improved as a result of all these changes? How did people live without contemporary institutions — and how can they live with them? What is the meaning and movement of the dynamic that animates modern life? What should a Christian think about the arrival of modernity?

And what about sociology? The world existed for a long time without it. Why do moderns feel they need it? Is the modern world so novel that it now requires a new science in order to understand itself? What gifts does sociology bear for humanity and even for Christianity? And what gifts does Christian faith have to offer to sociology to enrich its perspective and practice? These are the questions that animate this book.

The pages that follow take up a number of important themes. Part I considers why sociology and faith often express hostility toward each other, in spite of the contribution of Christians to the formation of early sociology (Chapters Two through Six). Part II probes the multiple traditions and perspectives in sociology, seeking to understand how sociology is unified primarily by the questions it seeks to answer rather than by widely shared agreements on the correct answers (Chapters Seven through Ten). Part III outlines tools and concepts that Christians use as they attempt to think faithfully about social arrangements (Chapters Eleven through Seventeen).

Thinking Christianly about society requires the delicate task of blending sociology and faith. This book is an invitation to the adventure of combining the heights of human thought about society with the depths of Christian faith. The mixture, we believe, can be an explosive and heady concoction.

Chapter One begins the adventure by providing an overview of the peculiar difficulties in studying society.

NOTES

1. Robert K. Merton, *Science, Technology, and Society in Seventeenth-Century England* (New York: Harper & Row, 1970); Eugene M. Klaaren, *Religious Origins of Modern Science* (Grand Rapids, MI: Eerdmans, 1977); R. Hooykaas, *Religion and the Rise of Modern Science* (Grand Rapids, MI: Eerdmans, 1972); John H. Brooke, *Science and Religion: Some Historical Perspectives* (Cambridge University Press, 1991).

2. Roger Bannister, *Sociology and Scientism: The American Quest for Objectivity, 1880–1940* (Chapel Hill: University of North Carolina Press, 1987).

3. Bruce Mazlish's *A New Science: The Breakdown of Connections and the Birth of Sociology* (New York: Oxford University Press, 1989) has provided many of the ideas contained in this following section.

4. Arthur Lovejoy, *The Great Chain of Being* (Cambridge, MA: Harvard University Press, 1936). See also Henry Steele Commager, *The American Mind* (New Haven: Yale University Press, 1950).

5. Shakespeare, *Troilus and Cressida*, Act I, Scene III, Lines 85, 106–108.

6. Franklin L. Baumer, *Modern European Thought: Continuity and Change in Ideas, 1600–1950* (New York: Macmillan, 1977).

THE BEAST IN THE COURTYARD

The road south from Kinshasa, Zaire, leads a quick two hundred miles to Kikwit and the welcome sight of the Kwilu Hotel. Broad steps sweep into the stone building. A restaurant, bar, and glassed-in atrium with lush plants beckon. The rooms are large, clean, air-conditioned, fitted with telephones, reading lamps, soft carpets, and private baths. It promises all the amenities of a Hilton or Marriott. The bath, already filled with cold water, and the candles by the bedside are the only clues that promise and reality may not correspond.

When a guest checks in, the receptionist asks for payment in advance in order to purchase diesel fuel for the electric generator. Even so, the electricity is turned off at 8 P.M. in order to save fuel. The large restaurant menu is filled with succulent choices. But guests get what they want only if they happen to want the one dish that is available the night they are there. And when they return to their rooms, the candlelight illumines unworkable taps, an unflushable toilet, a disconnected telephone, and an air conditioner that does not run.

Nonetheless, with a little flexibility, a stay at the Kwilu Hotel can be most refreshing. Mary Douglas notes:

Considering that it depends on its own generators, and that it has not enough credit with the Bank, and considering everything else that makes it difficult to use its medium technology appurtenances, it does remarkably well. Its management is to be congratulated on providing a comfortable, self-contained place for privileged travelers to rest.[1]

Sociology is a recently constructed building on the intellectual map. Along with other parts of modern science, it beckons with its broad steps, and it is full of promise and pretensions. Like the Kwilu Hotel, all does not work as advertised. This book is a guide, taking a look at the building that sociology is constructing and the amenities it offers.

Christians are interested in the reception that sociology gives the historic Christian tradition to which they are committed. What is it like to be a Christian while living and working as a sociologist? What possibilities exist for a distinctly *Christian* sociology? Does sociology provide for all the matters that Christian faith provided for in the past? Does it sharpen old questions and offer better answers or simply ask questions very different from those asked by Christianity? What language is spoken by sociology? Does the grammar of Christian faith translate into sociological discourse, or are they two mutually exclusive languages?

Approaching sociology for the first time can be somewhat intimidating. There are many floors, twisting hallways, suites of various vintages. The newcomer cannot be expected to know which of the promised amenities will work. Then there are the occupants—interesting characters who are long-term residents, others of more recent vintage, and new ones checking in all the time. Old portraits hang on the walls, some prominently displayed, others encountered only in small rooms off winding hallways, each with a story. Some are of prominent architects and builders of sociology, now forgotten or neglected. Many of them were Christians. Current residents often attempt to move the portraits about so that their favorites are more prominently displayed.

Part of the romance of sociology is the undisciplined nature of the relationships and conversations that happen among those who profess it. At times the jokes and arguments between sociologists can be as interesting as sociology itself. They even give clues as to what's wrong with the more imperialistic versions of sociology that pretend, in deluded moments, to have all the truth about human beings and their communities.

A guidebook such as this is no substitute for actually talking to these figures or reading some of their wonderful books. It is a rewarding experience to curl up with a well-written work of sociology, to follow the cadence of the words as they reveal whole new worlds of experience and insight into the wiles and ways of human beings living in their unsociably social manner.[2]

Sociology helps one realize how narrow and limited his or her own social experience is. It takes readers to other worlds of culture and customs, social habits and arrangements that lie beyond the horizon of their own experience and imagination. It poses large questions that demand the clear, coherent, careful answers on which the very future of modern civilization depends. It also points out how difficult it is to construct such answers.

Difficulties in Discovering Sociological Truth

Philosophers of science often divide these difficulties into matters that have to do with the knower (the subject) and those having to do with what is to be known (the object).

Difficulties with the Subject

One difficulty in getting good answers arises from the sort of creatures human beings are. At the very origins of the tradition of modern science, Francis Bacon (1561–1626) wrote about the "idols" that obscure a person's ability to see things clearly. His idols refer to factors that bias the process of trying to discover truth. He listed four classes of such distorting tendencies.

The *idols of the tribe* are those tendencies of thought ingrown in human beings as a species. People are prone to believe what pleases them and to discount what doesn't. They look for evidence that agrees with their own hypotheses and overlook contrary evidence. These are general or *universal* biases.

The *idols of the cave* result from the fact that each person is a member of a particular human group. An individual may be Caucasian, Asian, African American, male or female, liberal or conservative, religious or irreligious. Group loyalties give people *specific* biases. When they peer out at the world from their particular cave, they see things from the vantage point of that cave. Group affiliations affect how individuals feel about the larger social world. Sociologists spend a lot of time looking at these sorts of bias. A specialty called the sociology of knowledge traces the ways in which membership in and identification with specific groups shape the knowledge that people consider genuine and important.

The *idols of the marketplace* are problems created by the words, often the only words, that people have to talk to each other about reality. Language is the tool through which humans handle the world, labeling it, calling attention to certain features and not others. No one can think without words, and yet sometimes he or she can't think straight with them. Words have a range of meanings, and people keep changing the ways they use words.

This is a serious problem in sociology. Most of the words that sociologists use are everyday, common words. To be scientifically useful, they must be given more precise and unusual meanings. Yet even when that is done, there is disagreement on those meanings within the sociological community. Many of sociology's central concepts have multiple meanings—a point that can be proved simply by asking three or four sociologists to give clear definitions of "social class" or "culture."

The *idols of the theater* represent the human tendency to prefer older, more widely accepted ideas over novel, minority opinions. Familiarity breeds respect. Common sense makes the uncommon look nonsensical. Humans (even scientists) prefer the security of the respectable and socially confirmed to the insecurity of the different and novel. Two hundred million Americans can't be wrong. Or twenty thousand sociologists can't be wrong. When something is considered self-evident and is widely received as the truth, it becomes nearly impossible to question it or to give new answers to those questions, even with substantial evidence as support.

Christians see these subjective tendencies toward confusion and bias as rooted in human nature. As fallen *creatures* made in the image of God, people have magnificent capabilities to probe the marvels of creation and human life. They have a hunger for truth, beauty, and goodness. Yet as creatures they are finite, limited in their ability to see the full picture. Still, humans have a God-given ability to apprehend truth and live in harmony with it.

As *fallen* creatures, people are afflicted by sin. Sin brings about alienating quests that take people away from the larger reality that this world belongs to God and is designed to serve God's purposes. Because they are fallen, humans may repress the truth, create ugliness, and call the evil they do goodness. They confuse the limited for the unlimited, the imperfect for the perfect. They may even come to see the body as the soul, to confuse earthly time with eternity, and to put the human in the place of God. One of the effects of sin is to magnify the idols of the tribe, cave, marketplace, and theater. These idols become powerful forces within all communities (including those of sociologists and Christians) that seek to make sense of the world.

One cannot banish human sinfulness or Bacon's idols from the rooms of sociology simply by putting the adjective *Christian* alongside the word *sociology*. Being fallen is not something that ceases when a person becomes a Christian or a sociologist. Anselm's famous words apply to both Christian and secular thought: *Nondum considerasti quanti ponderis sit peccatum* ("You have not yet taken full account of sin").

The aim of this book is to further the conversation between sociology and Christians about their commonly shared social worlds so that more sociological truth can be discovered. We authors believe that this will lead to more fair play in societal affairs and to more people securing a fair share of the goods of this life and of the age to come. But this conversation requires more than simply an understanding of the weaknesses of humans as the subjects or knowers of truth. It also requires an understanding of the difficulties posed by what it is that sociologists want to know about—the object of sociological knowing.

Difficulties with the Object of Study

A second major source of difficulty in figuring out social worlds resides in the particular nature of those worlds. Social reality is extraordinarily rich and complex. What is more, it continues to change in ways and at a rate that exceed even the imagination of the most acute futurists. The Indian story of the elephant and the six blind people suggests the difficulties here.

The question in the story is simple: The king asks six blind men to say what sort of beast an elephant is. Feeling a tusk, the first says an elephant is like a mighty spear. Feeling the side, the second claims it is like a wall. The others in turn contribute their best knowledge: feeling the ear, one says it is like a fan; feeling the leg, a tree; feeling the tail, a rope; feeling the trunk, a boa constrictor.

Of course, there are several problems with this story as an analogy for sociology. The story relies on the fact that someone has the sight to know that all the blind investigators are incorrect, that the beast is actually an elephant and like none of the descriptions given by the blind. The story's point is that the reality is larger than the partial truths contained in any of the single descriptions or in all of them put together. Yet the only way one can know that the reality is larger and different is because someone is able to see the elephant. Still, there are aspects of the story that make it a helpful parable.

Sociology offers more than six accounts of what its beast is like. That's often a bit surprising and disturbing to the person who comes to sociology hoping to get a fix on society. If sociology is scientific, then why all the disagreements among sociologists about what society is, how it works, and what one can do about it?

One reply is simply that the very nature of science lies in the conflict of interpretations, the rough-and-tumble challenge of hypotheses confronting data that will falsify one or another notion. Another reply is that sociology is still a youthful science and has not yet settled some of its fundamental disputes in the way that physics and physiology have settled some of theirs. But there is an entirely different reply that can be illustrated by changing the story of the elephant in a rather dramatic way.

Imagine the problem for the six blind persons if the elephant were encouraged to take up the bad habit of running at top speed. Now the king would get very complicated reports. The person clinging to the leg would experience it as a jolting, dusty elliptical motion. The one on the tusk would be convinced he is on some amusement park ride. The one clutching the tail would be whipped about (and, if fortunate, not wind up too wet or smelly) and would conclude that no rope could do such things.

Setting the beast in motion would destroy some of the previous accounts and would make the task of coming to consensus about its nature even more complicated. Yet even this is not quite the picture of how societies work. Fortunately for biologists (and blind investigators), elephants, whether stationary or running, have the habit of remaining elephants for long periods of time. They don't suddenly begin shedding their elephant skins and turn into lizards, leopards, or loons.

Societies, unfortunately, have the habit of changing in ways that are disconcertingly rapid and dramatic, of splitting up into new social groups, of taking on new forms of organization—that is, new economic, political, and religious arrangements. Moreover, "single societies" often include many language, ethnic, and racial groups with very different religions, worldviews, and lifestyles. What would the blind investigators say if, as they clung to the running elephant, the tusk transformed into a paw with claws, the trunklike leg into an arm and hands, and the tail simply disappeared? How then would they imagine and agree on the nature of the beast?

This new image of the changing beast on the move more adequately portrays the problem faced by sociology. Sociology came into being at a very particular time and place. It got into business when the Western world was in the midst of an extraordinary societal transformation. Its first and continuing question, more than any other, concerns this transformation called modernization and modernity. Sociology, conceived in the eighteenth century and born in the nineteenth, responded to the emergence of modern society.

When sociology began, people had the sinking feeling that the world was changing more rapidly than ever before. In addition, it was generating social arrangements that were bad for large segments of the population. The horrible problems of the old order vanished, to be sure, but new ones were appearing that seemed even worse. Hope of returning to the old order or of moving quickly through the new to something better was scarce. So sociologists got to work, believing they could discover what was going on and gain control over the process of change. They thought they might be able to steer change in new directions, leading to social arrangements where all members of the human community could flourish in societies of peace, prosperity, and justice.

Sociology's beast, thus, was a very large, very complex "elephant" of old and revered ancestry. It had started to lumber along at top speed and in the process had shed its elephant skin, turning into some new beast whose shape, form, and capabilities were so new that no one had ever seen one before. Even in the present it continues to move and change dramatically. It is no wonder that there are disagreements among sociologists and very different accounts of what the modern world is like. Because societies are the sorts of things they are (and not atoms, aardvarks, or angels), discovering truth about them is a very different and more difficult endeavor than discovering truth in physics, biology, or even theology.

Beginning the Tour of Sociology

Two last notes before the tour begins: First, the building that sociologists have erected for themselves sits in its own intellectual neighborhood, butting up against several other buildings constructed by other social scientists (economists, anthropologists, political scientists, historians, psychologists). There is a lot of convivial exchange among them (as well as shouted epithets). All of them front the same courtyard where the beast called the "social world" is found. All of them study parts of it.

Sociology has no monopoly on human society or on truth about it. It learns from the other social sciences. Every human being inhabits a social world and has ideas of how social arrangements work. Sociology challenges people to test their ideas against a much wider range of social experience than they normally do, to clarify the ideas that they already have about society and its processes, and to listen to the ideas of other people who have tried to do just that.

Second, Christians have been a part of sociology from its beginnings.[3] They bring their own tradition of rational discourse to sociology. In the story of the elephant, they are not the sighted king who can settle the issue of the real truth behind the various theories of various blind investigators. In this regard, they are on the same footing as all other social investigators.

What Christians do believe is that there *is* a sighted King who has spoken and given certain clues as to the meaning and purpose of the universe and its human inhabitants. They believe that the King of the universe, who sees the whole picture, is revealed in history in the person, life, and death of Jesus Christ. By attending to Christ and understanding the Bible's message, Christians bring to the debate about society certain distinctive meanings and assumptions. These shape the issues they consider crucial and the theories they find compatible with what the King has said. But none of this gets them out of the messy job of hanging onto the lumbering beast as it continues to change nor does it relieve them of the difficult work of developing the widest consensus possible with others who are engaged in the same task.

So check in to Hotel Sociology—and come with us to grab hold of whatever wondrous beast it is that inhabits the courtyards of social science.

NOTES

1. Mary Douglas, "Distinguished Lecture: The Hotel Kwilu—A Model of Models," *American Anthropologist* 91, no. 4 (December 1989): 864.
2. This is from Augustine: "There is nothing so social by nature, so unsocial by its corruption, as this [human] race." *City of God* (Book 12, Chapter 27).
3. For example, Giambattista Vico, Frédéric Le Play, Paul Göhre, Albion Small.

PART I

The Confrontation Between Christian Faith and Sociology

Chapter 2

TO SEE IS NOT TO SEE

It's always a surprise, though it probably should not be: some medical doctors smoke. Psychiatrists have one of the highest rates of suicide. Marriage counselors have high rates of divorce. Speech teachers often are poor public speakers. And what about accountants who can't balance their checkbooks, or lawyers who are unethical, or intellectuals who are among the most unreasonable people?

No doubt these stereotypes are unfair. What is fair is the expectation that the highly competent should have insight into their own behavior. They should have enough wisdom to take their own medicine. Why shouldn't medical doctors be more careful with their health than their patients are? Psychologists should understand their own hang-ups. Accountants should be able to balance their own checkbooks. And sociologists should understand how their very opinions about society (and Christianity) are socially influenced.

Often this is not the case. Yet whatever sociologists say about how social arrangements affect human life and thought in general applies equally to the life and thought of sociologists. This is the principle of reflexivity.[1] It will come up several times in this discussion of sociology and faith. Jesus hints at this concept as well. Why is it that people often see the speck of sawdust that needs removal from another's eye while they miss the plank that is in their own (Matthew 7:3–5)?

Why Do You See the World *That* Way?

Sociologists are intent on exploring the connection between social groups and the ideas that these groups hold dear. Some ideas foster people's social, economic, and political privileges better than others. People usually find ideas attractive because those ideas further their chances of acquiring more wealth or greater status and respect. Often people see the world in a particular way because it makes their own group look good, not because the world really is that way.

Even the use of certain labels reinforces a particular view of the world. Some people are called terrorists while others are freedom fighters. One country's policy is said to defend freedom while another's is a case of imperialism. Pro-choicers look at those picketing abortion clinics and shout, "Religious fanatics disrespectful of human rights." Pro-lifers shout back, "We are preventing murder." Some see the poor as oppressed by the wealthy; others consider them lazy people who have made bad choices.

People create whole systems of ideas that paint portraits of the social world and what needs to be done to make it better. Conservative political ideas are most commonly held by those in the wealthier social classes. Conservative ideas favor the status quo and leave the wealthy at the top of the social heap. Liberal political ideas occur most commonly among members of highly educated, relatively low-paid groups (the "new knowledge class"). These ideas favor changes in the status quo, giving more importance and wealth to those whose livelihood is based on knowledge.

The ideas people adopt have profound effects on social patterns. Racism and sexism are good examples. If someone defines African Americans as genetically inferior to whites, he or she sets up a basis in ideas for not providing them with educational opportunities equal to those offered whites. (This is the situation in South Africa.) If a person defines women as emotional and weak, he or she can find excuses for keeping them out of positions where high-level decisions are made (as large corporations and national politics have done in the United States). Such a person might not even listen respectfully to women's arguments.

Sociology is a social endeavor, carried out by real human beings with families, jobs, political passions, religious and antireligious involvements. It has its own social organizations and reward system. Its roots are in the evolution of modern academics in the West. It shares in the penetrating strengths and debilitating weaknesses of Western institutions. Sociology seeks to make sense of social worlds, especially the social world of modern large-scale, industrial societies. What sociologists have to say about that larger world may say a lot about the social world of sociology as well. Sometimes what sociologists see reflects their own social interests more than social reality.

The reflexive principle dictates that theories used to explain social worlds in general must also explain one's own particular social world. Because sociologists conclude that groups adopt ideas advancing their own interests, it is only fair to suspect that sociologists probably do the same. If the ideas of sociology are true, then they must be true for sociology—and true for Christians as well. In other words, sociological notions can be used to understand sociology itself and to illuminate the relationship between faith and sociology.

The worlds of Christian faith and sociology tend, at times, to become hostile camps. This chapter documents indications of this hostility. Christian faith and sociology do not always see eye to eye. Why that is and what it says about both sociology and Christian faith is something that this book puzzles over. A healthy dose of reflexivity could cure large amounts of academic dyslexia.

The Dyslexia of Sociology

There are some intriguing sorts of selective amnesia evident in contemporary secular sociology. While secularists see some things wonderfully well, they have great difficulty seeing other things at all. This seeing and not seeing is just the kind of thing that sociology finds interesting in other social groups. Now it is time to do a sociological analysis of how the secular biases of many sociologists make them blind to some important realities. Here are three pairs of items that hint at the ways in which much of contemporary sociology has eyes to see but doesn't always see clearly.

Item 1: Who Was the Founder?

Most histories of sociology and many introductory texts say that the brilliant but eccentric Auguste Comte (1798–1857) was the founder of sociology.

A Frenchman living in the aftermath of the French Revolution, Comte (Isidore-Auguste-Marie-François-Xavier Comte, to be exact) puzzled over what was going on. He argued that the troubles of industrialism and democracy were due to the numerous contradictory religious, philosophical, and scientific ideas that were then competing for prominence. His prescription was to adopt a single comprehensive worldview based purely on science. A unified, harmonious civilization requires a single, animating worldview, he claimed. "Positive science," as he called it, would banish all unscientific ideas and worldviews. *A Course in Positive Philosophy* (1830–1842) was his six-volume written account of what this new science and civilization might be like.

Comte's writings created hope that people might be able to forge a good and stable world through science. His writings contrasted with previous Enlightenment thought and its largely negative critique of the past. Comte suggested positive social changes to correct the shortcomings of the modern social order. He wished to create a social science based on assured knowledge, rather than on uncertain superstition or untested speculation.

He believed that such science would eventually replace all religious and philosophical ideas about society as well as end all ethical and moral debates. At last humans would have scientific truth about how to create the good, the true, and the beautiful social order. Sociologists in alliance with captains of industry and natural scientists would design and run a new social order of peace, prosperity, and progress.

This traditional picture of the founding of sociology by Comte ignores at least one monumental fact. In 1730 the second edition of a startling work by an Italian Catholic, Giambattista Vico (1668–1744), appeared. In it Vico argued for the development of a new science that would unveil the laws governing the rise and fall of nations. This work came a hundred years before that of Comte.

Vico claimed that people can be studied in a manner different from the way physicists study nature. People relate to other people in ways unlike those of atoms relating to other atoms. The difference lies in the meanings and purposes found in the hearts of humans. Their existence is a great advantage, according to Vico. The presence of meanings makes the scientific study of humans even more precise than the study of atoms. Unlike physicists, who can never "get inside" matter itself, social scientists can "get inside" the events, actions, and structures involving human beings. Why Brutus stabbed Caesar and how this changed the political structure of Rome can be studied and understood. People are not puppets, controlled by impersonal forces inherent in nature. People are actors who choose—within certain limitations, to be sure—to do what they do. The science of society studies the hows and whys of human life.

Vico said that human behavior can be understood by a sort of empathetic reflection governed by a principle: *One understands only what he or she creates.* God created the physical universe. In the final analysis, only God understands it truly. He does so from within as its Creator, knowing its processes and also the purposes behind its existence. Physical science can understand bits of nature when it is able to recreate small parts of nature's physical processes and control the results of those mechanisms. Yet only God understands the whole.

Since humans are the creators of their social worlds—which consist of people's relationships with other people and of the institutions of education, politics, technology, work, religion, and so on—humans can understand them *as insiders*. Social knowledge is a type of self-understanding. Hence, people can have more comprehensive scientific knowledge of the forces and principles that govern human institutions than they can of the forces governing physical nature. The title of Vico's book signals his intent to found a new science of society: *Principles of a New Science Concerning the Common Nature of the Nations*.

Since Vico's idea for sociology was published a hundred years before Comte's, why is Vico not acknowledged as the founder of sociology? Is this a reflection of the bias of secularists who do not wish to acknowledge Christians at the very foundations of sociology?

Item 2: Is Religion Dead?

One of sociology's long traditions claims that religion is dying as the modern world is being born.

Auguste Comte took as scientific truth the notion that positive science would completely displace supernatural theology. Karl Marx saw the coming communist society as one in which people would all be atheists without any need for God or religious ideas. Max Weber, a German economist and sociologist, portrayed the modern technical world as being disenchanted—that is, as losing its mystery or sacred qualities. As humans enter the modern era, according to Weber, they explain more and more through science and reason, leaving less and less to religion and revelation. Émile Durkheim, the most important sociologist France produced, was aggressively secularist. The public values needed by modern democracy must have strong and convincing foundations. Durkheim was sure that religion could no longer provide these foundations, while a scientific sociology would.

Secularization is the major term for this "death of religion." Sociology texts frequently take it as an inevitable consequence of modernity. Secularization refers to the process in which increasing numbers of people stop being religious and increasing sectors of society and life go on without reference to religious values or ideas. Religious institutions and ideas decline in their importance in modern life as people become increasingly rational.

One of the ways in which this decline manifests itself is in the so-called war between religion and science. According to this hypothesis, the more science expands, the more religion vanishes—like water replacing the air in a bottle thrown into the ocean. Area after area of knowledge loses its religious controls. More and more is explained simply and directly in scientific terms. At times this process provokes stiff resistance from the religious. One thinks of Galileo, of the Scopes "monkey trial," or more recently of the struggle over creationism. Modern sociology often asserts that science will win in the end.

Indeed, some sociological findings suggest science really does weaken religion. Nearly all surveys indicate that people with higher levels of formal education characterize themselves as having lower commitments to conventional religious tenets. These include such Christian basics as the divinity of Christ, the existence of God, the Bible as God's revelation, life after death, and the necessity of belief in Christ for salvation.

Furthermore, the social prestige and political power of clerics and ministers have declined in the West over the past three hundred years. Most private colleges in the United States originated as religiously affiliated institutions. Many on the boards of trustees as well as the colleges' presidents and teachers were Protestant ministers. As reason and science pushed religion aside, the majority of those colleges became almost completely secular (examples include Harvard, Yale, Princeton, and Oberlin).

Other institutions show similar patterns of secularization. Once virtually all hospitals were religious in their origins and operation. Now most hospitals no longer maintain ties with the denominations and churches that founded them. The Young Men's Christian Association (YMCA) began as an explicitly evangelistic organization aimed at converting young men to Christ. Now local YMCAs resemble community centers whose activities are without religious content or intent.

However, as sociologists herald the death of God in the modern world, they tend to ignore the evidence to the contrary. What is startling in the United States is the combination of high levels of *both* religious *and* scientific activity. Levels of religious belief and involvement historically have been and remain comparatively high in this country. Surveys for the past fifty years show that between 66 and 76 percent of the adult population in the United States say that they are members of a church or synagogue.[2] They also indicate that, among adults, weekly attendance at religious services peaked near 50 percent in the mid 1950s, with the current level near 40 percent.[3]

Theodore Caplow, Howard M. Bahr, and Bruce A. Chadwick offer one of the few long-term comparative studies of a single community.[4] They conclude that "the trend of Middletown's religion in the past century has been inconclusive: the general level of religious belief and practice is not very different today from what it was a century ago, and the leading tenets of popular theology have remained virtually the same during the past half-century."

At the same time, science is well supported and even glorified in the United States. Take sociology as an example. The United States is where sociology has developed most vigorously, as of 1991. There are more professional sociologists (some 20,000[5]) in this country, more research projects (on any given day there are on the order of 1,200 surveys and polls taking place[6]), more money invested in sociology, and more graduate programs in the field than in any other society in the world. This is largely true of physical science as well. Scientists from North America dominate in winning the Nobel Prize in the natural sciences.

Admittedly, the status of science and religion in Europe creates a different picture. Modern science flourishes there, while religion is not doing very well. Significantly larger numbers of Europeans are involved only marginally in traditional religious institutions than is the case in the United States.[7] Comparative attendance figures during the 1950s and 1960s show worship attendance of 10 to 16 percent in France, about 15 percent in Great Britain, and 16 percent in Switzerland.[8] Statistics for the rest of the European countries show a similar pattern. More contemporary surveys yield similar results.

Here's the puzzle. If science and modern thought are what erode faith and religious practice, then they should do so most strongly in the United States and less strongly in Europe. Yet this is not what has happened. Why is the modern society with the strongest practice of sociology and the other sciences also the society with the highest levels of religious activity? And why don't secular sociologists acknowledge this contradiction to their theories of secularization more directly and honestly than they do?

Item 3: What Role Has Christianity Played?

Christianity fostered and encouraged sociology in its North American origins. Christians committed to social reforms spearheaded sociology as a profession here. A survey of those teaching sociology in American colleges and universities up to 1900 reveals that nearly 100 out of 298 had received some theological training.[9] Albion Small, the chair and founder of the first graduate department of sociology in the world, which was located at the University of Chicago, was the son of a Baptist preacher and was himself theologically trained. Most of Small's early appointments to his graduate sociology department had been brought up in clerical homes or had been ministers at one time. Of the early presidents of the American Sociological Society, Giddings, Thomas, Vincent, and Small were from ministerial families. Presidents Sumner, Vincent, Hayes, Weatherly, Lichtenberger, Gillin, and Gillette were Protestant ministers before they became sociologists.[10]

Even in Europe there are surprising and normally hidden connections between sociology and Christianity. Frédéric Le Play (1806–1882), a French Catholic scholar, wrote the first major empirical sociological study, *The European Workers* (1855), which ran to six volumes. Norwegians consider Eilert Sundt (1817–1875) their first sociologist. Educated in theology at what is now the University of Oslo, he was an ordained Lutheran minister. He pioneered sociological research into the social and economic conditions of the poor.[11]

In Germany, a young theology student inaugurated the study of the German factory workers by means of participant observation. Paul Göhre's *Three Months as a Factory Worker* (1891) shows the structural sources of family disintegration. It documents dual parent employment, the lack of privacy in crowded tenements, the impossibility of having even a single, common family meal a day, and the self-sufficiency of older children because of their employment in the factories. Later Göhre collaborated with Max Weber in a massive study of agricultural labor in the Eastern part of Prussia.[12] Göhre was both a committed Christian and an initiator of empirical sociology in Germany.

If religion and sociology make poor bedfellows, how is it that practicing Christians were active among the early originators of sociology? And why are these Christian roots largely unacknowledged in contemporary sociological histories?

Furthermore, surveys of contemporary academics in the United States show patterns of much less religiosity than the public in general. In one random survey of "leaders," scientists recorded far less religiosity than leaders in all other sectors of public life.[13]

QUESTION	"SCIENTIST"	"PUBLIC"
Ever read the Bible	64%	75%
Am a religious person	50	74
Frequently felt God loved them	31	73
Prayed frequently	27	57
Made a personal commitment to Christ	18	47
Attend church frequently	28	44
Frequently had a religious experience	8	25

This appears to support the notion that science erodes religious faith. However, there is more specific information contrasting the religiosity of academics by their discipline. Among academics, contemporary social scientists as a group are the most indifferent and hostile to religion. Among social scientists, 49 percent so reported themselves compared with 46 percent in the humanities, 41 percent in biology, and 37 percent in the physical sciences. In another study, a similar pattern is apparent.[14]

QUESTION	SOCIAL SCIENTISTS	HUMANITIES SCHOLARS	NATURAL SCIENTISTS
Do not believe in God	41%	36%	20%
Never attended church	48	45	34

Something is curious here. If it is science that conflicts with religion, then the natural or physical scientists should be the least religious, with the social scientists in the middle and those teaching humanities the most religious. Yet the pattern shows the natural scientists as having the fewest disbelieving God and the fewest never attending church. Those in the humanities are in the middle, and the social scientists are the least religious. The data do not clearly fit a theory of science itself eroding religious faith.

So again there is a puzzle. North American sociology starts with deep and cordial relations between Christian faith and sociology. Now it has many who say they are indifferent or even hostile to religion (and choose not to expose themselves to faith). Further, it is not the natural scientists who are the least religious but the social scientists. Those commonly acknowledged as the most scientific in the academy are also the most religious.

When these three items are brought together in summary form, they raise some rather uncomfortable questions. Why does sociology, invented at least as early as the eighteenth century by a Catholic Italian scholar, consider a nineteenth-century secular French intellectual as its founder? Why do many of the central contributors to sociology keep writing religion's obituary when religion continues to show remarkable liveliness? Why, in a so-called war between science and religion, does the strongest center of indifference or hostility to religion lie in the social sciences rather than in the hard sciences (the physical or natural sciences)? Why, in the one country where sociology is the most vigorous, did sociology begin largely as an applied Christian endeavor, only to lose that connection? And why is it now an aggressively secular discipline with Christians underrepresented?

In sum, why are many contemporary sociologists more likely to be antireligious than other academics? This book suggests that a good answer can be found by studying sociology with the tools of sociology. If groups adopt ideas congenial to their own larger social interests, maybe this indifference to religion reflects some compelling social interests of sociology.

Looking Through Both Eyes

The chapters that follow undertake to solve some of these puzzles. Not a few think that it is foolish to try to negotiate a harmonious relationship between faith and sociology. Suspicions are strong on both sides of the faith-sociology divide. It is not unusual to hear someone say that putting Christianity and sociology together is very likely to ruin one of them, if not both.

Those who are religious, especially the more conservative or orthodox, are likely to see social science as dangerous to their faith. Among fundamentalist Christians, sociology is often seen as competing with the principles of the Bible and as a promoter of "secular humanism." As one teacher at a Christian high school expressed it, "I have doubts about psychology . . . because it is man trying to understand man. I also reject anthropology and sociology because they are man-centered."[15]

So on one side, there are sociologists loudly denying their discipline's Christian roots and vigorously contesting attempts to reconnect sociology with a Christian outlook. And on the other are Christians saying that the sociology department is the chief residence of the devil in American universities, a perpetrator of relativism, liberalism, atheism, socialism, and whatever other "-ism" is damnable. (This charge isn't true. The devil has many addresses, some of them religious!) Unfortunately, two errors don't add up to a single truth.

We think it is time to allow people to look through both the eye of faith and the eye of sociology. There is a depth in modern society that can be seen only when we look with both eyes.[16] To see through the eye of faith has become more difficult because of the place the modern world gives to religious commitment. Chapter Three sketches the dramatic changes that have affected religious faith in the past four hundred years.

NOTES

1. "I shave myself" is a reflexive statement. (In contrast, I can also shave others, as barbers formerly did with their long, straight razors, and carpenters shave doors with planes.) In a reflexive statement, the action is performed by the actor on himself or herself. Some psychologists say that religious ideas about God are a projection of the inner wishes and emotional conflicts of the personality. The reflexivity principle suggests that it is just as valid to consider the psychologist's idea that "the idea of God is a psychological projection of the personality" as itself a projection of the psychologist's inner wishes and emotional conflicts.
2. The Gallup Poll, *The Gallup Report: Religion in America* (Princeton, NJ: Gallup Organization, 1987).
3. George Gallup, Jr., and Sarah Jones, *100 Questions and Answers: Religion in America* (Princeton, NJ: Princeton Research Center, 1989), p. 204.
4. Caplow, Bahr, and Chadwick, *All Faithful People: Change and Continuity in Middletown's Religion* (Minneapolis: University of Minnesota Press, 1983), p. 280.
5. Herbert Gans, American Sociological Association Presidential Address, *American Sociological Review* 5, no. 1 (February 1989): 1.
6. Morton Hunt, *Profiles of Social Research: The Scientific Study of Human Interactions* (New York: Sage, 1985), p. 98.
7. Post–World War II Gallup polls indicated that 94 percent of Americans believed in God; England registered 83 percent; Holland, 80 percent; Sweden, 80 percent; Denmark, 80 percent; France, 66 percent. Charles D. Kean, "God, Gods, and Dr. George Gallup," *Christianity and Society* 13 (1948): 17–19.
8. Hans Mol, ed., *Western Religion: A Country by Country Sociological Inquiry* (The Hague: Mouton, 1972), pp. 180, 232, 517. Other comparative statistics

on baptisms, belief in God, religious marriages, and so on show lower levels than those found in U.S. studies.

9. J. Graham Morgan, "The Development of Sociology and the Social Gospel in America," *Sociological Analysis* 30, no. 1 (Spring 1969): 52.

10. Anthony Oberschall, "The Institutionalization of American Sociology," in A. Oberschall, ed., *The Establishment of Empirical Sociology: Studies in Continuity, Discontinuity, and Institutionalization* (New York: Harper & Row, 1972), p. 198.

11. Priscilla Reinertsen, "Report of a Sociological Pioneer: Eilert Sundt," *Journal of the History of the Behavioral Sciences* 6 (October 1969): 360–369.

12. Anthony Oberschall, *Empirical Social Research in Germany 1848–1914* (New York: Basic Books, 1965).

13. Reported in Robert Wuthnow, *The Struggle for America's Soul: Evangelicals, Liberals, and Secularism* (Grand Rapids, MI: Eerdmans, 1989), pp. 144–145.

14. Reported in Wuthnow, *The Struggle for America's Soul*, pp. 146–147.

15. Alan Peshkin, *God's Choice: The Total World of a Fundamentalist Christian School* (Chicago: University of Chicago Press, 1986), p. 75. William Helmreich, in *The World of the Yeshiva: An Intimate Portrait of Orthodox Jewry* (New York: Free Press, 1982), pp. 143, 223, indicates similar aversions among Orthodox Jews.

16. Richard Perkins, *Looking Both Ways: Exploring the Interface Between Christianity and Sociology* (Grand Rapids, MI: Baker Book House, 1987), provides an excellent account of the benefits of this dual vision.

Chapter 3

PUTTING RELIGION IN ITS PLACE

Don't you hate it when someone cleans up the mess called your room or desk? What looks like chaos is actually "complex order." It matters little that others can't find the clothing, the book, or the phone number. You know exactly where they are. But not after someone has "straightened up."

The world that existed prior to modernization was an orderly place, though at a distance it looks a bit chaotic. The people who lived in it could feed themselves, marry and mate, learn and work, worship and heal, sing and cry. Wars, famines, pestilences disrupted life, as did inventions, new lords, and new laws. Nations rose and fell. The slow accumulation of small changes created pressures that led to the larger transformations that are chronicled in history books. Yet the people who lived in the centuries preceding the industrial revolution felt themselves at home.

The Civilization with the Church at Its Heart

The Western world grew up in close connection with Christianity. Its rulers and intellectuals trained in schools that were founded in the early cathedrals and cloisters of the fourth and fifth centuries. The Church nurtured most Western thinkers. They articulated a vision of the world that held faith and thought in integral and complementary relationship. Religion provided an overarching picture of the universe into which (in principle) every element of life fit, from a sparrow to the sovereign, from work to weddings, from art to avarice.

It was not a completely uniform social world. No society is. There were disaffected people and people who held ideas very different from the dominant religious worldview.[1] Minority groups (such as the Jews, Waldensians, and Humiliati) coexisted in uneasy tension with the majority. Their differences with dominant views acted as potential seeds of change. Yet possibilities for change existed even among those who held tightly to the ruling cultural and social patterns. Worldviews never pass from parents to children without some changes. There is an immense difference in outlook between the religious elites—those educated and sophisticated in matters of faith and theology—and commoners.

The popular beliefs and practices of commoners frequently reflected a folk religion combining faith and popular superstitions. Magic, rather than science, competed with religion. Nonetheless, there was a publicly acknowledged place for religion in the premodern world, which gave it special status and importance. Often the most highly educated individual in the community was the parish priest or pastor. He was a powerful and respected person. The ideas of Christianity were trusted lighthouses and buoys by which to navigate life, no matter the weather or the tide. When the Church spoke about public concerns, people listened carefully.

Christian faith provided the most stable, eternal verities on which everyone could count. Agricultural techniques might slowly change, fashions evolve, musical styles emerge along with new instruments and composers, national borders shift, rulers rise and fall, cities grow. Yet the Christian faith was a stable, orienting framework. It kept human life in contact with the drama of salvation of which the present was but one small scene.

In most communities, a church building or cathedral stood at the town center next to the public square, symbolizing the centrality of the religious. The church tower overlooked a community serving a God who loved all its members. Religion penetrated all aspects of societal life and thought.

Christianity possessed significant insight into the traditional society it had helped to bring into being. The chaos of the medieval room was actually a complex order. For the most part, Christianity knew where to find things and where things belonged. It developed sophisticated social philosophies, and its theology offered insight and evaluation on a wide range of social patterns that were characteristic of that time. But a new day has now arrived.

The Dwarf Church Among Skyscrapers, Stadiums, and Shopping Malls

Modernization rearranged everything. Sociology, economics, and political science resulted from needs that moderns had in the face of growing social complexities. People keenly felt the confusion created by the upheavals of social and economic revolutions. The rising bourgeoisie (middle classes) had to make sense of a world that didn't appear to be as sensible as the one it had replaced. They invented and supported sociology and other social sciences.

For instance, think what would happen if you lived in a comfortable room for several centuries. One day you came home and discovered new roommates. Some of your precious items were gone. The rest of your things were now stacked into a small corner, and you were told to keep them separate from the rest of the furniture. Concurrently, you discovered that the lenses in your glasses, ground to very precise specifications, no longer gave proper focus. The result would be massive disorientation. Something of that sort happened to the Church as the modern world came into being.

The dwarfing of church buildings symbolizes this change. The physically dominant buildings that pull communities together are no longer church edifices. Instead, skyscrapers have risen as the temples of business and government. Huge stadiums provide a major theater for the drama of modern life. There teams enact parables representing the survival of the fittest in place of the older drama of the cosmic struggle for salvation. Finally, the bright lights of shopping malls declare consumption as the pinnacle of the good life.

Though it is hard to date the beginning of the modernizing process, the period of the late fifteenth and early sixteenth centuries is a good candidate. That was when the modern world order began to show its distinctive features. After that, a new social system appeared whose characteristics intensified and broadened into a global system, leaving few corners of the world untouched.

Modernization refers to "the institutional concomitants of technologically induced economic growth." There is no such thing as a "fully modern" society.[2] The United States is a modern society, yet it continues to modernize further with no clear end point in view. Modernization encompasses a variety of dramatic changes. These include increased uses of inanimate energy, the mechanization of productive capacities, the continuing enhancement of technical apparatus for accomplishing the everyday tasks of society, and so on. What is of interest here are several of modernization's effects on Christian faith.

Creation of a Marketplace in Religion

Modernization constructs new patterns for distributing products as a result of a vast expansion in productive capacity. In contrast to feudal European society, modern Western societies possess an immense array of products that move with great freedom across national and continental boundaries. Impersonal forces of the marketplace, rather than the personal choices of a feudal lord or prince, guide economic behavior. The result is an explosion of widely available new products. The average modern shopper in market-dominated economies faces a wonderland of choices.

This experience in economic goods is symptomatic of a much larger process. Modernization means the movement in many realms of life from a world of few choices to one of many. The name for this is the *pluralization of the life-world*. Pluralization refers to the gradual vanishing of the singularity, integration, and stability of the life-world of traditional society. At one time, the place, people, options, and symbols governing choices for individuals were highly cohesive and stable. Life was a "one-possibility" reality (or at least a "few-possibilities" affair). Now it is highly pluralistic. People encounter a much wider range of choices than they used to when it comes to goods, occupations, values, religious notions, cultural expressions, symbols, and meanings. The "old cultural store" from which people could secure what they needed for life has added whole new rows of shelves and thousands of new products.

At one time, people lived in highly bounded and limited social worlds. Restricted choice was a reality. In a word, necessity ("that's just the way it is") rather than choice characterized experience. Most had no conception of alternatives nor expectations that the world could be different. Change occurred—but it was a slow accumulation of rather trivial adjustments that only added up to major modifications over several centuries. In ages past, most people did not experience change as the intrusive, uncontrolled presence that they do today. Moderns often respond to change with what Alvin Toffler calls "future shock."[3] This is the disorientation experienced when new changes come so rapidly and continuously that people lose a sense that anything has permanence.

Pluralization is more than an awareness of new and un-dreamed-of possibilities; it also involves the technical capability to realize them. Variety is everywhere. The well-equipped kitchen now produces Italian pasta, stir-fry in a wok, sushi, and French pastry for dessert. People no longer assume they will walk in the shoes of their parents, taking up their occupations or jobs. Nor will they characteristically inherit the "family homestead" or even recite the same prayers to the same gods. What a person becomes is much more dependent on individual choice than ever before. Residence, marriage partner (or none), whether and when to have children, what religion to follow and how actively, which political ideas to endorse—these have become choices, unending choices.

This does not mean that making these choices is without structure or order. Family and friends still exert pressures on the individual to consider some choices as wonderful and others as detestable. Children from Catholic homes more often than not become Catholics. Many southern whites retain a distinctive way of speaking and looking at affairs. Children from working-class homes often end up in working-class positions. Class, gender, and racial barriers limit many cultural and social opportunities and attitudes. Yet in spite of the way objective features of modern arrangements shape choice, people still sense that they possess a larger degree of freedom than did people in traditional societies.

Peter Berger gives us a feel for this:

The national airline of Indonesia calls itself by the name of Garuda, the mythological bird of the Ramayana. The name, which is emblazoned on its airplanes, is appropriate. The traveler flying over the Indonesian archipelago with its myriad islands may well feel himself to be borne on the wings of the original Garuda. Which makes him too a quasi-mythological being, a god perhaps, or at least a demigod, soaring through the sky with unimaginable speed and served by machines of unimaginable power. Down below are the mere mortals, in their small villages and fields. They look up and they watch the gods fly by. Occasionally the traveler will touch down among them, but even then he rarely mingles with them. He has important business in the big city. . . .

The jet traveler in the Third World is a pretty good metaphor of modernity. He moves on the same planet as those villagers, and yet he moves in an altogether different world. His space is measured in thousands of miles, theirs by the distance a bullock cart can go. His time is expressed in the controlled precision of airline schedules, theirs by the seasons of nature and of the human body. He moves with breathtaking speed; they move in the slow rhythms set long ago by tradition. His life hurls itself into an open future; theirs moves in careful connection with the ancestral past. He has vast power, physical as well as social, more or less at his command; they have very little of either. And, while he is not a god in that he is mortal, his life-span will very likely be much longer than theirs. Seen in the perspective of such villagers, modernity is the advent of a new world of mythological potency. Modernization, then, is the juxtaposition of this new world over the old worlds of traditional man—a cataclysmic and unprecedented event in human history.[4]

Objectively, pluralization means that a vast array of new possibilities are now present in the culture. Subjectively, pluralization means that individuals no longer have strongly affirmed, predetermined identities. Who they are is no longer largely given with their gender, family, occupation, religion, or ethnicity. Identity is something constructed by the choices one makes from the modern cafeteria of possibilities.

In a traditional society, people not only know who they are but everyone else does too. The social groups relating to them treat them in ways that affirm their identity. In modern society, people go through an identity crisis (sometimes several times as they move through the passages of life). At any given stage, their sense of identity can be riddled with self-doubt. The achieved identity is often fragile, transitory, and largely unknown to many people with whom they interact.

Furthermore, religious identity is a "one-possibility" affair in most traditional societies. Even after the Protestant Reformation, each European state or principality adopted an official, established religion on the basis of *cuius regio, eius religio* ("whoever reigns, his [religion] is the religion [of the realm]"). Usually, premodern European settings embodied a single political structure accompanied by a single religious structure.

The arrival of the modern world brought a smorgasbord of Christian denominations and other religious groups, as can be seen most dramatically in the United States. Now congregations and denominations compete for members and status in a "religious marketplace." This has changed the nature of religious leadership as well as the relationship of religion to all other institutions. Without a monopoly, religious groups no longer speak with a single voice on crucial issues. The average person, faced with this proliferation of religious choices, can conclude that religious groups are either all equally true or all equally false. It is not unusual now for someone to think that religion is a matter of preference (rather like one person preferring Hondas while another likes Lincolns).

Pluralization results from a variety of processes. These include the expansion of technological control with the consequent multiplication of occupational specializations, the enormous growth of the cities bringing masses of people with differing social and cultural roots together, the development of geographical and social mobility, and the rise of modern communications. People have come together from small-scale, highly stable, relatively closed communities into large-scale cities. There they have to deal with incomprehensible strangers in workplaces and jobs created since the youth of their parents. One response to pluralization is a sharp redrawing of the split between private and public.

Hiding the Unseemly and the Personal

It is sometimes disturbing for moderns to discover how uncouth their ancestors were.[5] In premodern Europe, body noises were taken for granted, not considered embarrassments. Table manners were "not civilized" and included eating with one's fingers, spitting on the floor, and blowing the nose into one's hands. Husbands and wives conceived children in one-room hovels with little privacy.[6]

One of the marks of modern society is the rearrangement of space through the creation of zones of privacy. Now places are defined for changing clothes and allowing the body to relax and satisfy its various needs for scratching and belching. This creation of a gulf between the private and the public reflects the high amount of discipline required for sitting at a desk or for running a machine. The discipline introduced into the regulation of all bodily functions and presentation of the self in public places is part of expanded controls over people in productive and public activities. Even the private realm comes to be more highly defined and regulated. Redefining physical space is only one part of a larger transformation.

The name for this dramatic shift is the *process of privatization*. Privatization is a solution to some of the problems created by modern society.[7] Social and cultural life is split into public and private arenas. The boundaries between the two have not been and are not stable and impermeable. Matters spill over from one to the other. Nonetheless, the tendency is to separate elements of the life-world into one or the other. This includes placing certain sorts of ideas or even intellectual traditions into one or the other.

The public realm includes the central political and economic institutions. Here people are to behave as generic human beings, as citizens or workers without regard to their race, gender, religious involvements, or family status. In the public realm, people are to present a rather disciplined, sanitized, groomed self for activity and interaction.

A legal apparatus grew up to define civil liberties and rights that accrue to anyone who is a member of a given nation-state. These laws secure rights for all citizens to act in the public realm. Abstract, impersonal values govern interpersonal relations. In the public arena, family and personal connections are theoretically irrelevant. What counts is the task, the contract, the job slot, or the role a person is playing. Only a part of that person is involved. The public world is a fragmented one in which people exercise reserve and remain anonymous in many settings. It is a place where people monitor themselves to ensure that they meet various norms of public decorum. One must shove the "true self" into a role in which he or she conforms to expectations that do not fully express who he or she is.

The private world, while circumscribed by the public, is a realm where all one's personal distinctiveness appears. The private is the sphere of friendship, of personality, of voluntary religious involvements, of family, of hobbies and interests. The specific values of intimacy, commitment, self-disclosure, and uniqueness govern interpersonal relations. Here the wholeness of each person can express itself. People do not treat others with the sort of reserve that they exercise in the public. This is an arena where most matters are the free choice of individuals, even though at times some of these free choices (such as marriages and divorces) must gain recognition in the public arena.

Nor does the private realm require that people discipline their bodies or their presentation of themselves in the way the public does. One can be "oneself," let one's hair down, have bad breath, make embarrassing noises, see people without makeup. These things do not matter because the individual is not acting as the agent or representative of some public institution. One can say what one thinks and not parrot the line of one's public role and identity. One can use language and tell stories that would elicit shock and disapproval in the public arena.

In the public arena, political and economic institutions, as well as "objective culture," have grown in size and complexity over time. Objective culture refers to all the things that people produce, such as music, automobiles, language, tools, legal systems, philosophy, novels, movies, science, and so on. This is a notion developed in detail by the German sociologist, Georg Simmel (1858–1918).

People experience the public arena as dominated by immense bureaucracies and organizations beyond the knowledge or control of the ordinary person. These are run according to an infinite web of rules and legal decisions that bind people, policies, and products into an ongoing process. It appears futile to hope that the individual can affect these bureaucracies or organizations in any significant sense. People experience the modern world as so complex that they cannot piece together a picture of the whole or of how they relate to it. This is the problem of "invisible complexity."[8]

In other words, people begin to see the public realm as beyond their comprehension and control. The tendency is to turn inward and operate in terms of individualistic orientations. The values of utilitarian individualism encourage people to use or manipulate the public realm in order to advance their private interests. This perspective sees society as arising from a contract entered into by individuals so as to create space for the competitive, peaceful striving after desirable goods.

Too much of this sort of individualism and self-interest as the rationale for participation in the public arena eventually undermines this realm. It creates pressures to protect the public institutions from private, personal manipulation. The public arena becomes overly institutionalized, governed by more and more explicitly stated norms and contracts, administrative regulations, and legal precedents. These become such a thicket of agreements with so many people interested in maintaining affairs that rapid or even slow change becomes difficult. Public institutions no longer seem to have the flexibility necessary to humanize their processes. People feel alienated and overwhelmed by them, even though the purpose of these institutions is "to serve the public."

Nor can people reshape these institutions quickly even when studies prove that they are having disastrous consequences. For some time, this society has known the major sources of both acid rain and the chemicals that deplete the ozone layer, threatening the world with the "greenhouse effect." Yet the major actors are so highly institutionalized that changing them takes billions of dollars and decades of effort by government, business, and voluntary associations.

The growth of objective culture is another way of portraying the effects of modernization in the public arena. People experience objective culture as growing in absolute size with increasing modernization. Every decade dictionaries are updated with thousands of new words. Libraries continue to expand with forty to fifty thousand new titles published every year. And these figures represent net growth, since every culture discards elements at the same time that it adds new ones. Some words become archaic and are no longer used, while new ones come into common usage. Yet the result is an enlargement of culture because more new items come into being than there are old ones that vanish.

Objective culture also multiplies the number of its components. Those who grew up in the 1950s remember approximately five types of music: rock and roll, jazz, blues, country, and classical. Now there are more than five types of rock music alone, and new genres of music continue to appear. Fifty years ago there were no computers, much less a vitally growing industry with multiple computer specializations. Who would have even dreamed of computer music?

Objective culture appears to people to have its own life, with its parts intertwined in a powerful, self-contained world beyond their control. Their own subjective culture grows smaller and smaller in relationship to the objective. Subjective culture refers to that part of the objective culture that individuals effectively draw into their own personalities and use in their own lives. This includes a person's usable vocabulary, the books he or she reads, the music one is acquainted with. As a result of this overpowering objective culture, people commonly experience feelings of alienation, insignificance, and powerlessness.

Individuals who feel fragmented in the large-scale, impersonal public world turn to the private realm to find stable meanings and identity. However, as modernization advances, this process is less and less viable. The private world increasingly becomes under-institutionalized, with fewer traditions or fixed guidelines to help people make choices. The private world has also become pluralized. It is littered with alternative family structures, a potpourri of religious options, disintegrating traditions, and the rupture of long-term social ties due to mobility.

In a pluralized private world, moral standards are seen as valid only when they are expressions of the fervent choice of individuals. The old morality said, "Do the will of God" or "Do what is right." The new morality says, "Do your own thing" or "Be true to yourself." But there is no clear content to guide the self in doing "its own thing." This produces an intense subjectivization and individualization of the private. People are thrown back on themselves to create or find the meanings and identity they need. The modern person is, in Peter Berger's apt word, "homeless." For many, not even religion provides a home in a heartless world.

In many modern societies, religion is increasingly confined to the private world. Both nonreligious and religious persons consider religion to be an institution principally concerned with private issues. In the United States, these are issues of the family, sexual morality and other bodily disciplines (such as alcohol consumption), pornography, and personal virtues such as honesty, wholesomeness, and self-discipline. The private arena is a realm where values are chosen rather than a realm of facts or claims about truth needing adjudication through public discourse. When confined in this way, religion becomes incapable of encompassing all the meanings or conferring the identity that people need.

Furthermore, the pluralizing of religion generates a veritable cafeteria of conflicting religious choices, leaving the religious consumer wondering which is the best product in the church market. Competition from nonreligious sectors in giving order to the private realm comes from such professions as psychiatry and counseling. They too seek to help the individual find meaning and self-definition. The "cure of souls" is no longer the exclusive province of the pastor or priest.

By contrast, sociology developed as part of the objective culture placed in the public realm. Here facts and truth govern affairs, rather than private value choices. This way of defining affairs makes sociology a public, fact-based profession and religious faith a private, value-based commitment. To interrelate the two is to yoke a whale and an elephant together, a rather difficult if not absurd endeavor.

In sum, privatization pushes religion out of the public arena. It restricts it to the small corner of the modern life-world that is labeled private. It interprets it as an arena of commitments to certain values, not as a reality-oriented or factually based sort of rationality. The public and the private, facts and values, science and religion are all matters that moderns compartmentalize.

The Naked Public Square

Privatization of religion is accompanied by the stripping of the public realm of the influence and symbols of the religious. This process of *secularization* means that religious ideas and structures lose their potency to shape and sustain a common public world. Religious groups no longer control various sectors of society (such as education, government, or economic relations). These sectors of life are enacted without the use of religious symbols.

Many contemporary sociologists are convinced that secularization is accompanied by processes of resacralization or desecularization. So while prominent features of religious life and symbols may be declining, in other parts of the society new religious groups and symbols are being created. It may even be that people relocate sacredness from religious symbols and personalities to secular ones (as in the cult of Mao Ze-dong in China during the 1960s or in the "religious" attitude many have toward their national flag or favorite professional sports team).

At one time, virtually all schools in Western societies were staffed by religious orders. Cathedrals and monasteries housed schools, and the medieval university had its origins in these religiously based schools. Local bishops invested rulers with power; popes did the same for emperors. The church dictated laws against certain economic arrangements, such as charging interest on loans.

At the end of the Thirty Years' War in Europe (1616–1648), the term *secularization* referred to the transfer of real estate and other property from the church to the state. It now refers to several aspects of modernization. These include the declining percentage of people committed to a religion and the rise of secular worldviews that perceive history and nature without relationship to God, the removal of required indoctrination in religion from public schools, and the banning of Christmas crèches on public property.

Secularization sums up the obvious changes in the place and importance of religious ideas, symbols, leaders, and institutions since the Middle Ages. Religion simply is not as taken for granted, as imposing, or as plausible as it was when it was a dominant presence in the culture. The religious world is now a smaller part of a greatly expanded objective culture. In addition, there are now hundreds of Christian denominations to choose from (instead of only a few) as well as many other religious groups and cults. The components of the religious world have multiplied, making it a many-possibility reality. This pluralization contributes to certain declines in the potency of religion in everyday life.

Furthermore, though initially grounded in Christian ideas of the world as God's creation, Western science now has an autonomous and prominent place in modern objective culture. The Enlightenment of eighteenth-century Europe reoriented science as a project whose only goal was knowledge, not the worship of God through knowledge. It made it secular in its outlook. It is not difficult to point to figures and movements that consider science to be a replacement for religion.[9]

As pointed out earlier, some analysts confuse the shifting place of religion in the modern world with its pending demise. Prominent social thinkers like Auguste Comte and Karl Marx issued death certificates for religious faith. Numerous others have done the same only to be surprised that the patient refuses to die. Certainly the pulse and presence of religion have changed in the modern world, but change is not the same as disappearance.

Secularization affects the intellectual elite far more than the average person. In the 1960s, secularization theory reached a high point. Harvey Cox (a sociologically trained theologian at Harvard) authored a best-selling book, *The Secular City* (1966). It declared that moderns no longer needed the supernatural and other unmodern religious notions. Moderns were completely secular, he

said. Other theologians agreed and started a movement known as
the "death of God" theology. Contemporaries of his, living and
working at Harvard in the same period, knew that he was describing his own friends, not the average person on the streets of
Boston. The urban Bostonian was still actively religious, but this
was somehow unknown to Harvey Cox. Later Cox rediscovered
the spirituality of modern society and declared religion alive and
well.[10]

Christian Faith and Sociology in the Modern World

These pages on pluralization, privatization, and secularization
offer only a sketch of a few of the central aspects of modernization. Nonetheless, this is enough to reveal some of the central
features of the relationship between faith and sociology.

Christian intellectual concepts and ideas served as starting
points for the development of many of the modern intellectual
disciplines, including sociology. While the Enlightenment reacted
against the political and religious environment in which it developed, it articulated many ideas that have unacknowledged ties to
the Christian heritage. The idea of progress, a secularized version
of Christian visions of eschatology, is the most notable. The
Enlightenment also stimulated the creation of the social sciences
in a secular mold.

Christian faith once was a major player in public discourse
about all realms of life and history. Modernization changed that.
It pluralized the life-worlds of those who lived in its midst,
making multiple choices and possibilities a pervasive reality.
Religious pluralism marks the modern world as well. This pluralization means that religion and religious ideas are experienced
differently in the modern world than they were in the traditional
world. It also means that religious outlooks must be justified and
argued in a new intellectual marketplace where they are no longer
the major players.

In the twentieth century, the tendency to privatize religion has intensified. Moderns are prone to redefine religion as a personal value choice appropriate for the private realm but not for the public. With so many religious ideas and groups, the unity of civilization no longer comes from a shared religious tradition. The hope has been to bring about a unity through facts made persuasive for all by science, regardless of a person's private values. Sociology has its place among the family of intellectual disciplines considered factories of public facts and thus generators of civilizational unity. Sociologists normally portray their field as "value free." They claim that sociology is a public discipline and that private matters (such as values and religion) must not be mixed with it.

Secularization accompanies privatization. The dominant modern culture increasingly segregates religious symbols and perspectives from the public arena. This relocates the presence and place of religion. At times religion is a coconspirator in this secularization, giving up the public realm willingly in exchange for freedom to operate purely in the private.

Authentic Christian faith cannot be comfortable with these arrangements. Jesus is Lord of all creation, all peoples, all history, and all dimensions of human life. Part of the tension that Christians experience in the modern world is that their faith is a permanent rebel within modernity's neat polarities. Christian faith cannot accept the division between the public and the private, the secular and the sacred, science and faith, facts and values. These dichotomies may point to important distinctions and closely guarded boundaries, yet they are boundaries that Christian faith acknowledges by violating. It makes nonsense of its own identity if it does not embrace the whole world and relate the wholeness of its message to all dimensions of life. When it does, it often finds sociologists among the loudest objectors to its crossing over into "public matters of science." Why that is and what it means for Christian sociology are the topics of the next chapter.

NOTES

1. Emmanuel Le Roy Ladurie, *Montaillou: The Promised Land of Error* (New York: George Braziller, 1978).
2. Peter Berger, Brigitte Berger, and Hansfried Kellner, *The Homeless Mind: Modernization and Consciousness* (New York: Random House, 1973), p. 9.
3. Alvin Toffler, *Future Shock* (New York: Random House, 1970).
4. Peter Berger, *The Heretical Imperative* (New York: Doubleday, 1979), pp. 1–2.
5. Norbert Elias, *The Civilizing Process*, Vol. 1: *The History of Manners* (New York: Urizen Books, 1978).
6. Elias, *The Civilizing Process*, pp. 148ff on nose blowing, 156ff on spitting, 163ff on customs about the bedroom and privacy.
7. J. Anthony Walter, *A Long Way From Home* (Exeter, England: Pater Noster Press, 1979).
8. Robert Bellah et al., *Habits of the Heart* (University of California, 1985), p. 207.
9. Such as E. O. Wilson, Evan Vogt, Stephen Jay Gould. The British Society for Social Responsibility in Science explicitly seeks to replace religion with science. Many practicing scientists in the British and American Association for the Advancement of Science take this position.
10. Cox, *Religion in the Secular City* (New York: Macmillan, 1987).

Chapter 4

PUTTING SOCIOLOGY IN ITS PLACE

W igs for gentlemen, telescopes, and facts: these are three outstanding inventions of the seventeenth century. Each began a set of fateful changes that continue to produce more changes today. Each tells something about the place of sociology in the modern world. Each helps answer some of the questions this book is exploring.

Wigs became a mark of professional status. Telescopes ushered in an age of skepticism about appearances. "Facts" became the most sought-after item to settle disputes about truth. This chapter considers the rise of professions and of sociology as a profession in the modern world. The next chapter looks at sociology's affinity with the telescope's ability to shatter trust in appearances. It also explores its claim to be a profession that produces "social facts" (and nothing but "social facts").

Pinning the Wig on the Professional

Wigs are archaic, going back at least to the threatened pate of the thin-haired ancient Egyptian. They enter history as a means of protection from the Egyptian sun. The funny little white number, still worn today by British judges and barristers, got its start in the seventeenth century.

The first seventeenth-century wigs simulated real hair. These gave way to formal periwigs or perukes, with large horizontal curls above the ear and longer hair gathered in queues at the back and tied with a bow. Wigs were expensive so people never wore them as an everyday thing, the way jeans and sneakers are worn now. So popular was the style that men began wearing their own hair in a manner that imitated the peruke. The pictures of the founders of the United States show some good examples.

After the novelty wore off and wealthy aristocrats had given them up, wigs remained popular among the emerging professional class. They came to mark a gentleman of substance (only later were women allowed into professions) whose specialized knowledge should command community respect. Wigs became a status marker much like the white lab coat of the scientist, which says, "I am a professional. I know whereof I speak."

One of the major characteristics of the modern world is the way professions dominate life. There are professions that heal bodies, design homes, extend the frontiers of knowledge, manage assets, litigate untidy relationships, save souls. Yet why should occupational groups with their schools, licenses, associations, and journals control the development, acquisition, and application of specialized knowledge? Why have human beings given their bodies and souls to professionals? Dozens of professions like engineering, architecture, counseling, accounting, and sociology are new, adding their expertise to the ancient professions of medicine, ministry, and law.

Sociologists are not characters found in the ancient or medieval worlds. Auguste Comte coined the name *sociology* in the nineteenth century, long before it became a bona fide profession. The eccentric English bachelor, Herbert Spencer, more widely read and known than his contemporary Charles Darwin, popularized this new science. To understand sociology's place in the modern world requires understanding some of the problems it faced as it became a recognized profession. This in turn requires knowing a bit about how professions come into being in the first place.

King of the Mountain

Central to all professions is the claim of jurisdiction over a particular domain of life and the exercise of control within it.

Medicine is an ancient and well-recognized profession. Its jurisdiction is over issues of disease and health. But a claim of jurisdiction is just that: a claim. It often does not completely settle the issue of who has the rights and the authority to control an area of knowledge and skill. Or even how to define what that area is about.

Even within medicine there have been disputes about what good medicine is and who its best practitioners are. This past century witnessed battles royal among medical doctors, allopaths, osteopathic doctors, chiropractors, and herbalists. Now even nurses and pharmacists vie for some of the spheres that doctors have claimed for themselves. Money is at stake. So too is a moral claim for status and authority in the larger community.

The outcomes of the various battles among those who claim expertise vary from society to society. What appears natural at any given point is in fact the product of a long historical process of slow change. Behind every profession is a history of decisive struggles among different claims. Often some genius appears and shapes a profession, becoming an exemplar for practitioners. Of course, professions also inevitably adjust to the worldview and cultural matrix of a given society. Control over a given area of expertise is thus very much a matter of cultural agreements and social struggles, rather than a natural, automatic outcome of a claim to knowledge.

Lawyers claim control over legal matters, psychiatrists and psychologists over mental health, journalists over "the news," clergy over religious matters, engineers over the design of various physical utilities. Such claims are regularly contested, and the boundaries of a profession's territory shift over time. Most professions ensure control by excluding others from practicing the same task. This is done by securing legislation to get rid of those whom the professionals define as quacks, charlatans, and con artists. It is also common to create rigid entry requirements based on long courses of education and training with stiff examinations. All of this is advantageous to a profession. Restricting and controlling entry into a profession limits the number of people living off the same economic pie. It also guarantees minimum levels of professional competence (or incompetence, depending on one's experience with the members of a particular professional group).

Jurisdictional boundaries can change dramatically as rival groups challenge them. One profession can even displace another. Complementing the traditional professions of law, medicine, and ministry are a host of new professions designed to cope with the changing landscape of life in modern societies. Psychology and sociology are a pair of such professions, rooted in the chaos created by the shift to modernity.

A Tale of Two Professions

Professions arise in response to human purposes and problems. By definition, they are bodies of people with expert knowledge focused on solving distinct human problems. Modern society has its own constellation of characteristics. The dramatic expansion of professions relates to the rise of pluralization, the explosion of objective culture, and the way modern technology places a high value on efficiency. One fascinating story concerns the rise of the professions of individual life-problem counseling, now dominated by psychologists.[1] It is also a story of changes in the role that religious professionals play in society.

Careers and the Life-Problem Professions

Andrew Abbott claims that the nineteenth century had no general conception of "the problems of living." Until a person conceives of such problems, he or she cannot even think of taking them to a professional for solution. To be sure, people in the nineteenth century and earlier experienced marital conflict, disappointed dreams, poor social skills, neurotic habits, financial crises, and other similar problems. But when these things occurred, one mulled them over with friends and family or with one's physician, lawyer, or member of the clergy. Advice was given, but there was no notion that such advice was "professional counseling."

The only group with a professional construction for personal problems was the clergy. They claimed jurisdiction over specifically religious problems. Religious issues, however, were seen as interwoven with many of the other sorts of crises that afflicted their parishioners. The one large issue of salvation encompassed all other problems facing the individual. The advice given by clergy to people with problems was weighty and powerful. It concerned more than simply grief over lost companionship or trauma over a fall into poverty or legal wrangles. Rather, it concerned one's very relationship to God in the midst of the troubles of life.

Three factors intensified the awareness that personal problems were something requiring professional help. The first was the spread of the notion of career and of career success and its uncertainties. Under the impact of modernity, life became something to plan and manage. Pluralization of the life-world meant that people faced wide ranges of occupational choice. A person's life path became open to many possibilities. The task of living meant choosing wisely what one was to be and do. This engineering of one's life makes a good definition for the term *career*.

Furthermore, people have to deal with "multirelational synchronization."[2] This term refers to the process of balancing a multiplicity of relationships within several sorts of "life careers" (marrying, having children, pursuing an occupation, managing finances, enjoying leisure time, owning real estate). A sort of master life plan governs the timing and investment of self in these various components of one's life. The nuclear family, shrinking though it is, becomes a base from which to design this life plan. From within the family, people try out scenarios, replan when obstacles occur, and seek help from experts, such as travel agents, financial brokers, or job counselors.

Traditionally, people's lives followed the social scripts prescribed for the roles they had been given by birth and culture.

People now have more control in composing their biography. Professionals help those having difficulty writing their own script. Furthermore, as professions are born and become large, powerful groups, they begin to write the primary public script for career success in their own ranks.

The second factor that highlighted the need for professional help with personal problems consists of the sweeping social changes that accelerated and magnified these problems. Such changes included the rise of the modern bureaucratic organizational structure, the growth of the centralized, activist state, the increased social and geographical mobility, the appearance of millions of immigrants who became an underclass in urban areas, and the release of women from nineteenth-century restrictions, allowing them to participate in the public arena. These changes confronted people with new problems at a time when the old bonds that had held them and helped them cope were weakened. No longer were friends and family available throughout the long stretch of one's life. Traditional clerical advice was inadequate in the face of these new problems.

The third development in the rise of life-problem professions consists of the evolving changes in the practice of medicine and the organization of health care. Medicine increasingly based itself on experimentation in biological and clinical practices. More and more problems were drawn into a medical model. This model sees people's problems as rooted in the physical realm (such as in chemical imbalances, micro-organic disease agents, or degeneration of the nerves).

People registered the stress of modern life physically as well as psychologically. The medical profession developed a model of "nervousness" to cover these disturbances with their bodily symptoms. Quite naturally, physicians considered these problems to be within the jurisdiction of their profession. Neurologists (specialists in the nervous system) labeled these bodily symptoms as a "syndrome of general nervousness." They defined it as a medical problem, curable by medical techniques. People under extreme pressures had "nervous breakdowns." However, so pervasive was the problem thus defined that the few specialized neurologists could not handle the flood of troubled people.

At the same time as neurological definitions of life problems gained acceptance, psychiatrists began to be active outside the mental hospital. With more than enough nervousness to go around, psychiatrists claimed a share in handling these personal problems. "General nervousness" was, after all, a large bin into which doctors placed a variety of different emotional and somatic (physiological) life disturbances. Within a few decades, the whole definition of these matters changed to specifically defined "neuroses." In contrast with former diagnoses, neuroses were psychological rather than physical problems. Defined this way, these problems did not need the intervention of a medical doctor.

This psychological orientation now dominates the professions focused on personal problems. There remains a set of personality disturbances rooted in organic causes. Psychiatry (where medical training is required) continues to claim those as its exclusive territory. But other groups have muscled in on them. Personality adjustment does not require a knowledge of or skill in physical medicine. Psychotherapists, psychologists, and various types of counselors took up personality adjustment techniques. They have come to dominate the professions that claim life problems as their territory.

During the rise of these new professions, the clergy remained front-line professionals. They dealt with life problems most frequently and often first. Yet they were gradually shoved into a smaller province of task competence, and they eventually yielded many of their former advice areas to the new professionals. Furthermore, life problems lost most of the moral and religious meanings they had carried in the 1850s, except for those people who remained highly devout.

Clergy accepted a psychologically oriented definition of personal problems. Seminaries added courses and even doctoral programs in pastoral counseling. Training became primarily psychological rather than theological in these areas. Still, despite much professional psychological training, clergy are not given the status of insiders in the professions focused on life problems. The payments of medical insurance or Medicaid go to *health* professionals who must be psychotherapists or licensed counseling professionals, *not* to clergy. Nor are clergy liable for the misuse of expert knowledge or malpractice. Suing clergy for inept counseling does take place, but none of the suits has as yet succeeded. The courts do not consider clergy as authentic professionals in this sphere. The privilege of losing such suits is reserved for the "real" professionals.

Nonetheless, the role of the clergy in the parish changed due to competition with the life-problem professionals: much more of the cleric's time is now taken up with counseling of various sorts than was the case in the nineteenth century. The nature of that clerical counseling has also shifted. Personal problems are not as frequently taken as one strand in a larger religious and moral issue that places a person before God. Life crises may not even elicit probing to discover what God might be saying to a person or a community. Instead, they are occasions for probing the personality and its dysfunctional organization. The goal is to revise one's coping strategies in order to enhance a self-chosen career path. Life-problem solutions are technical solutions, dealt with in their own terms, often without reference to God, the spiritual world, or even moral questions.

What life-problem counseling did not deal with well was the larger societal context that generated the "syndrome of general nervousness." Its task was limited to aiding individuals in the quest for career success and personal happiness. The social context was taken for granted. Another profession was needed to deal with the "syndrome of general modernity" that provoked so many occasions for personal distress and disturbance.

If All Else Fails, Invent Sociology!

Sociology, along with economics, political science, and anthropology, first donned the mantle of a profession in the nineteenth century. It tried to make sense of the many changes that created needs for such new professions as counseling. In many ways, sociology was designed to find an antidote for the social disintegration of modern societies.

Sociology is not the beginning of careful reflection about society. All the great philosophers of both East and West have articulated thoughtful insights into the fashioning of community life. Virtually all major theories of social life are present in the ideas of the ancients.[3] One marked distinction between social theories and theories of the physical sciences is the vastly longer shelf life of social ideas. As Giambattista Vico highlighted, humans' insider knowledge of the social world is much more penetrating and direct than their outsider understanding of the physical universe. People have accurately seen some of the basic structures and dynamics of social life for a very long time and have expressed them in cogent terms.

To read Aristotle's musings on biology is to enter a thicket of confusions and virtually useless information, given the advances of modern biology. By contrast, studying his *Nichomachean Ethics* and *Politics* brings insights and explanations that still illuminate social life, even given all the advances in the social sciences. Yet it is also to survey a way of thinking about the social world that is no longer sufficient. Three factors contributed to a shift from an occasional, philosophical musing about society to a professional, scientific approach.

Newtonian Science

The first factor was the dramatic success of Newtonian science. It is difficult now to understand how spectacular Sir Isaac Newton's methods and results looked in the intellectual landscape of the seventeenth and eighteenth centuries. Newton (1642–1727) took speculation and philosophical rumination and turned it into science. Where there had been insight and sharp disagreement, he brought clarity and decisive conclusions. By the magical alchemy of an empirical, mathematical methodology, he transformed natural philosophy into natural science.

In the wake of this success, hope soared that the same could be done to *moral* philosophy (the area dealing with human action and social arrangements). The vision of a Newton-like penetration of reason into the social world fueled sociology and the other social sciences. They hoped to organize the chaos and complexity of social life by discovering a few laws. Controlling the great tidal forces of history would enable humans to build orderly, rational, prosperous, peaceful, and just societies. Thus, the birth of sociology resulted from a wedding between this hope for social progress and the techniques of science. The term *sociology* meant a natural science of society, using the approach of physics and producing the same assured conclusions. Sociology was to end age-old disputes about the best arrangements for societal organization.

Capitalism and the Bourgeoisie

The second factor contributing to the rise of sociology was the rise of a liberal, bourgeois capitalist world system. What provided clientele for professions of experts working on solving the problems of society was the new world of industrialization and modernization. Modern capitalism began its gradual emergence around 1500. The group central to its dynamism and triumph was the bourgeoisie. Originally this group consisted of artisans and merchants living in the medieval towns of France; they were a middle group between the peasants and the landlords. In alliance with the kings, they uprooted feudalism and aided in the centralization of government. Then they supported principles of constitutionality and natural rights and progressively secured political, commercial, and personal liberties against the monarch's power.

Their number greatly expanded during the industrial revolution. Over time, the bourgeois class became divided between the "high" bourgeoisie (industrialists and bankers) and the "petite" (or petty) bourgeoisie (tradespeople and white-collar workers).

Their social philosophy aimed at expanding individual freedoms. It saw capitalist-industrial forms of social order as superior to their alternatives. It prefered private property and private economic action as well as political and legal equality.

What the bourgeoisie wanted was a predictable, rational social world in which to pursue economic and commercial activities. They solved this problem in part by pressuring (and even revolutionizing) political arrangements. This meant setting up stable codes of enforceable laws for contracts. It led to bills of rights to prevent the government from arbitrary intervention in private economic affairs. It created larger territories under single political entities so that markets could grow to national and eventually international size.

The bourgeois solution also involved creating a new cadre of professional experts on society. The bourgeoisie conceived of society in a very specific way. For them, the powerhouse of change in society is its economic—especially its technological—side of productivity and distribution. Both Adam Smith and Karl Marx agree on this fundamental point. As technology evolves, it brings into being new fields of endeavor and new occupational roles. This in turn leads to the obsolescence of old economic roles and groups. New groups, organizational structures, and even social classes rise to prominence. This inevitably results in new needs among the masses, who are arranged in new occupational and class groups. New political demands and legal pressures register these changing interests and needs.

Essentially, the bourgeoisie sees society as a three-story house. First comes the foundation: the economic and technological level. Then, building on that foundation, comes the social level. The third floor, resting on the social, consists of the political. A threefold division of professional expertise results: economics, sociology, and political science. In this arrangement, no one was given responsibility for understanding the whole of modern society or for the way various societies come together in a globally interdependent world economic system.

Further, the higher up one moves in this scientific household, the "softer" the practice of science. At the foundation, disciplines dealing with technology are the most scientific, economics a bit less. Sociology, dealing with the effects of the technological and economic, is even less scientific. Its subject matter is less quantifiable and deals with phenomena that are related more to the ideas and choices of people than to objectifiable, publicly-shared "facts." Political science is the least scientific and coherent of the three, with the least ability to exclude values from its analysis.

With the big three in place, the other modern professions dealing with human social arrangements were given their appropriate roles. Anthropology has the primary task of understanding premodern societies where the economic, social, and political realms are not as distinct as they are in modern societies. (There are, however, many anthropologists who also study cities and peoples in industrial contexts.) Modern societies take from these premodern groups raw materials for industrial factories as well as cheap labor and land. Colonization and subsequent decolonization have brought profound changes in these nations, and anthropologists have been kept busy documenting many of these changes.

History's task, on the other hand, is to collect and keep records of the past straight. Psychology finds its niche in helping moderns hold their personality and families together in the midst of an ever-changing, high-pressure society.

The Centralized State

The third factor shaping the emergence of sociology was the development of the technically oriented activist state. A centralized state, seeing its task as an active promotion of the welfare of all its citizens, is a modern development. Currently, most research funds for sociology (as well as for economics and political science) come from governmental sources. These funds aim less at the applied side of fixing society (now largely the job of social workers and community organizers) than at providing basic information on "social facts" and trends. Sociology also provides explanations as to how modern societies work. Others have the responsibility to take what sociology discovers and put it to good use.

Several of sociology's early practitioners existed outside the academic world. Very rapidly, however, sociology became a profession with most of its members in universities and colleges. As a new academic specialty in a competitive context, it faced stiff resistance. Older university disciplines did not like having a new one around trying to claim limited resources. Nor did they appreciate a new voice or a new perspective where theirs, by hoary tradition, had reigned supreme.

Thus, sociology had difficulty becoming recognized in academia. In the central university system in France, the first chair with the name *sociology* in it didn't appear until 1909. In Great Britain, sociology was substantially confined to one university until the 1960s, when it suddenly caught on. Only now is sociology taught in most British colleges and universities. By far the greatest success for the sociological profession was in the United States. Yet Harvard had no department of sociology until 1930. Princeton established a separate department only in 1960. Amherst appointed its first sociology professor in 1968.

The actual role that sociologists play in helping to order society is another measure of the competitive environment. Sociologists are not "big shots"; economists and lawyers are clearly more influential at present than sociologists. There is no Presidential Council of Sociologists equivalent to the Council of Economic Advisers in the United States. The two major instruments that industrial societies use to order society are markets and states, neither of which require sociologists as chief advisors.[4]

A distinctively sociological approach to the issues and crises of modernity hardly influences people's common lives. Enormous energy and seriousness are given to protecting and strengthening markets or to elaborating and revising the legal and administrative functions of government. Missing in action is a concern for one of the distinctive subject matters of sociology: civil society (which includes such things as families, voluntary associations, churches, and cultural institutions). Markets and states that function well occur only within a context of a strong civil society. Yet civil issues are downplayed in most initiatives created to reform and restructure industrial societies. The major entrées on the menu call for the work of economists and legal and political experts. Sociological services are present only as garnishes.

The net effect of the competitive environment is a sociological inferiority complex. Sociology's status is less secure than that of the humanities or the natural sciences. In part this explains sociology's aggressive nature. It constantly has to prove itself a worthy profession in a context where other experts question its importance. This also lies behind its inclination to imitate the physical sciences and thus appear more expert through the use of arcane mathematics and language that is difficult to understand. It even motivates tendencies toward demeaning other sources of possible insight into human social arrangements, especially those that resemble the humanities. In this environment, the suggestion that the Bible might offer insights into the social order is treated as worthy of nothing more than scoffing by sociologists already battered by other competitors.

The general culture of the United States is profoundly antisociological. One of the major products of the modernization process in the West is a robust individualism. Individualism is a multifaceted phenomenon, and people use the term in sometimes contradictory ways. One side of it is the "belief in the inherent dignity and, indeed, sacredness of the human person."[5] Many legal codes and declarations of human rights in the modern world enshrine this notion. It represents an important accomplishment of modern civic life.

Another meaning of individualism is "a belief that the individual has a primary reality whereas society is a second-order, derived, or artificial construct."[6] This view of the individual sees all social processes as directly rooted in the activities and nature of individuals. To understand the problems that people experience is to see the choices they make as individuals as the source and solution for societal ills. The typical American religious mind-set strongly reinforces this view. By viewing religious commitment in a highly individualistic manner, Americans tend to see all elements of a person's fate as tied to his or her own responsible (or irresponsible) choices.

At virtually any North American high school graduation ceremony this value system is in full display. The valedictorian commonly attempts some insightful rhetoric along the lines of "Society is nothing more than the sum total of the individuals who make it up. Each of us, as individual members of this class, will determine what this great country will be in the years to come."

The mainstream of sociology challenges this second sort of individualism. The sociological spirit considers society to be as real as individuals. It suggests that society determines what individuals are every bit as much as, and sometimes more than, individuals determine the nature of society. At times, American sociology also gets itself in trouble with an opposite extreme—that of denying human freedom. This is known as the "oversocialized" view of people, taking individuals to be nothing more than the sum total of their environmental influences. In such a view, individuality actually disappears.

Fortunately, most sociologists do not get carried away with either extreme. On the whole, sociology distinguishes between individual troubles and social issues. Individual troubles are viewed as matters that result from traits specific to individuals and their personal relationships. Solutions to these troubles appropriately take place at the individual level (and personal counseling often delivers real help). Some people are unemployed, for example, because their levels of personal discipline and skill are so low that they cannot meet the demands even of low-skill jobs. Such individuals need new motivation, better skills, and stronger self-discipline.

Almost every sociologist, however, also recognizes that social issues and problems stem from the characteristic structuring of society. If an economy is stagnating in a depression, there will be hundreds of thousands of qualified, motivated individuals unable to find employment. If a social structure systematically discriminates against racial minorities, no amount of change in personal motivation and educational skills will secure desirable jobs for those minorities. If the number of families needing low-cost housing is large and the availability of such housing minuscule, there will be homelessness. It does not matter how responsible and desperate low-income families are about finding homes. These are hard notions for a culture of individualists to grasp.

Romping Uninvited in Other People's Houses

Actually, sociology is a rather wigless profession. It commands neither the prestige of the natural sciences nor the acceptance of the life-problem counseling professions. People accept the idea of counseling to deal with personal problems (and will even pay $100 an hour for someone to listen to them). Many still wonder whether sociology can offer any worthwhile "social counseling" or whether it is able to suggest ways to improve social arrangements. What makes sociologists even more unpopular is that life counselors give advice only when sought while sociologists dispense their wisdom whether invited to or not. Thus, sociologists' contributions to the storehouse of collective wisdom frequently goes unappreciated. Often critics are vociferous in saying that sociologists shouldn't be messing in other people's business.

The problem is that social appearances and reality often differ considerably. Actually, that's one reason sociologists are needed. In the movie *Mississippi Burning,* the surface calm and harmony between African-Americans and whites in Philadelphia, Mississippi, hides violence and repression. The disappearance of two civil rights workers shatters the appearance of peaceful contentment. Members of the white power structure assure outsiders that the trouble is due to outside agitators. For the blacks, the murders are a dramatic revelation of the way the social system actually works. Investigation turns up the presence and power of the Ku

Klux Klan, operating out of the sheriff's own office. The appearances fostered and supported by the white power structure shatter, but not until after there have been violent repercussions for anyone telling the real story.

Most of science engages in correcting people's surface impressions of reality. Sociology often has the uncomfortable job of revealing differences between what people want to believe is happening in society and what actually is going on. That is the story for the next chapter.

NOTES

1. Andrew Abbott, *The System of Professions: An Essay on the Division of Expert Labor* (Chicago: University of Chicago Press, 1988), Chap. 10.
2. Berger, Berger, and Kellner, *The Homeless Mind*, pp. 71–74.
3. Alvin Gouldner, in *Enter Plato* (New York: Harper & Row, 1966), puts Plato forward as the first great social theorist of the Western tradition. A similar argument can be made for Confucius in China.
4. Alan Wolfe, *Whose Keeper? Social Science and Moral Obligation* (Berkeley: University of California Press, 1989).
5. Bellah et al., *Habits of the Heart*, p. 334.
6. Bellah et al., *Habits of the Heart*, p. 334.

Chapter 5

HALLUCINATIONS OF
DIRECT ENCOUNTERS

"**S**ince a babe was born in a manger, it may be doubted whether so great a thing has happened with so little stir."[1] This is the way Alfred North Whitehead introduces Galileo. What profound changes began with the silent wonder of the astronomer gazing heavenward and the stunned silence of a public still convinced that the sun revolved around the earth.

The first practical telescopes appeared at the beginning of the seventeenth century. When the world absorbed Galileo's findings, the shock was immense. The sun did not revolve around the earth.

Not only did the Church eventually have to admit that it had wed itself to bad science and bad interpretations of the Bible but the whole Western mind reeled. How was it possible that so many for so long had been so misled by the most certain and positive testimony of the senses? If Galileo was right (and he was), then reason and human senses were capable of monumental deceptions. How could seemingly direct encounters with the real world turn out to be no more reliable than hallucinations?

Telescopes and Shock Therapy for Common Sense

The philosopher Hannah Arendt states that one significant result of the invention of the telescope was the rise of the "school of suspicion."[2] The telescope provided incontrovertible proof that appearances and reality can be two very different things.

René Descartes (1596–1650), the French philosopher, spelled out the implications of this with his famous method of radical doubt. To gain reliable knowledge, according to Descartes, one must doubt all that can possibly be doubted until he or she finds something that cannot be questioned, something indubitable. Descartes's own indubitable was the famous *Cogito ergo sum* ("I think, therefore I am"). The act of doubting, he reasoned, requires a doubter. Therefore, one cannot deny or doubt the existence of the doubter without falling into contradiction. Starting from the indubitable foundation of the existence of the thinker, Descartes attempted to develop a philosophy of clear and certain postulates.

His philosophy led to a dualism that marked modern thought: there are some things absolutely certain because they are true by definition (these are tautologies). There are other things only probably true because they are known by means of untrustworthy sensory experience. Sensory experiences may not be what they appear to be. The telescope taught humans to doubt the information coming from their senses, although not entirely—not for what are called facts.

The German philosopher, Immanuel Kant (1724–1804), refined Descartes's scheme. He said that ultimate reality is unknowable. One can only know things as they appear to be. What they actually are in themselves is beyond the reasoning capacity of human beings. Among unknowable things are notions of purpose and what the philosophers call "final causes."[3] Human knowledge encompasses only what human senses perceive and human concepts give order to. So what is knowable about nature, human nature, and the nature of social reality includes only "efficient causes" (the directly observable relations of causation). Ideas about their ultimate purpose or final causes are mere opinions. Science cannot say anything about them. People can know *how* things work, but they cannot know *why* things exist.

Sociology came into being when the natural sciences had achieved spectacular results by following this set of ground rules for reasoning. Systematic skepticism meant challenging all accepted ideas about the particular subject matter dealt with by a science. Explaining nature scientifically required the elimination of any statements of its purpose. Nature was no longer seen as a good creation of God or as the theater where the drama of salvation was enacted. Nature was part of a world conceived as a deterministic web of forces that were governed by laws—but without anyone or anything creating those laws. Experimentation enabled scientists to test alternative models of the laws of nature. Mathematics provided a precise, abstract language in which to represent the relationships discovered. Research excluded the particular opinions and values of the scientist, who attended directly to the way things appeared within the scientific gaze.

Nineteenth-century sociology modeled itself on the practices and principles of the natural sciences. Over the years, it has increasingly adopted quantitative methods. It now designs its data collection in quasi-experimental forms and seeks universal, abstract laws of social life. A "value-free" ideal governs its research. It insists on settling its disputes based on the weight of unbiased, objective facts. This has not always led to good science or good sociology. There is no doubt, however, that it has expanded human knowledge and understanding of social arrangements. Unfortunately, social realities do not permit the sort of experimentation that some physical phenomena do. Of course, not all physical sciences use experimentation either. The course of the stars and plate tectonics, to cite two examples, are no more subject to controlled experimentation than are the economic relations of nations. Yet this limitation does not prevent good science, as much of astronomy and geology prove.

However, there is one crucial difference between sociology and the physical sciences. Sociology cannot keep notions of purpose out of the process of understanding human beings and their social arrangements. Genuine understanding requires some notion of the purposes guiding people as they create institutions. This includes the purposes that people assign to their own lives. These purposes shape the reasons by which people act and the vision they have for institutions. People hold strong ideas about why and what they are doing as they act in their social world. Yet appearances and reality are not always the same. People deceive others. They even deceive themselves. They may not willingly or honestly share with an investigator their true reasons for engaging in certain patterns of behavior. Their purposes in doing things may be concealed even from themselves. There may well be forces acting in social settings that are beyond the comprehension of the actors involved. Once investigators say what they think is going on, the actors may change their behavior, change their story, or even suggest that the investigator is deceived. Fortunately for physicists, atoms cannot evaluate the scientists who are trying to determine what goes on inside atoms. Unfortunately for sociologists, their subjects can glare back and say exactly what they think of sociologists and their ideas.

Sociologists tend to be skeptical of what people think is going on in their social worlds. Social common sense frequently is scientific nonsense. Social groups create myths, illusions, and ideologies that mislead. The grammars of social cooperation mask processes of actual conflict and coercion. In such cases, the misleading is deliberate, enabling people to work together without having to confront the actualities of oppression, deception, and injustice. When sociologists disagree with appearances as socially defined by groups, they become unpopular (as unpopular as Galileo was when he disagreed with the bad science of his day).

Science is inherently debunking because of its skeptical attitude. This creates ongoing debates with various publics as discoveries conflict with long-held truths. Ideas that debunk social illusions are an acute problem for sociology. The people who live within the processes and relationships that sociology characterizes and explains know parts of their reality more completely and acutely than the social scientist. They also are more misled about aspects of it than the social researcher. Sociology deals with affairs that are close to the everyday experiences of people. For that reason, sociology generates intense and protracted debates. It is one thing to claim that, contrary to appearances, the world is not flat. It is another to claim that there is evidence that churches teach wives to be subservient to husbands because of the economic advantages gained by men. People are more likely to understand and be upset by social findings and their interpretation than by the highly technical, mathematically obscure findings of physics.

Prestige and authority also enter into the picture. Science as such is the most highly valued sort of knowledge in the modern world. In the popular mind, physical science is more authentically scientific than the life or social sciences. Consequently, laypersons and physical scientists are less hesitant to challenge social scientific findings than to challenge the findings of the physical sciences.

Some consider the social sciences to be ideological in ways not true of the natural sciences. Yet this perception is most certainly wrong. Just look at the ways natural science and Christian notions of what the Bible entails in its teaching have interacted ideologically. Celestial mechanics was ideological in the time of Galileo and Copernicus, as geology was in Lyell's day. These sciences have all come to seem less ideological as opponents of their findings have changed their interpretations of what the biblical accounts entail. Christians changed their interpretations because the grounds for the claims of Galileo and Lyell were persuasive within the proper competence and limitations of science. Christian convictions include the notion that God made this world and that it all belongs to him. Whatever is scientifically substantiated, whatever is a warranted conclusion about the state of affairs of this world authentically merits the concurrence of Christians. Such science tells Christians more than they previously knew about the sort of world God made and still upholds by his power.

On the other hand, arguments between Christian faith and science do occur. There are several possible options for settling them. Sometimes Christians mistake the appearances of biblical texts that are theological in force and phenomenological in form as scientific statements.[4] Christians now uniformly agree that this is the case with Psalm 19:5–7 as to the motion of the earth: "The sun comes like a bridegroom out of his chamber." Christians no longer suppose that this phrase was ever meant to offer a scientific account of the revolution of the sun about the earth.

Sometimes, however, conflict arises over the larger network of beliefs that properly undergird science itself. Some wed science to a worldview and a tradition of rationality that exclude God in principle or that deny the authority of Scripture as the inspired Word of God. In this case, the issue is a much larger one concerning which worldview and tradition are most compatible with science. Thoughtful Christians (for good historical reasons) continue to claim that Christianity is the most fruitful and adequate worldview for nourishing authentic and creative scientific work.

There are scientists who use science beyond its area of competence, setting it up as an ideology in opposition to authentic Christian faith. There are Christians who use biblical truth beyond its competence, setting it up as an ideology against good science.[5] Some preeminent scientists have said that science has replaced their religious faith. Edward O. Wilson, the famous entomologist and sociobiologist, went through the ritual of accepting Christ while his Baptist congregation in Pensacola, Florida, sang "Softly and Tenderly Jesus Is Calling." Two years later, enraptured by the elegance and scope of the theory of natural selection, he gave up Christian faith. For him, evolution was a competing, not a complementary, theory to that described in Genesis.[6] In effect, he was converted from Christianity to secular science. Wilson continues to treat science as excluding faith.

So long as one interprets Genesis as teaching a creation of six twenty-four-hour days no more than ten thousand or several tens of thousands of years ago, then scientific theories will appear contradictory to faith, and scientific information may well produce conversions *from* Christian faith rather than greater praise of the Creator *within* Christian faith. So long as one takes science to require a purely naturalistic, secular worldview, so long will religious truth appear contradictory to science. We are not trying here to settle what is good science or good biblical interpretation in geology and biology. There are serious problems on both sides of the current debate.[7] We are illustrating how science and faith can appear to be mutually exclusive alternatives.

Sociology exemplifies the scientific tradition of skepticism about appearances, and for that reason it is a contested and contestable discipline. It participates in a modern world where doubt is more respectable than dogma and where open-mindedness means questioning all beliefs. As a profession, sociology considers uncovering social facts one of its major tasks. As a science, it must state the facts and nothing but the facts. Yet the contemporary notion of facts is itself a creation of the modern world.[8]

Please Pass the Facts

Pluralization is a marked feature of modern life. Descriptively, it is one of the factual characteristics of the modern social world. Normatively, an ideology of pluralism supports pluralization. Acknowledging the immensely increased diversity created by pluralization, pluralism celebrates that diversity as something that should be approved and cherished. Society should be open to all sorts of people, cultures, races, religions, values, and ideas. Tolerance becomes a paramount virtue in a pluralistic society. This does not mean that there is total openness. Intolerance and dogma are not tolerated.

Of course, there is something intrinsically Christian in celebrating certain sorts of plurality. Cultural tolerance is a part of the Church's identity as a community that is intentionally universal. The Church is a multicultural reality. It opens its arms to all peoples without erasing or diminishing cultural distinctions. This is part of Christ's commission to make disciples of all nations.

It is a different matter when pluralism also means religious pluralism. This is the idea that all religions are equivalently true or false or that all lead their adherents to the same God. Equally objectionable is moral pluralism. This refers to the claim that there are only changing ideas of right and wrong, no truly objective moral standards. All must decide what is right for them, and whatever they decide is what is right—for them.

The ideology of pluralism, however, normally does not make distinctions among cultural, religious, and moral diversity. It considers religious and many moral matters to be matters of personal choice and commitment and thus properly private and pluralistic. This is one of the reasons modern secularists are so vociferous in their objections to pro-life people who are attempting to secure public legislation about abortion. For them, such legislation would affect a religious and personal choice that is properly private. To legislate against abortion is to confuse the public and the private.

Pluralism does have one acknowledged limit, however. The notion of facts is a very widespread one. Most of this society's education, science, and jurisprudence base themselves on it. Those who celebrate open-mindedness and tolerance as virtues of pluralism do not mean to extend this attitude to facts. As Lesslie Newbigin says:

A teacher who asks [a] class whether Paris is the capital of France or of Belgium will not appreciate the child who tells him that he has an open mind on the matter. The principle of pluralism is not universally accepted in our culture. It is one of the key features of our culture . . . that we make a sharp distinction between a world of what we call "values" and a world of what we call "facts." In the former world we are pluralists; values are a matter of personal choice. In the latter we are not; facts are facts, whether you like them or not.[9]

Sociology itself is after facts. That is one of the reasons its central journals and graduate training programs put such stress on high standards of evidence, rigorous methodology, and quantitative tools for analysis. After all, since social appearance and social reality can diverge, then determining what the facts are is not a direct or simple matter. Sociology as a profession buttresses its claim to expert authority with various rituals of objectivity. Many of them are sensible and essential and have led to dramatic improvements in the way people understand the world. Others seem far more related to intimidating nonprofessionals and securing status within the profession itself. Specialization and increasing doses of quantification do not necessarily lead to significant or useful information about human beings or social institutions. Sometimes it seems as though massive amounts of research are carried out only to prove things that seem trivial.

The sins of sociology, however, are not solely sociological sins. They are sins of modern academia and should not draw attention away from the real virtues of sociology. There is elegant and excellent sociology. It has given humans the incomparable gift of much greater understanding of their social worlds. That sociology has not delivered a world of peace, prosperity, and progress as the nineteenth century hoped it would should not overshadow what it has actually accomplished.

Sociology offers an enormous cornucopia of facts. Anyone reading a massive introductory text knows that. Some findings are more surprising than others (although one generation's surprises become the next generation's common sense). In the modern world, sociology lines itself up on the fact side of things. Just what does this mean?

Whatever Happened to Good Old Facts?

The seventeenth century invented the modern notion of facts. The idea went something like this: "Facts" are brute actualities littering the landscape of reality. Human minds are blank slates onto which experience writes these facts. What appears in the mind are the traces of these infinitely multiple encounters with the facts of reality.

Not all of these fact encounters are wide-awake, carefully attended experiences. Nor do facts make themselves apparent in a direct fashion. Some appear in ways that can introduce very misleading ideas into human minds (for example, the stick thrust into the water appears to bend; the sound of a train's whistle appears to change in pitch as it approaches and then rushes past). Mistakes and errors creep in. Still, language, concepts, and ideas are all composite products of experience.

Science is a highly disciplined method for focusing the mind on facts. Science allows facts to speak their truth into humans' dim awareness, and it corrects for the differences between appearance and reality. It provides a neutral way of mediating conflicting understandings of the facts by establishing an objective method that settles decisively what the facts are.

In its most powerful form, this notion led to the nineteenth and early twentieth century's positivist theory of science. Positivism is a sophisticated philosophy and ideology of science. It denies the validity of any nonempirical elements in knowledge. Thus, sensory experience, mathematical logic, and observation are the only avenues to true knowledge, ideas, and concepts. All metaphysics (questions about what is ultimate in reality) are to be thrown on the garbage heap of history as unscientific. They are another sort of "knowledge" similar to poetry or art, and have nothing to do with science.

In positivist models, all forms of science are to follow a single method that is modeled on a natural science grounded in empiricism. Human knowledge is singular. There are not several types of knowledge (scientific, existential, religious, moral). Only that which is verified by the strict canons of an objective, empirical science is knowledge. All else is mere opinion. There is but one path to knowledge and one sort of knowledge: science. "Facts" and "values" in this account are two radically different sorts of realities. Empirical knowledge of things as they are is logically separate from moral knowledge. Moral knowledge comes from evaluating things by what they ought to be. "Facts" are about actual states of the real world; "values" are about how people feel or ought to feel about the real world.

It is not difficult to see positivist themes as strongly congruent with the ideology of pluralism and the modern boundaries between facts and values, the public and the private, and science and religion. Unfortunately for positivist theories of science, this clear distinction between facts and values is misleading and false in actual scientific practice. Science today is in a postpositivist period with a new watchword: "No observations without presuppositions."[10] What this means is that no responsible scientist now conceives of the mind as a purely passive recipient of brute empirical experience. Empirical experience does not result in mental ideas that mirror the structure of the external world in a purely objective and direct fashion.

Scientific knowledge, along with all other kinds of knowledge, is dependent on certain nonscientific, metaphysical presuppositions. Some of the presuppositions in all systems of knowledge are values. Science itself operates according to a set of empirically unverifiable norms and values. The primary goal of all science is the extension of certified knowledge.[11] This endeavor is supported by two sorts of values. Science places technical or cognitive value on empirical adequacy (for some sciences, this means the ability to predict phenomena) and logical consistency. It places moral or social value on universalism (the impersonal evaluation of research and evidence), communalism (the free flow of information), disinterestedness (the curbing of personal bias in research), and organized skepticism (the suspension of judgment on a matter until the evidence is conclusive).

The cognitive values and norms specify how to study the subject matter. The social norms structure the relationships between fellow scientists and the public. A scientific profession extends collegial recognition when a work meets these values and norms. When a work also displays originality while contributing to an extension of the knowledge of the science, it is recognized as good science.

The practicing scientist knows what many laypersons do not. Good science is a practice that follows a set of values. In addition, good science is not a blind expedition into the world looking for a new load of brute facts. Good science happens on the basis of prior ideas about the world and an intention to put that set of ideas to the test. *Theory* is the name for that prior set of ideas. A theory is an interconnected web of propositions and presuppositions about given states of affairs in the world. A theory offers to explain those states of affairs. Some theories are simple and elegant and explain many things. Einstein's $E = mc^2$ is among the most famous theories. Others are more complex. Robert Michels's "iron law of oligarchy" is a good example.[12]

Michels's theory claims that an elite minority controls power no matter how democratic the ideology of a group might be. Beyond this simple claim, the theory contains a series of other propositions. These offer details that support and explain the basic claim. They include propositions about the tendency of groups to split between their mass base and the small group that dominates. Other statements describe the social psychology underlying the veneration of leaders as well as the efficiency and benefits of having few decision makers for meeting challenges that threaten group survival. Another proposition deals with certain individuals' lust for power and privilege, which motivates the monopoly of instruments of domination, and so on.

The political sociologist no less than the physicist undertakes observations of the "real world" within a tradition of theories and concepts. Traditions focus attention, structure the questions asked and answered, suggest what sorts of evidence might be important or even crucial. What turn up as "facts" are the products not only of what is there to be seen and heard in the "real world." "Facts" are noticed and interpreted because of what the tradition of a given science suggests is there to be seen and heard. "Facts" are always combinations of experiences of the real world and the interpretative schemes brought to those experiences. "Facts" are given the status of facts only within a given theory tradition (also called a *paradigm*).

This is a highly simplified explanation of why the seventeenth-century definition of facts and the scientific tradition based on them are no longer valid. Philosophers are still at each other's throats about the logical details of how science actually arrives at knowledge. There are a number of philosophical accounts as to what a "fact" is and how it differs from a "value."

Sociologists cannot pretend to solve the philosophical issues involved here. But sociology has a unique contribution in making sense of how science happens. Sociologists examine the actual activities and practices of people to see if what they say they do is what they actually do. Sociologists of science study scientists to see empirically how scientists use facts and values. A number of such studies show the variety of ways in which science involves far more than simply gathering facts.

Karin Knorr-Cetina, for example, studied a microbiology lab. Her results offer scientific evidence for the way in which physical science is a social construction.[13] Something is a social construction when its existence is the result of the activity of a social group. Some things are pure social constructions in that every facet of them can be traced back to the creative activity of a group (the French language is an example). Other social constructions are a reshaping and refining of a naturally occurring reality—for example, the purified chemicals used by a biology lab. The research materials used by the microbiologists are not substances that someone can simply find in nature. Rather they are "socially constructed." The source materials are artificially grown and selectively bred by a group of people under controlled conditions. The substances used are highly purified products purchased from a few industrial companies. Without other social groups creating and selling these substances and organisms, they would not exist.

The questions posed to those materials are also socially constructed. They are developed through consultations among the various researchers. This involves deciding what is already known and what is theoretically interesting in microbiology. The questions that get asked are the result of a social process of debate and negotiation.

The physical set-up of the experiments is the result of a social tradition of available techniques, earlier investigations, and what are taken to be their outcomes. The jumble of information that pours out of the readings from the lab instruments in the experiment is often ambiguous. Lengthy arguments about what has actually been seen occur among the investigators.

The elegant paper summarizing the research in a scientific journal gives the appearance of a process that was unproblematic. The findings look like unambiguous experimental results developed by objective observers. What the smooth rhetoric masks is the empirically demonstrable process of social agreements that mask the complexity of the actual experiment. Nothing is said about false starts, failed experimental attempts, ambiguous data interpreted in only one of several possible ways, and so on. The sociology of science confirms the notion that there are no "brute facts" but only what scientists, given a scientific tradition, take to be facts.

This social and cultural foundation of science does not prevent it from creating precise and powerful sorts of knowledge. Scientific activity is a tremendous aid to the fallible common sense of human beings. Science becomes dubious when it pretends to be infallible, rather than simply a less fallible knowledge than common sense. Science has not fulfilled the seventeenth-century drive for facts and nothing but the facts. That does not denigrate its value or importance. No knowledge available to humans fits such a model of facts. Knowing that science is a social construction enables humans to be less messianic in their hopes about what factual knowledge actually is and can do. It also means they can challenge the hard-and-fast division of the world into facts and values or into science and religion. These things are not identical matters, but neither is there an unbridgeable gulf between them.

Another benefit of the sociology of science is humility. Virtually all introductory texts and elementary works in sociology and other sciences hide the amount of controversy and uncertainty that exists in these fields. It is much easier to recruit a new generation of scientists from college students when they feel they are embarking on a journey that quickly arrives at fully certified truth grounded in incontrovertible facts. The myth of seventeenth-century factuality is a common way of dressing up twentieth-century findings in introductory texts. A little knowledge in the sociology of science goes a long way toward recognizing this shell game.

Fortunately for the practicing sociologist, the philosophical issues underlying the nature of facts and values or science and religion need not be tidy before getting on with social research. But they are very important matters when one seeks to build a bridge from Christian faith to social science and back. Then the footings for careful thought need to be strong in both faith and science. A philosophy of social science and clear-headedness on the nature and function of worldviews are crucial.

Facts and Civilizational Unity

Facts remain an important commodity, even as a scaled-down, provisional, theory-connected account of the state of affairs of the world. People cannot live or think without facts. Yet it must always remain clear what facts are and what they are not. They are mental maps of the world and of history. They are socially constructed accounts of real events and actual states of affairs. They are not isolated, brute actualities, unconnected to values or worldviews. They are used to explain what people believe, but they are always socially arranged accounts of the real world, and they serve social interests. Atheists can arrange them to make it appear that there is no God. Christians can arrange facts so it appears (to them) that there is a God.

The next chapter maps some ways in which sociology and its social facts involve and use values and worldviews. The reader must not misunderstand what is being said here. None of this discussion pretends that sociologists or Christians can do without facts. Facts simply cannot do all the tricks that the seventeenth century tried to train them to do.

Facts, however, cannot be banished from Christian sociological thought. That is a cheap response to a very real state of affairs in sociology. Many sociologists practice sociology as a secularized discipline that excludes religious facts and assumptions. They do so on the supposed basis of the facts of sociology. Sociologists who suppose that any person with rudimentary intelligence and two or three sociology courses should abandon faith are victims of the ideology of pluralism and probably positivism. The authentic dispute that these sociologists have with Christian faith is not genuinely over facts or facts versus values, with sociology firmly in the fact corner. Rather, it is over what worldview or symbolic universe provides the rationality tradition within which one can make sense of the full range of human social experience.

There are, of course, disputes over facts as well. Some contest the facts of the history of God's activity in creating the nation of ancient Israel, or the facts surrounding the incarnation and life of Jesus Christ. These are authentic disputes that must be settled by carefully marshaling the evidence as to the authenticity and reliability of the witnesses who reported these events in the texts of Scripture. But much of the debate is not genuinely at this level. Rather, those who dispute Christian faith come with a prior conviction that certain kinds of "facts" cannot be facts at all. If they appear in the eye-witness reports, the eye witnesses are pre-judged wrong by definition. These people are actually engaged in a dispute about the nature of reality and the sort of universe they live in.

Such a dispute is actually over the appropriate relationship between religious and scientific knowledge. However, the tension between Christian faith and sociology has an unusual sharpness to it. If sociology is of any use, it ought to help understand that tension. Thus, one needs to look with sociological eyes if one wishes to explain the concentration of indifference and hostility to religion in the social sciences. The next chapter does just that. Such understanding will help show how a positive and constructive relationship between Christian faith and sociology is possible.

78 / CONFRONTATION BETWEEN FAITH AND SOCIOLOGY

NOTES

1. Alfred North Whitehead, *Science and the Modern Mind* (Baltimore, MD: Pelican, 1926), p. 12.
2. Arendt, *The Human Condition* (Chicago: University of Chicago Press, 1958), pp. 260–263.
3. "Final causes" explain something by looking at the goal or end for which a thing exists or was brought into being. Aristotle distinguished four "causes," and their relationship can be seen in this example: Michelangelo (the "efficient" cause) sculpted his *David* by making changes in marble (the "material" cause); these changes created marble formed so as to show the characteristics of a strong young man (the "formal" cause) in order to produce an object of beauty (the "final" cause).
4. John Calvin, in his *Commentaries on the First Book of Moses, Called Genesis* (Grand Rapids, MI: Baker Book House, 1984), Vol. 1, p. 86, put it simply: The spirit of God in Scripture seeks to enlighten all humans, learned and unlearned. The Bible's subjects are matters intelligible to all. So Moses "wrote in a popular style things which . . . all ordinary persons . . . are able to understand."
5. Howard J. Van Till, Davis A. Young, and Clarence Menninga, *Science Held Hostage: What's Wrong with Creation Science and Evolutionism* (Downers Grove, IL: InterVarsity Press, 1988).
6. Robert Wright, *Three Scientists and Their Gods: Looking for Meaning in an Age of Information* (New York: Harper & Row, 1988), p. 123.
7. Phillip E. Johnson, *Darwin on Trial* (Downers Grove, IL: InterVarsity Press, 1991).
8. Alasdair MacIntyre, in *Whose Justice, Which Rationality?* (Notre Dame, IN: University of Notre Dame Press, 1988), pp. 357–358, says "fact" in English renders the Latin *factum*, a deed, action, or event. Such a notion was, of course, around prior to the seventeenth century. What is new is the notion of "fact" as a realm "independent of judgment or of any other form of linguistic expression so that judgments or statements or sentences could be paired off with facts, truth or falsity being the alleged relationship between such paired items."
9. Newbigin, *The Gospel in a Pluralist Society* (Grand Rapids, MI: Eerdmans, 1989), p. 7.
10. W. G. Runcimann, *A Treatise on Social Theory*, Vol. 1: *The Methodology of Social Theory* (New York: Cambridge University Press, 1983), p. 56.
11. Robert K. Merton, *The Sociology of Science* (Chicago: University of Chicago Press, 1973), Chap. 13.
12. Robert Michels, *Political Parties: A Sociological Study of the Oligarchical Tendencies of Modern Democracy* (New York: Collier-Macmillan, 1962).
13. Karin Knorr-Cetina, *The Manufacture of Knowledge: An Essay on the Constructivist and Contextual Nature of Science* (New York: Pergamon Press, 1981). See also Bruno Latour and Steve Woolgar, *Laboratory Life: The Social Construction of Scientific Facts* (Beverly Hills, CA: Sage, 1979).

Chapter 6

GUERRILLA WARFARE
AT THE BOUNDARIES

If dogs and cats were trying to speak the same language, then they would be famous for miscommunicating. Dogs signal friendliness by wagging their tails. Cats signal nervousness by switching their tails. Dogs signal hostility and readiness for attack by a low noise in their throats. Cats show their friendliness and relaxation by a low noise in their throats. Growling and purring mean very different things in the communication pools of different species.

Humans are like cats and dogs. They live in different symbolic and communication pools. Gestures of friendliness or honor in one group of people may be gestures of hostility and shame in another. This is part of the meaning of cultural differences. However, humans are also not like cats and dogs. The differences between human communication pools are not in the genes. Cultural differences are learned differences. Humans can participate authentically and fully in more than one communication pool by learning the meanings and behavior of a second or third culture. People can even become bicultural to such a degree that they can help establish new patterns within different cultures.

In some ways, the tensions between Christian faith and secular sociology are tensions between two different communication pools. The meanings and evaluations each gives for the "same things" can be quite divergent. Christian faith makes the supernatural activity of God central to its identity. It believes that there is one unique human, the incarnate Son of God, whose life and ministry, death and resurrection provide the pattern of meaning for human existence. His teachings, culturally contextualized for first-century Palestine, are nonetheless transculturally valid, a message for all peoples and all times.

In Christ's life, Christians find the Archimedean point, the yardstick that measures all other yardsticks. In him, the eternal became temporal, the infinite finite, the absolute relative. Yet that relative, finite, temporal appearance displayed to the world the eternal, infinite, and absolute reality. These are positives within Christian faith. They speak about the empirical but also go beyond the merely empirical or purely scientific. They speak of metaphysical matters without denigrating or denying the empirical or the scientific.

Secular sociology reverses many of these valuations. Within its communication pool, the supernatural as such is not a legitimate subject matter. Sociologically speaking, the absolute is an impossible notion. All that people can know is the infinite play of finite, humanly constructed worlds of meanings and civilizations. Metaphysics may be fine for philosophy and theology but not for sociology. Sociology speaks of the empirically describable, of the socially observable and the scientifically validated. It studies what is intersubjective (shared by several subjects) in a public, secular fashion.

Where Christianity says that the world has meaning and purpose with its history heading for a God-given goal, sociology will not specify any meaning to the world and history. Some secular sociology even goes beyond science and sees the large sweep of life and history as occurring by chance—that is, it is purposeless, directionless. To the secularist, the world is absurd. In this view, sociology studies how humans have created meanings out of meaninglessness, purposes out of nothing, and direction out of drift. These claims are clearly more than scientific. They are philosophical or theological statements about the world.

Such differences show up in the way the two communication

pools speak about Jesus. Sociology is quite willing to assert the actuality of a Jesus movement in the first century. Historical and textual evidence indicates a movement led largely by itinerant artisans and journeymen and located in the towns and villages of the eastern provinces of the Roman Empire. Its dynamic fed on the decay of the old parochial religions and the widespread receptivity to universal ethical monotheism. What sociology is unwilling to assert is that the dynamic of this movement springs from the power of the Holy Spirit. Nor will sociology say that its object of worship, Jesus of Nazareth, is the incarnate and now resurrected and exalted Son of God. This would go beyond what is permissible, given its normal assumptions.

This chapter seeks to understand more about communication pools. It looks at why sociology has difficulty acknowledging some of its Christian roots and relating to contemporary Christian faith. To do this, the chapter begins by exploring the nature of what sociologists call symbolic universes and plausibility structures. Then it turns to questions about the border hostilities that sometimes flare up between sociology and faith.

Naked Ape or Mortal Angel

The most important element in any communication pool is language, even though there are other ways, such as kinesics, by which people communicate meanings. Kinesics is a system of gestures, postures, and facial expressions. The words, "What a lovely dress," can say one thing while the sly wink that accompanies them hints at a different meaning. Scratching the head or knotting the brow suggests doubt or puzzlement. A smile may signify friendly communication.

People also convey meaning through tone of voice, changes in pitch, and forcefulness or loudness of speaking. Vocalizations are another means of communication: laughing, wailing, the scream of pain, the use of sounds to demand certain behaviors. "Shhhh" is a way to quiet things down. Clicking the tongue indicates a judgment about misbehavior. Humans have developed extraordinarily elaborate systems of signs and symbols so as to communicate with each other. These include color schemes, clothing styles, lighting patterns, genres of verbal and written materials, social rituals, music, and so on.

Distinctive linguistic capabilities have traditionally served as the moat surrounding the human spirit, separating it from lesser animals. In Genesis 2, Adam named various animals, signifying the domination of humans over them. A common language facilitated the cooperative attempt to storm heaven at Babel (Genesis 11:1–9). John's Gospel begins, "In the beginning was the Word, and the Word was with God, and the Word was God." Anthropologists and sociologists traditionally see the quality and nature of human linguistic abilities as the clearest boundary between human beings and the animal kingdom. Some say this distinctive linguistic ability is what defines human beings.

Yet having language in the full human sense is not an either-or situation. It is more like having a large, versatile tool kit of the most intricate sort. In it are tools that are also used in lesser zoological quarters. Only recently have studies begun to unlock the "languages" of animals: the fancy waggle dance of bees indicating the source and distance of nectar, the distinctive songs and body language of birds, the various croaks and harrumps of bull frogs, the chemical messages ants send to one another. Animal communication turns out to be more complex and of a higher level than was thought only thirty years ago.

It is also apparent that animals learn parts of both their language and behavior. Without hearing elder white-crowned sparrows, offspring grow up to sing rotten mating calls. The long-billed oystercatchers of the Atlantic and Pacific open their feast in one of two ways. Either they bang the shell until it breaks or slip in their bill to snip the muscle that locks the shell shut. Any oystercatcher is capable of both techniques but none uses both. It is one or the other, learned from parents. Some animals can learn to use human language. Recent studies place several primates on the same level as small children in their human language learning and use.[1]

The gorilla Koko, for example, knows about four hundred words. She does not vocalize them, for none of the nonhuman primates have the throat equipment essential for such complex oral communication. Those gorillas who do use human language—along with several other primate cousins, notably chimpanzees—speak by using variations of American Sign Language (ASL), which is used by the deaf. Koko signs up to 180 words in an hour. Not only do these primates use ASL signs with accuracy but they can also create new strings of words to communicate ideas not taught them by humans.

On first seeing a duck, Washoe (the most famous "talking" chimp) coined the name "water bird." Brazil nuts were "rock berry." Koko's new word for the zebra was "white tiger" and for a Pinocchio doll, "elephant baby." On seeing an orange for the first time, Lana, knowing symbols for apple and the color orange, put together the request, "Tim give apple that is orange." Lucy was given a radish for food. For three days she simply designated it "food." Then, spontaneously, she created a new name for it as "cry hurt food."

The long-term study with Koko suggests an ability to remember and talk about past events and feelings. She even has a capacity to lie and show a playful cantankerousness. Francine Patterson and Ronald Cohn write:

One day my associate Barbara Hiller saw Koko signing, "That red," as she built a nest out of a white towel. Barbara said, "You know better, Koko. What color is it?" Koko insisted that it was red—"red, Red, RED"—and finally held up a minute speck of red lint that had been clinging to the towel. Koko was grinning.

Another time, after persistent efforts on Barbara's part to get Koko to sign "Drink," our mischievous charge finally leaned back on the counter and executed a perfect drink sign—in her ear. Again she was grinning. Sometimes Koko will respond negatively, but without a grin—leading me to believe her intent is not to joke but to be disobedient.

She seems to relish the effects of her practical jokes, often responding exactly opposite to what I ask her to do. One day, during a videotaping session, I asked Koko to place a toy animal under a bag, and she responded by taking the toy and stretching to hold it up to the ceiling.[2]

The surprise that primates are closer in their communication skills to humans than was imagined thirty years ago should not overshadow the limits of their language tool kit. Even with extensive training, their language use is rudimentary. Herbert Terrace of Columbia University concludes that learning among these primates has advanced nearly to its highest levels. Their short utterances never race on to produce sentences and paragraphs as they do in the three-and-a-half-year-old human. Primates do not expand on what their human companions say, as do human children. Nor do they develop the genuine ability to take turns, essential for sustained conversations. Even the most sophisticated training program does not take the nonhuman primates beyond the linguistic performance levels of a young human child.

The lines between human and animal communication pools may well blur even further in the future. Nonetheless, it is clear that in the wild, animals (even primates) get along just fine without a full human language tool kit. By contrast, the human is unable to do without a full kit in the wilds of Tokyo, Philadelphia, or Nairobi. Why this should be and what difference it makes speaks volumes about human beings. Humans are creatures who operate by means of and within a world of symbols. They exist in and by their cultures. Christian faith ties this uniquely human linguistic and symbolic capability to the human likeness to God. Human beings are not naked apes but mortal angels.

Symbolic Universes

Why this necessity for the world of symbols and culture? The answer lies in the relative "world openness" of the human being.

Compared with other animals, human programming does not include a set of strong instincts limiting humans to a single, species-specific environment. There is no single human world in the same way that there is a tick, worm, turtle, cat, horse, or ape world. While learning and intelligence are involved in the cat or ape world, the relationship of these animals to the environment is comparatively rigid and fixed. Catness or horseness is highly predictable wherever one travels or even whatever type of cat or horse might be one's fancy. The American cat will quickly fit into the Albanian, Afghani, or Argentine cat world.

By contrast, the biological limits of human behavior are comparatively nonspecific. This provides an open platform for forging effective adaptations to many environments, both physical and social, across a broad spectrum of possibilities. In consequence, the human has developed an enormous variety of adjustments, spreading virtually to every possible environment. Humans live in a kaleidoscope of social patterns, values, and customs, with at least five thousand different language groups.

The average American traveling the globe is a fish out of water in the human worlds of Albania, Afghanistan, or Argentina. The human world learned in the United States only sets him or her up for "culture shock" in these other communication pools. (Culture shock is the disorientation experienced when customary patterns of communication and behavior do not work in a new group where norms and values are markedly different from one's own.) A cat traveling with this American doesn't experience such culture shock but quickly gets down to cat business wherever the master or mistress may go.

Actually, it is more accurate to speak of human *cultural* worlds, since there is no general human world. No human world is ever shorn of its cultural particularities, any more than a human being can be without a specific gender, race, or ethnic type. Humans are always raised within a specific cultural world. When someone speaks of "human traits" or "human nature," he or she is trying to imagine what it might be like to meet Mr. or Ms. Human without the clothing and influences of any particular culture. What would a real Tarzan be like?

That fellow humans are always found in the context of specific cultures should not be surprising to any wide-awake, educated person. These different cultural worlds serve as large communication pools. Yet there are often boundaries between communication pools within the "same" culture. We put quotation marks around the word *same* because even social scientists are not always in agreement about where to draw the line to separate one culture from another. Sometimes differences are a matter of "subcultures." Boston Brahmins and black Mississippians, San Francisco gays and Texas Southern Baptists display subcultural differences—that is, variations on the general American culture. Other differences are a matter of the special formalization and elaboration of everyday communication patterns, such as those found in chemistry, medicine, and philosophy. It is this latter type of difference that is interesting here. Peter Berger and Thomas Luckmann paint a helpful picture of this type of difference.[3]

Most of the time, whatever the culture, humans live in an "everyday life-world." This is the world shared by all members of a society. It operates according to several principles. It is the "here-and-now" world, an arena of immediate family and friends, coworkers and contemporaries. Normally one experiences these people as "more real" than people who are geographically or historically distant. One's present activities are also more vivid and attention grabbing for him or her than most past activities. People live in the here and now in terms of a standard sense of space and time. Whether or not a person has a date for Friday night can be an overwhelming existential issue, more important for the moment in this person's personality than the tens of thousands of people who are dying in a hot war on another continent. Each human exists in one three-dimensional place and one moment of time, moving forward into a not-yet-finished future.

Humans order the everyday life-world in very pragmatic ways. The concern is not with settling philosophical mind benders

("How do I know I exist?" or "Give irrefutable proof that the universe is not the dream world of a dozing giant turtle"). The everyday world is where people work, cooperate, eat, play, laugh, love, and argue. It is a place of basic existential involvements designed to cope with immediate, practical matters. It takes place in the wide-awake time in which one takes for granted that things are pretty much as they seem. Roads don't turn into the backs of boa constrictors and swallow up cars. People can't fly without mechanical help. Tuesday will last only twenty-four hours. Term-paper assignments get done by reading and writing.

Part of the ordering of the everyday life-world is its division into "spheres of relevance." Experience is divided into compart-ments organized around the sorts of skills, knowledge, and tasks involved: car driving, partying, making a living, test taking, parenting, maintaining health. By compartmentalizing life into spheres of relevance, people screen out a vast array of nonrelevant knowledge. This reduces the level of complexity one must cope with when he or she sets out to accomplish a specific pragmatic task.

The vocabulary of a language often reflects the paramount spheres of relevance of a culture. The Nuer of the Sudan have more than four hundred words to describe the cattle they herd. Eskimos have dozens of words for snow. English allows its speak-ers to name numbers up to monstrous sizes, and English speakers have developed a prodigious set of mathematical symbols.

Accordingly, the everyday life-world is a routine, orderly world enabling people to cope within their culture. It also empowers them to relate to others on a common basis. Routines pattern human behavior, though the content of this standardization varies from culture to culture.

To be sure, the ordinary course of events and of life is often not simply ordinary. Extraordinary events and turns of fate raise issues and questions not handled by the routines of the everyday life-world. These range from night terrors (the most vivid form of nightmares) to the inexplicable burdens of death (whether one's own or those of thousands in a massive earthquake). Every human being faces the puzzles of morality and questions about the destiny of the earth and the meaning of all things. Even the clumsiness and crudeness of the techniques and tools people use to solve ordinary problems lead them to wonder whether there might be better ones. These are matters that they have difficulty making sense of within the ordinary course of life.

For answers or understanding, people turn to more formalized ways of reasoning and knowledge. What they take for granted in ordinary affairs is not taken for granted in formalized reasoning. Even the obvious is examined and placed into larger "symbolic universes." Religion and science are two important examples of formalized reasoning and knowledge. Several intermediate levels of insight and knowledge act as factories of meaning as one moves upward from the everyday to the most comprehensive level of the symbolic universe. Much that is explicit at the highest levels of formalized knowledge is implicit in ordinary language use. Simply to label a person a criminal or a best friend is to evaluate and give meaning, and it suggests appropriate ways of relating. To call something a tragedy conjures up images of uncontrollable events that have ended a promising life senselessly or fortuitously. The word *tragedy* tells the listener that this is an event whose meaning, if there is any, is beyond ordinary explanations. Thus, the labels used in everyday speech carry with them implicit ways of viewing things, already suggesting larger worldviews.

Above everyday language and labels is a more explicit level of proverbs, maxims, or wise sayings that provide explanations and theoretical rules of thumb. "To err is human, to forgive is divine." "Time is money." "A bird in the hand is worth two in the bush." "Buyer beware." These summarize and concentrate experience into memorable, easily retained form. Almost never does someone think of testing these proverbs to see whether they are always true.

Then there is the even higher, more formal level of explicit theories that deal with institutional sectors such as economics, politics, religion, or society. The law of supply and demand is an explicit theory of the marketplace about price fluctuations. That revolutions are likely to occur during times of economic improvement and political liberalization is an explicit theory.[4] Here are two other examples: inequalities in income and wealth first increase sharply, then decline sharply, and then remain comparatively stable as technological modernization and economic growth occur.[5] The growth in sophistication and size of technology (with the associated requirements for large sums of capital and long lead times in planning) leads to increasing intervention of the state to regulate the risks of demand.[6] Such theories summarize more complicated bodies of experience and, unlike proverbs, are subject to observations, debate, and testing.

At the highest level are symbolic universes. These are "bodies of theoretical tradition that integrate different provinces of meaning and encompass the institutional order in a symbolic totality."[7] Symbolic universes function to capture meaning in the most complete, comprehensive manner. Gathering together large bodies of information and wisdom, symbolic universes do things such as relate everyday life-world concerns to long-term ideals. They also suggest the relationship between economics and religion, aid in the integration of the self with the ultimate meaning of life itself, and so on. This is somewhat equivalent to a weltanschauung, or worldview.[8] Pervasive faith assumptions about what is "really real" structure symbolic universes and worldviews. They answer questions about what ultimate reality is like, what the meaning and purpose of the universe are, how one knows right from wrong, and what a human being is.

A symbolic universe is not necessarily something firmly crystallized into clearly stated elements that are known to most people. Nor is it always logically integrated. It may include various tensions caused by incompatible ideas. For example, most people today want to affirm both independence and interdependence in human relationships. Yet they sense conflict and tension in valuing both, and they vacillate between asserting their independence and reaching out for connectedness to others. Most of the time, human beings do not know how all their various values and principles fit neatly together. A classic illustration lies in the struggles that modern Americans have in relating to their parents. Data indicate that children living with parents until their mid-twenties, returning after college for several years, wish to be treated as adults yet continue to be dependent upon parental help.

The symbolic universe of modernity is a loosely assembled and constantly reassembling set of reality definitions. The premodern symbolic universes were often more highly crystallized, slower to change, and more integrated. With these distinctions in mind, we can now more clearly identify the key players in the dialogue between sociology and faith.

Sociology and How It Fits into the Secular Symbolic Universe

Sociology is a set of explicit theories about society wedded to the modern, secular symbolic universe and organized by the professionalized standards of science. Sociology moves beyond the everyday experience that most people have with society and seeks formalized, tested understandings. By seeking realities beneath the appearances of everyday social life, it challenges many common ideas. Sociological knowledge is different from the everyday lifeworld cunning that helps people navigate practical affairs but that may have little to do with how the overall social structure operates.

Sociology does not aim at providing a symbolic universe. Its self-given task is not to give overarching, ultimate frames of reference for determining the meaning of life or the moral status of social structures. Instead, most sociologists see their task as giving a value-neutral account of the symbolic universes and social structures within which various human groups live. Sociology itself supposedly does not have a symbolic universe. This notion that a group or category of knowledge need not be tied to any symbolic universe is part of the symbolic universe of modernity.

It is an ideological masking of sociology's alliance with values such as pluralism, scientism, and positivism. The effects of this often-hidden alliance are, nonetheless, clear. Sociological pronouncements frequently have powerful moral and even religious overtones. Furthermore, as traditional codes of morality disintegrate, the social sciences increasingly assume the role of providing moral languages and guidance for modern life. Economics does this for the market. Political science defines normative codes for the state. Sociology does the same for what has traditionally been known as "civil society"—that is, the family, voluntary associations, religion, and other social groups that are not economic or governmental in nature.

Christianity and How It Defines Its Own Symbolic Universe

Christian faith is both a set of explicit theories and a symbolic universe in its own right. It exists in tension with the modern, secularized symbolic universe. Christian faith exists both at a lay level in congregations and at the level of professional theology. It moves beyond everyday experiences by acknowledging the presence of the hidden Kingdom of God, that transforms both personal and social life. It challenges unbelief, injustice, idolatry, falsehood, spiritual counterfeits, and immorality. Its principal dispute is with whatever minimizes God's place in the world. Thus, Christian faith challenges whatever damages or distorts creation, preventing it from fulfilling its God-given purpose of plenitude and blessing. It opposes whatever diminishes any human being and treats him or her as less than a bearer of the image of God.

In the modern pluralistic world, knowledge and belief systems are precarious simply because so many differing ones compete for a hearing. The growth of professions is one of the ways that people manage pluralism. Professions advance claims that they hold expert knowledge (explicit theories and practices) and accredited rights to truth in given spheres of relevance. Sociology adopted the structures and habits of a profession and is frequently jealous about its claims to be the real expert on social arrangements. Theology and biblical studies have also become professionalized. They share the habit of claiming areas of life as their exclusive domain. Some of those claims overlap not only with sociology but with a wide range of other professionalized disciplines. This is a sure formula for conflict.

For knowledge to be plausible under the conditions of pluralism, it must be more than the outlook of professionals. It must become a part of the accepted outlook of wider circles of the public. "Plausibility structures" refer to the processes and social patterns that make given theories and symbolic universes subjectively believable. The stronger the plausibility structure, the stronger one experiences a set of theories and beliefs as sound or solid truth.

Plausibility Structures

Plausibility structures are networks of social relationships that enable the people within them to have a strengthened sense that their conclusions are true and right. When significant others react affirmatively to the ideas and actions that make up a symbolic universe, their responses reinforce shared categories and perspectives. In other words, people who share the same symbolic universe talk about the world in the same terms, rather than challenging those terms, and this creates a sense of strong plausibility. This is why "birds of a feather flock together." If one wants to swim in a particular communication pool, one must stay in its conceptual lanes and obey its lifeguards.

There is no truth or symbolic universe that survives without some such plausibility structure. For the sciences, including sociology, the plausibility structure includes professional associations, journals, meetings, colleagues in the same department, books, and intensive socialization (such as through Ph.D. programs). These elements help to ensure that practitioners of the discipline share the same explicit theories and criteria for evalu ating good scientific thought. The editors of the journals, the "referee system" for judging articles submitted for publication, disciplinary awards, and the doling out of research money are also part of the plausibility structure. They help establish a degree of consensus and uniformity in a given professional sphere of knowledge and activity. Only through the interactions of sociologists with each other does sociology become real. If one hangs around with sociologists long enough, the stuff they talk about will begin to seem really important and believable, no matter how one felt about it before.

Within the larger sociological symbolic universe and plausibility structures are smaller plausibility structures, built around schools of sociological thought. Some of the more prominent include Marxist, feminist, functionalist, conflict, symbolic interactionist, and social behaviorist sociology. The more technical term for these substructures is *paradigm*. (Paradigms are discussed further in the next chapter.) Members of these smaller plausibility structures often publish their own journals and organize symposia articulating their point of view at national meetings. Frequently they control certain graduate departments where they socialize new sociologists into their point of view as they teach them the broader discipline. They seek to persuade other professional sociologists to adopt their point of view. They also aim at persuading more of the general public to use their particular brand of sociology.

One mark of the success of a profession is when nonprofessionals adopt the language of the profession (even if lay understandings are rather murky). Psychology's plausibility is enhanced when nonpsychologists begin to talk about self-image, ego strength, obsessive behavior, phobias, or rationalization. If inflation-deflation, trade deficit, money supply, and the law of supply and demand are everyday terms, then economics will appear to be an important and valuable endeavor. Sociology has managed to get terms such as social class, deviance, life-style, socialization, and bureaucracy into common parlance.

Boundary Skirmishes

Now a few of the basic questions presented earlier can be answered. Why are the skirmishes more frequent and intense between sociology and Christian faith than between faith and other academic disciplines? How does one explain the comparatively high levels of indifference and even hostility to religion among sociologists?

One explanation says that the difference in degree of hostility is a function of the scholarly distance of a subject matter from religion. Physicists and mathematicians do not deal directly with religious phenomena, while those in the humanities and social sciences do. Conflict in theories is more likely the more the subject matter overlaps. This explanation in effect says that religion is part of the subject matter of sociology and that when sociologists study it scientifically and objectively, they conclude that it is irrational, nonsensical, or otherwise incompatible with good sociological thought.

Unfortunately, this explanation is not particularly persuasive. It implies that most sociologists spend time studying religion. On the basis of what they discover, they conclude that religious claims or theories and sociological patterns of reasoning are incompatible. Choosing the sociological patterns as superior, they become hostile to religious categories and activities. The problem is that only a minority of sociologists actually study religion (fewer than 10 percent of professional sociologists list religion as a specialization). Further, a common complaint in articles assessing the status of the sociology of religion is that sociologists who are religious dominate this specialization.[9] Thus, the data suggest that hostility toward religion is not the result of conclusions based on careful study. The majority of sociologists who are hostile seem to avoid taking religion seriously as an object of study.

A second explanation argues that science itself is a precarious sort of knowledge. It needs strong plausibility structures that affirm and validate it. Scientists are a special social group that sustain skeptical and critical attitudes toward appearances and strengthen their confidence in their theories by communicating primarily with each other. They develop their own communication pools with special insider vocabulary, stories, jokes, and heroes. They are not immune to the tensions that result from conflicts with the larger lay public; rather, part of their communication involves putting down those who are not insiders in their own communication pool.

Further, professionals communicate with each other through codified theoretical paradigms. These paradigms define what research a discipline considers to be important. They exemplify ideal patterns of reasoning and argumentation. They specify the chief concepts and indicate the criteria for evaluating scientific work and distributing awards.

The degree to which a field is highly codified varies. Theoretical physics and mathematics score high in codification. Social sciences and the humanities are much less codified. As Robert K. Merton and Harriet Zukerman put it, "codification refers to the consolidation of empirical knowledge into succinct and interdependent theoretical formulations."[10] The "hard" sciences are more codified. Much less experience and the mastery of a smaller volume of information is necessary to become a productive scholar in the hard sciences than is true for the "soft" sciences. In such disciplines, experience and command of a mass of descriptive facts are essential for productive scholarship.

Less codification has a number of effects. There is less agreement in a less codified discipline than in highly codified ones. This disagreement is apparent in disputes over which explanatory strategies are ideal. Multiple schools of thought vie for privileged status. There are higher rejection rates for submitted articles to the central journals. For these reasons, the claim of a sociologist to a discovery or to validated knowledge is much more precarious than claims in highly codified sciences. The public is less able to judge the quality of the work. Even fellow professionals have difficulty deciding the merits of certain work in the discipline.

How then are theories and explanations in less codified fields validated? How do scientists in these fields come to consensus and draw boundaries about their knowledge as superior to lay knowledge (which is also low in codification)? Since insecurities over which findings and which researchers are exemplary add to internal conflicts, what effects does such disagreement have on the profession's social dynamics?

Other mechanisms come into play to buttress the sense of a separate and superior status vis-à-vis everyday lay knowledge. Robert Wuthnow writes:

> The argument I wish to suggest here is that scientists, especially those in the less codified disciplines, rely frequently on values, attitudes, and life-styles to maintain the reality of science by setting up *external boundaries* between themselves and the general public or those who represent the realm of everyday reality. In other words, scientists who lack clearly codified paradigms and strong communication networks turn to symbolic modes of differentiating themselves from everyday reality in order to maintain the plausibility of their scientific orientations—orientations that are inevitably precarious in relation to the paramount reality of everyday life.[11]

For the professional in a discipline with low codification, a lack of religious commitment or adherence acts as a means of setting up boundaries. It helps to distinguish these professionals from the larger public, who tend to be more highly religious. In the highly codified disciplines, the need for boundary maintenance is not as great. The internal agreement of the field creates stronger plausibility structures. Highly technical, abstract language is common in such a communication pool. Not even very highly educated laypersons can understand the discourse. The differences between an initiated member of a highly codified discipline and everyone else are very clear. This becomes quickly apparent to any uninitiated person who tries to participate in the discipline's communication pool. Additional boundary markers are superfluous.

In the less codified disciplines, what sets expert knowledge off from lay knowledge is far less clear. Thus, boundary mechanisms beyond those that are part of the internal communication pool are necessary. Refusing religion is one of the ways to mark the social expert off from the naive layperson. Of course, this is not the only boundary mechanism. The tendency for sociologists to be politically liberal and to adopt unconventional life-styles also acts as a boundary mechanism. Lack of religious commitment is only one of several markers sustaining the plausibility of sociology.

This second explanation suggests sociological reasons for why sociologists forget or deny their Christian roots. Such behavior relates to felt needs within the discipline to strengthen its plausibility structure and to legitimate its endeavor by affirming its ties to the secular symbolic universe of modernity.

This analysis, if true, applies to the communication pools of the Christian faith as well. Christian communities also operate with codification schemes (creeds, confessions of faith, theologies, commentaries) that resemble those used in the humanities more than those in the sciences. As sociology and other modern professions have gained power and prestige, the formalized sector of Christian theory making has declined in power and prestige. Christian journalists and theologians also display assertive and aggressive boundary-maintaining mechanisms, at times taking unfair potshots at sociology and the other sciences. There are several ways in which Christian theological thought and practice try to maintain the boundaries of faith.[12]

Fundamentalism solves the boundary problem by seeking to create closed, parallel institutions (such as Christian schools, colleges, and Bible schools; separatist congregations; and the Christian yellow pages). It denigrates key aspects of the sciences and adopts life-styles that strongly set its followers off from the larger culture. Evangelicalism takes a more accommodationist approach, seeking to participate in the larger pluralistic culture. It affirms science yet weds its thought to an explicitly orthodox version of Christian theology. Liberalism chooses to adopt much of the symbolic universe of modernity. It trims the religious claims of Christian faith, attempting to show the compatibility between a demythologized Christian symbolic universe and that of modernity.

At present, the evangelicals show the most promise of a rapprochement between Christian faith and sociology. Most fundamentalists are content to stay in their trenches and reject sociology. Sociology seems to them irredeemably yoked to a secular symbolic universe and hopelessly infused with non-Christian assumptions. Liberals so trim Christian faith that it is no longer clear what is left of Christianity to integrate with sociology. Liberalism either corners religion into its own unique symbolic terrain, unrelated to science, or surrenders the territory whenever contemporary science speaks loudly.

This account does not settle the larger issue of where the truth might lie in the midst of tensions between faith and sociology. Yet at least it provides some clue as to why boundary skirmishes are so much more energetic in sociology than in statistics or theoretical physics. One more important observation having to do with symbolic universes needs to be made here.

The Grass Is Always Greener

At its center, sociology is a professional, formal set of explicit theories and practices dealing with social phenomena. It also has a particularly intimate tie to modernity. Its professional origins stem from the rise of the modern world, and its subject matter deals with the breaking up and remaking of social connections in the modern world. More important, secular sociology weds itself to modernity through a symbolic universe that validates pluralism, privatization (especially of "religion"), and secularism. When a sociologist concludes that religious assumptions are incompatible with scientific and sociological assumptions, he or she is allowing the symbolic universe and plausibility structure of modernity to operate. In that symbolic universe, there is no God, no purpose behind the universe, no destiny infusing human history. Those who run in these circles simply take all of these things for granted.

Science does not function without connections to some symbolic universe any more than grass grows for very long without roots in good soil. Christians cannot ask for a science with a neutral worldview. There is no such science, and Christians need to be aware of this. When science concludes that God is not at work in the universe or that there are no transculturally valid moral standards, these conclusions are not the results of "pure science." Similarly, when sociology concludes that all knowledge is socially relative, it is expressing the effects of its intimate connection with the pluralistic, secular symbolic universe of modernity.

Furthermore, given modernity's symbolic universe, many sociologists consider the notion of a Christian sociology to be both wrongheaded and positively dangerous. For them, religion is a private matter of values, not something dealing with facts important for sociology. Values are many. They concern matters of individual, subjective choice, unjustified by reason. Science (and sociology) are matters of the public realm—that is, matters of facts. The practice and rationality of sociology, for them, are not a matter of values but of facts on which all reasonable people can agree.

The large dispute between the Christian faith and secular sociology is over symbolic universes. Christians claim that the symbolic universe of Christian faith, along with its plausibility structure, includes science in a way that the symbolic universe of modernity, with which sociology frequently allies itself, does not include Christian faith. Faith is a broader and more penetrating worldview and practice than a sociology allied with modernity. Because of that, Christians will continue to contribute to social science, even if many social scientists choose to be indifferent or hostile to Christian faith. The ideological alliance with modernity is not the only possible alliance for sociology. There are other symbolic universes with which it can fruitfully ally itself.

In Part I, some of the reasons sociology and faith quibble have been illuminated through a sociological analysis of the rise of the modern world and sociology as a profession seeking to understand that world. Constructing a positive relationship between Christian faith and sociology requires a deeper understanding of both. Part II begins this process by considering the variety of perspectives found in sociology.

NOTES

1. The primates Washoe, Koko, Lana, and Lucy are some of the better-known language users. Francine Patterson and Eugene Linden, *The Education of Koko* (New York: Holt, Rinehart & Winston, 1981).
2. Quoted in William A. Haviland, *Anthropology*, 5th ed. (New York: Holt, Rinehart & Winston, 1989), pp. 283–284.
3. Peter Berger and Thomas Luckmann, *The Social Construction of Reality: A Treatise in the Sociology of Knowledge* (New York: Anchor Books, 1967).
4. James S. Coleman, *Foundations of Social Theory* (Cambridge, MA: Harvard University Press, 1990), p. 472.
5. Peter Berger, *The Capitalist Revolution* (New York: Basic Books, 1986), p. 46.
6. John Kenneth Galbraith, *The New Industrial State*, 4th ed. (Boston: Houghton Mifflin, 1985), p. 5.
7. Berger and Luckmann, *Social Construction of Reality*, p. 95; Berger, Berger, and Kellner, *Homeless Mind*, pp. 108–109.
8. James W. Sire, *The Universe Next Door: A Basic Worldview Catalog*, 2nd ed. (Downers Grove, IL: InterVarsity Press, 1988). In *Discipleship of the Mind: Learning to Love God in the Ways We Think* (Downers Grove, IL: InterVarsity Press, 1990), Sire defines a worldview as "a set of presuppositions . . . which we hold . . . about the basic makeup of our world" (pp. 29–30). Most of such presuppositions are pretheoretical (that is, one never really thinks about them or seeks to justify them by rational argument).
9. Jeffrey Hammond, "Toward Desacralizing Secularization Theory," *Social Forces* 65, no. 3 (March 1987): 587–611; Myer Stratton Reed, Jr., "Differentiation and Development in a Scientific Specialty: The Sociology of Religion in the United States from 1895 to 1970," unpublished Ph.D. dissertation, Tulane University, 1975, pp. 82ff.
10. Merton and Zukerman, "Age, Aging, and Age Structures in Science," in Robert K. Merton, *The Sociology of Science* (Chicago: University of Chicago Press, 1973), p. 507.
11. Wuthnow, *The Struggle for America's Soul: Evangelicals, Liberals, and Secularism* (Grand Rapids, MI: Eerdmans, 1989), p. 153.
12. Mark Ellingsen, *The Evangelical Movement: Growth, Impact, Controversy, Dialog* (Minneapolis: Augsburg, 1988); chapters 4–5 explain the major distinctions between fundamentalism and evangelicalism.

PART II

The Varieties of
Sociological Experience

Chapter 7

SOCIOLOGICAL PARADIGMS

W̲hen surgeons step to the operating table, surgical tools of various shapes and sizes surround them. The modern scalpel, forceps, retractors, clamps, needles, probes, laser instruments, and so on result from a long tradition of tool-making innovation. Each tool solves a surgical problem.

The surgeon's skill is also the product of very old traditions. Behind the surgeon are centuries of accumulated insight combined with the most recent advances in medical knowledge and education. Equally significant is the evolution of hospitals and licensing boards over the past two thousand years or more. Then there is the more recent funding of research facilities. Other social constructions important to medicine include the web of laws and regulations meant to protect against malpractice and the various insurance arrangements that pay for certified procedures. A division of labor between specialized doctors and nurses gives order to the work done. Tens of thousands of hours spent poring over books, listening to lectures, watching videos and live operations as well as practicing procedures have created these persons who tear at the patient's flesh.

Traditions are not an invention of conservatives bent on turning the clock back to the Middle Ages. They are the very stuff that makes contemporary achievements possible. The reason moderns can see more truth than their predecessors is because moderns are dwarfs standing on the shoulders of giants.

Without musical traditions, there would be no jazz, rock, salsa, hymns, or gospel songs. Ancient constitutions and bills of rights structure the democratic traditions out of which contemporary Western public life is woven. Someone invented the words used today. Others reshaped and redefined them and handed them down. Cotton shirts are possible only because different people discovered the qualities of the cotton plant, learned to make thread, figured out how to weave it into cloth. Cultures are living traditions. Without traditions humans would not and could not be human.

Traditionalism is another matter. Traditionalism enshrines past practices and ideas, condemning innovation and change. Yet traditions stay alive only so long as they are mixtures of both continuity and discontinuity with the past. Who would wish medicine to be what it was even fifty years ago? Yet today's medicine grows out of the medical traditions of fifty (and 250) years ago. As a living practice, it benefits modern humans because it includes both the insights of the past and more recent developments. Remove from it everything developed and learned before the twentieth century, and it would collapse. Yet without the advances of the twentieth century, medicine would stand helpless against conditions that could kill hundreds of millions.

Furthermore, as disease and health matrices change, medicine must change. Doctors and researchers managed to put down measles and tuberculosis with herculean struggles, only to have AIDS appear. What makes change possible are the infinite small changes that have happened in the past, leading up to this or that particular innovation. In other words, innovation is possible because of an accumulating, living tradition. New challenges are what make innovation necessary.

Modernity has often been seen as an acid that dissolves all traditions. This image is not accurate. Modernity does destroy traditionalism (and evokes traditionalist movements of protest).[1] It also has the tendency to turn into an ideology of modernism that views affairs as good simply because they are new or recent.

Modernism is to modernity what traditionalism is to tradition. Often the ideology of modernism, taken up as a giant hoe to uproot traditionalism, cuts the very roots of the traditions that nourish modernity. The major threads of modernity as a continuing tradition include a number of disparate items. These include liberal democratic political thought, bourgeois individualism, ideologies of progress and enlightenment, values of technological innovation, and universal education.

Traditions are like the tools of the surgeon. People must learn how to use them and discover what they are good for. It is foolish to assume that one instrument will be equally adept at cataract replacement, heart surgery, amputation of a leg, and removal of a polyp from the lower intestines. Similarly, sociology is a living tradition of scientific thought and practice. It organizes explicit theories about social phenomena. For it to be useful, one must learn its practices and knowledge base. How effective is it for dissecting social systems and laying bare the processes of social give-and-take? The sociological tradition contains several streams of thought that differ from each other and that suggest widely variant perspectives on social worlds. These are sociological paradigms.

Can You Paradigm?

The year was 1947. Thomas Kuhn was spending the summer preparing lectures on seventeenth-century mechanics for the fall term at Harvard. To set the stage, he traced the subject to its source in Aristotle's *Physics*. He puzzled over how such a brilliant mind could be so consistently wrong about the nature of the physical world. What suddenly struck Kuhn was that he was trying to pour Aristotle's thought into the modern molds of atoms, molecules, and quantum mechanics. How would the physical world appear if one adopted Aristotle's worldview? One of Aristotle's key assumptions was that bodies seek the location where they belong according to their nature. Under this perspective, Aristotle's conclusions that physical bodies have various sorts of spirits made eminent sense. Heavenly bodies rise in accordance with their airlike spirit, while earthly bodies have spirits that cause them to fall.

Matters are puzzling or sensible only within a given set of assumptions about the world. This insight set Kuhn on the path of what he came to call paradigms. Like other humans, scientists negotiate their everyday scientific life-world using a framework of presuppositions that they do not question most of the time. All scientists operate within a sort of intellectual gestalt that influences the perception and understanding of the object of study.

Kuhn's book, *The Structure of Scientific Revolutions*, created a sensation when published in 1962.[2] He said that people have a distorted image of science. The impression of a gradual, incremental accumulation of certified scientific truth combined with the conception of science as a purely rational enterprise neglects the ways in which scientific inquiry actually happens.

Scientists work within a framework of presuppositions. At a given time in a particular scientific community, there is a dominant or paramount framework that guides scientific work and training. This is what Kuhn called a paradigm. Scientists get attached to their paradigms. Once they use a paradigm for some time, they have difficulty seeing their subject matter in any way other than as the paradigm allows them to see it. When new ideas or even inconvenient data appear, the proclivity is to reject them or explain them away rather than change the paradigm. When scholars change paradigms, it is a time of high drama and a lot of shouting. Scientific traditions do not just develop gradually. Instead, their history is one of scientific revolutions involving the spilling of buckets of intellectual blood.

Kuhn arranges the typical pattern of development of a particular scientific tradition into several stages. First, an area of knowledge is *preparadigmatic*. During this time, there is little agreement on what the subject matter is or on the sorts of methods to use.

Disagreement exists over standards for evaluating attempts to discover and articulate knowledge. Various schools of thought exist, and they do not agree. Following this is the emergence of a *paradigm*. This refers to "universally recognized scientific achievements that for a time provide model problems and solutions to a community of practitioners."[3] A paradigm is a model or standard of scientific achievement in a given discipline. The history of science is a history of the careers of various paradigms. A paradigm guides research during a period of *normal science*. This is a time of widespread consensus among scientific practitioners on the basic core of their field. This basic core includes the field's symbolic generalizations (such as laws), metaphysical commitments, values, and exemplars. Exemplars are classic examples within a particular science (perhaps some elegant experiment or piece of reasoning) that typify excellent science.

In physics, the preparadigmatic period was that existing before Isaac Newton. Newtonian mechanics became the first integrating paradigm for physics. After that, until Einstein, mechanics developed as a "mopping-up exercise," filling in the details and gaps in Newton's theories. Evolution is the contemporary integrating paradigm for most biologists. Virtually all current work in biology uses and integrates its findings as revisions and extensions of the notions of natural and kin selection.

Because of the consensus within a paradigm during normal science, scientists engage in "puzzle solving." They fill in the cracks in the paradigm and apply it to new areas. They do not spend much time challenging the paradigm itself or examining its metaphysical commitments. Eventually, the puzzle solving leads to the discovery of discrepancies or anomalies. These are findings that are incompatible with the reigning paradigm.

When these discrepancies are important or frequent enough, the discipline enters a crisis period, which Kuhn calls the time of *extraordinary science*. Rival paradigms appear as alternatives to the dominant one. These new paradigms are not always accepted. The discrepancies may only be apparent ones, with the old paradigm eventually explaining them. Or the rival paradigm may not offer as good an explanation of other facets of the issue as the old one did. Or it may be unacceptable for other reasons. A scientific revolution occurs when the dominant paradigm is overturned and replaced by a rival. Kuhn speaks of shifting from one paradigm to another as a revolution because the change often appears to be rapid. It happens through the accumulation of younger scholars who accept the new paradigm in the face of resistance from older dominant scholars. As the older scholars pass from the scene, the new paradigm assumes control.

The process is not a neat, rational one in which logic and evidence decisively persuade all experts. Rival paradigms are very different ways of looking at much the same reality and data. Because their assumptions differ and their major concepts have different meanings, Kuhn believes that paradigms are incommensurable. This means that a scholar cannot fully translate his or her paradigm into another's terms or compare the merits of both against some independent standard. Persuasion to accept a new paradigm is more than a matter of rational discourse and empirical proof. The shift from one dominant paradigm to another is a social and political event, involving the ousting of powerful advocates of the former paradigm. In other words, paradigm change is intellectual "gang warfare." One way of looking at things prevails until a stronger, younger group of scientists gangs up on the older ones and defeats them.

Scientists convert from one paradigm to another in a way similar to people converting from one religious worldview to another. The shift in outlook is more like a dramatic switch in viewpoint than a gradual process of reasoning through to the truth. This process can be seen in the historic struggles of astronomy coming to accept a heliocentric view of the solar system. Or in the shift from Newtonian to Einsteinian physics. Or in the adoption of evolution by biology. Personal relationships, the prestige and commitment of scholars to the old paradigm, the politics of the community of scientists—all play a role in the switch. In short, the development of a scientific tradition is largely a sociological process. It depends on plausibility structures, commitments to the values of symbolic universes, and a socially enforced consensus about dominant paradigms.

Kuhn does not argue that the process of paradigm change is purely subjective and irrational (though some sociologists and philosophers of science do). Crisis in science happens because discrepancies between paradigms and the investigated reality do occur. Nature does not always fit people's expectations and paradigm-structured perceptions. Scholars cannot always stuff reality into the categories of a given paradigm. Yet no one can ever know that reality except through the use of paradigms.

One implication is that facts may well fit several paradigms. This leaves unsettled the issues of which paradigm might be closer to the truth or which is a better model of reality. What finally settles the choice between rival paradigms at a given point in time is the plausibility structure of a discipline. It often enforces more agreement and certainty than the actual data and the paradigm warrant.

Paradigmitis or Imaginization

Kuhn's scheme emerged from a comparative study of the history of several of the natural sciences. Because of their subject matters and the highly codified quality of their discourse, achieving consensus in a single paradigm marks the emergence of normal science in them. It is a different matter for the less codified sciences such as sociology with its more complex subject matter. That complexity is captured by a comment from Charles Beard: "After all, physics, complex as it may be, is relatively simple as compared to a subject which includes physicists and physics and everything else mankind has ever said and done on earth."

Sociology is a relatively young science as compared with astronomy or physics. It still has several perspectives that seek to unify the field and show they can make sense of all the "facts." Some of them create problems for a Christian sociology because they adopt assumptions that seem incompatible with faith. Examples of these assumptions include deterministic views of human behavior, materialistic assumptions about religious realities, relativistic views of knowledge and truth, and reductionist principles that efface the integrity of the human level of phenomena. Many of these assumptions derive from an alliance with the ideology of modernism and scientism. Nevertheless, one must consider every perspective on its own merits, spelling out its assumptions and stating its preferred methodology and data. Only then can one fairly evaluate the conversation of the various sociological schools of thought.

Christian thought must explore and appreciate the valid insights currently spread throughout the full variety of paradigm candidates active in sociology. Depending on one's point of view, this multiplicity is either a cursed disease ("paradigmitis") from which more infusions of science are essential as a cure, or it is a necessary feature of sciences that deal with a multifaceted reality—a reality that requires imaging the social world through multiple perspectives ("imaginization"[4]).

How many paradigm candidates are there in sociology? Depending on the analysis, there are five to a dozen perspectives vying for dominance in research and summaries of what sociology is about.[5] Most textbooks boil this diversity down to three heavyweight contenders as a simplified way of introducing nonprofessionals to sociological paradigms. This book uses a similar threefold division as a simple way of illustrating some of the diversity in sociological traditions. We freely acknowledge that the sociological tradition is much more complex.

Examples of Sociological Paradigm Traditions

Sociological paradigms include several interconnected elements. We suggest as important a paradigm's philosophical roots, its exemplars and images of the subject matter, and its notions of human nature as well as the nature of society. Paradigms also include images of the nature of science and an account of preferred methodologies. Here, paradigms are taken to be collections of explicit theories that organize the formalized knowledge of a social science. One can often also identify typical sorts of ethical and political concerns that comport well with a specific paradigm. Because a paradigm is a web of interconnected ideas and evaluations, its relationship to Christian faith is never a simple matter. Consider the following paradigm traditions, which stress order, conflict, and diversity.[6]

The Rage for Order

Above all else, this tradition says, society is an organic, collective, cohesive reality. What impresses careful observers using this paradigm is the way in which patterns of regular social interaction and interdependent institutions serve underlying social needs.

The most important philosophical roots for this tradition lie in Plato's *Republic* and Thomas Hobbes's *Leviathan*. The classical exemplar is the famous French sociologist, Émile Durkheim (1858–1917), especially as represented by his books, *Rules of the Sociological Method* (1895) and *Suicide* (1897). Durkheim considered the subject matter of sociology to be "social facts." Roughly speaking, social facts are large-scale social structures and institutions along with their effects in the consciousness and actions of human actors. Durkheim analyzed as social facts the division of labor, moral customs, the rates of suicide in differing social groups, education, and religious beliefs and practices. Social actors experience a social fact as external to them. At the same time, the social fact exercises a sort of authoritative, obligatory control over their thinking and acting.

Language is a good example of a social fact: it is both outside and inside individuals and precedes a person's existence. If individuals are to communicate meaningfully with each other, they have no choice but to use the grammar and vocabulary of a language. Language is also representative of the primary forces that hold a society together. These are ideal (as opposed to material) forces; they include values, attitudes, and collectively shared worldviews. These forces are, as Alexis de Tocqueville put it, "habits of the heart."

Human nature in this perspective is self-interested, individualistic, and competitive. Without checks on inner human passions and urges, a community would disintegrate into hostile, suspicious mobs of warring individuals. What most effectively limits and disciplines human wants is reason. Reason appears either consciously in a social contract in which people voluntarily give up some of their freedom for the control of government, or it works unconsciously through an "invisible hand" in social arrangements that punish people who do not seek the most rational ways to secure their interests.

In this tradition, inequality is natural. People are born with innate differences in gifts, motivation, and capabilities. This shows up in variations in social worth. Because humans are by nature inclined to disorder, strong social bonds are essential. The nature of society is that of interdependent institutions with a supportive set of norms and values that bind people into a cohesive whole. The most common metaphors for this vision of society are those of the living organism and the system. In either case, the images stress the unity of the social whole and the self-correcting functioning of the social organism when its parts properly interrelate. A stable but dynamic equilibrium is created when every part or element contributes to the survival and health of the whole.

This is not to say that the functioning of the social organism is purely automatic. Skilled knowledge and wisdom must be mobilized and used in key decision-making roles. For the sake of the health of a social organism, there must be specialization and division of labor. There must be identification of some positions and people as more important for the survival of the social totality than others. Hence, social inequality is natural, essential, and legitimate since it rewards those with greater social worth with higher power, prestige, and privileges. Such differences motivate the most qualified to take those social roles that are important for sustaining the society.

Social harmony comes from sharing norms and values. Social change is primarily a gradual, evolutionary process. In fact, forced social change represents a grave danger to the restraints on individuals that are essential to healthy and harmonious social organisms.

The practice of sociology in this paradigm is markedly similar to that of the natural sciences. Sociology is systematic, empirical, and quantitative. It seeks predictive power. Social facts are as objective as any other sort of scientific facts. Sensory-based knowledge and rigorous observation lead to quantitative measurements of variables and to the establishing of lawful relationships between them. The ideal is that of positive science: completely objective knowledge, neutral toward all values, concerned only with describing the facts and developing explanatory laws. The preferred methods are the interview questionnaire and the survey. In many ways, this has been and remains the dominant approach of North American sociology.

The Rigors of Conflict

In this tradition, struggle, warfare, competition, battle, rivalry, and contest are emphasized as central aspects of the human experience. Inequality is not so much the result of natural differences as it is due to the exploitation and repression of one group by another. Look closely, adherents say, and it is clear that the most fundamental reality in society is conflict.

The philosophical roots of this tradition lie in the works of Polybius, Machiavelli, and Hegel. An important exemplar of this paradigm is Karl Marx (1818–1883). The subject matter, as in the order paradigm, is social facts. However, the focus is much more historical and comparative, looking for the dynamics of basic societal changes. Most adherents of this perspective see technology and economic forces as driving and structuring social reality. Material forces are at the center of history. Ideal forces such as law, worldviews, ideology, and shared values derive from and reflect material forces.

Human nature is seen positively, as innately good, creative, cooperative, and sociable. It is inherently perfectible yet distorted and alienated under the conditions of an exploitative, class-divided society. People are naturally rational. Through proper experience and education they can realize their inherent goodness and creativity. They do this primarily by engaging actively in productive physical activities. Effective labor in the material world masters the forces of nature and contributes to the collective welfare. Most people do not experience this sort of existence. Their work activities are boring, alienating, competitive, trivial, mindless, and undertaken only to "make a living." Because of the conditions imposed by class conflict, work is not an expression of their gifts and freedom but a necessity for survival.

Society embodies structures of institutionalized inequality. The vast differences in wealth, power, and status deny the social nature of human beings. Powerful people exploit racism, sexism, ethnicity, and class differences to deny a fair or just distribution of the goods of this world. This is done so that a small elite group can have more. The result is a social order laden with conflict between groups with opposing interests. What this boils down to is that the rich control the key matters of societal life. The rich are able to exploit the poor because the poor must work at lousy wages in order simply to survive. This sets rich and poor against each other and often sets poor against poor in competition for the few jobs available.

The ongoing conflict over wealth and power drives a constant process of change. Any existing order contains the seeds of its own eventual destruction and the embryo of its successor. A class of revolutionaries is perpetually created in opposition to those in charge. The legitimacy of the status quo is constantly in question. The transition to a society favoring the good and creative nature of humanity comes through overthrowing the present order. Social harmony is only a facade that hides deep divisions between the haves and the have-nots.

In this perspective, science exists to change an alienating world into one that is more rational, just, and inclusive of all its members. Science as purely neutral and objective is an illusion. Science is always used in the service of some social group's interests. The so-called objective sociology as practiced in the order paradigm is seen as a middle-class, capitalist sociology. It serves capitalist interests, providing a scientific legitimation for a repressive, irrational, alienating, hierarchical, and oppressive world. Marxist sociology would even claim that such sociology does nothing more than show rulers how they can continue to hang onto their control over the weaker classes.

The goal of good science in the conflict paradigm is not universal, abstract laws. What social science discovers are time-specific laws of the movement of history. They are historical laws because social laws change as societies change. The sociological laws of the localized, feudal, agrarian world of the Middle Ages differ from laws governing the capitalist, industrial, internationally connected world of today. The coming revolution and classless society will usher in new sociological laws. These will transform people and social interaction, releasing all the repressed creativity of human nature. Understanding these scientific laws of society removes the illusions and ideologies that hide the cruel reality of repression of the weak by the strong. An authentic social science aims at applied, value-oriented understandings of social phenomena in the service of banishing injustice, alienation, poverty, racism, and sexism. Its methods include those used by the older paradigm with the addition of methods more typically found in history.

Many Definitions, Many Worlds

The diversity, heterogeneity, and complexity of human social worlds impresses a third sociological paradigm. No single set of forces, groups, or social structures exists in any society; rather, there exists an astounding diversity. Neither order nor conflict is basic in social arrangements. What is fundamental is the human actor, capable of collectively creating many different social worlds and cultures with immense complexity.

The philosophical roots of this paradigm lie in the works of Kant and Nietzsche and in the philosophy of pragmatism. One influential exemplar is Max Weber (1864–1920) with his books, *The Protestant Ethic and the Spirit of Capitalism* (1905) and *Economy and Society* (1922). George Herbert Mead (1863–1931) and Alfred Schutz (1899–1959) are other exemplars. The subject matter of sociology is social action—that is, human behavior structured and motivated by meanings. People interact in terms of meanings that they collectively give to their situations, to the roles they play, and to the symbols they use as they interact. This paradigm focuses its research on the ideas, emotions, values, and life-styles that motivate people to act.

The primary features of human nature in this paradigm are intentionality (goal orientation) and freedom. Human nature is socially constructed out of the patterned meanings and role relationships of the society into which a person is born. However, social conditions do not determine one's behavior. Even as fully socialized adults, individuals remain purposeful creatures, able to distance themselves from their roles and enact those roles in new, creative ways. A person's conduct is a reflection of his or her culture and of conscious, contemplated modifications to that culture. What people do is the result of their decisions, including decisions to conform to or change their cultural patterns.

The reciprocal orientation of individuals to each other is what the term *society* means. People do what they do in part because they can predict how others in society will respond to their behavior, and thus they act accordingly. Social norms teach individuals what to expect from other members of their social groups. The essence of society consists of collectively shared definitions and perceptions of the world. These definitions structure the interaction of teams of human actors carrying out roles embedded in institutions and organizations.

People, however, do not always share the same world of meanings. Society is heterogeneous and diverse. It incorporates different subcultures and interest groups, and this often causes trouble. Even members of the same social group disagree over which life-styles and customary behaviors to validate as legitimate. Pluralists do not assume that society is either structured by a value consensus and equilibrium (the order paradigm) or by a conflict of classes (the conflict paradigm). Society includes both clashing groups (not just classes) and pervasive, unifying subcultures.

This vision of society is profoundly ambivalent, seeing it as an ongoing antagonistic cooperation of groups. The heart of the struggle is over differing definitions of the world and differing life-styles and how to settle claims for power and prestige. In fact, society expresses the profound dualism of the sociability and self-assertion found in human nature itself.

Managing human life through the use of worlds of meaning is crucial to this paradigm. This makes its object of study very different from the objects of physical science. To speak of social facts as one might physical facts is highly misleading. In human cultural worlds, facts are not simply given. They are socially constructed through the meanings that people give to events. These meanings invariably are many and diverse.

Social science must consider the multiple realities of the social world. It not only must explain social action through laws (just as astrophysics explains the movement of the stars) but it must also understand social action by comprehending the meanings and purposes behind it. Hence, its method is interpretative in a way that is similar to the interpretative procedures of the humanities. It is not legitimate to group sociology with either the natural sciences or the humanities. It is a third sort of knowledge, sharing some features in common with the natural sciences and some with the humanities.

The pluralist paradigm begins with individuals and their consciousness. Its research aims at discovering how social actors interpret their world and, through interaction with others, construct stable social worlds. Pluralists often prefer qualitative research over quantitative. This is because they aim at getting inside the meanings and motivations of typical social actors. The paradigm requires that researchers be empathetic, able to see and feel experience as do members of the group they are studying. Preferred methods include participant observation and in-depth interviews, although not to the exclusion of surveys.

Sharing results with the actors investigated is crucial for assessing objectivity in this paradigm. Objective accounts describe the meaningful worlds of social actors well enough so that those actors agree it is a fair characterization. Such an account not only captures their everyday life-world but also reveals the explicit theories and symbolic universes they use to guide and give meaning to the ways they connect to the physical universe, other humans, and God.

Often scientific work in this tradition aims at enhancing the freedom of social actors by clarifying the meanings that structure their interaction. Much research in this tradition focuses on marginal and deviant groups. Most of it seeks to broaden tolerance levels in a pluralistic world and to enhance the participation of marginalized groups in the social constructions of the dominant cultural traditions of a nation. Many anthropologists work within this paradigm. Their research leads naturally into defending smaller tribes and cultural groups threatened by the spread of modernity and the rise of nationalism. In the face of strong pressures for uniformity and conformity to dominant national and world patterns, the pluralist tradition seeks to make room for alternative ways of life.

And Many, Many More

These three simple examples of sociological paradigms are part of three larger streams of sociopolitical thought. The order paradigm has many affinities with conservatism. It trusts the wisdom of the overall social system to correct itself if left alone.

The conflict tradition resonates with radical and revolutionary thought. Its urge is to tear down contemporary sources of inequality and oppression. The pluralist paradigm is an expression of classic liberalism and its vision of reforming contemporary institutions to enhance individual freedoms and protect the weak. Social science paradigms do not come in tidy packages. Theorists within these traditions actually vary widely in the political deductions drawn from their work. This is only a sketch of general tendencies that illustrate the web of interconnecting matters tied together in sociological reasoning. To be fair, we must say that there are many more paradigms. Further, specific theorists within each of these research traditions often put a particular spin on the paradigm that can result in surprising variations and extensions.

If there is to be conversation between sociology and Christian faith, it will happen only when the various sociological perspectives are taken seriously. Understanding sociology as a family of paradigms, none of which unifies the field, fosters a spirit of freedom and adventure. In looking at any piece of sociological work, one needs to ask:

1. To what general paradigm does this belong?
2. What are its assumptions about the nature of human nature? Are these spelled out or implied?
3. What is its view of the nature of society? What does it see as the relationship between the individual and society?
4. What is its view of the nature of science? What does it see as the goals and possibilities of science in sociology?
5. What methodologies does it prefer? What do these methodologies reveal about social worlds? What do they miss revealing about social worlds?
6. What value orientation stands behind this work? Does it imply or advocate a vision of the moral obligations of social actors? Does it offer some account of a better world than the one currently described?

These few questions, if answered carefully, will clarify the claims made by sociological work. First, one must hear what a paradigm says about a given social world. Only then can it be related to what Christian faith says about human beings and the social worlds they inhabit. When sociological traditions have been understood, then their usefulness in understanding contemporary peoples, cultures, and the social arrangements that structure life on this planet becomes obvious.

To See Is Not to See

One final note: human vision is limited. One can see only what the eyes turn toward. Everything behind one's head is out of sight. Even with twenty-twenty vision, the human eye can see only a part of the spectrum of light. What is actually seen depends on how close an object is and on what one is paying attention to.

Sociological paradigms are like detailed tourist maps and books, telling novices (and experienced travelers) where the best sights are. Some suggest looking at social worlds up close and personal, spending time with small groups and the tiniest details of interaction between two or three people. Work following this map is called microsociology. It dissects personal interaction and small-group dynamics. Others suggest that the best views of social reality are extensive panoramas, Grand Canyons of time and civilizations within which small groups and details are not even visible. Work along this line is known as macrosociology. The rise of capitalism, the sociology of agrarian civilizations, the analysis of the role of the state in social revolutions—these are the sorts of topics considered in macrosociology.

Our conviction is that these are not either-or directions. The sociological imagination needs the full range of paradigms in order to help people see the marvelous complexities that are present in human social experience. Sometimes one needs to know how great macrostructures and processes of global reach shape human life.

At other times, one needs laws dealing with face-to-face interactions within particular organizational settings. It all depends on the goal and purpose of one's research.

It is also true that a given paradigm, a given methodology, a given researcher, or a given period in the development of the discipline can lead to one-sided perspectives and conclusions. Sight and blindness are often Siamese twins in social science. The next chapter considers a case study in social research, an example of sight and blindness. It demonstrates the limitations of paradigms. It shows how the ideology of the symbolic universe of modernity can influence what is seen and not seen, even by one of the twentieth century's acknowledged masters of social research.

NOTES

1. Bruce B. Lawrence, *Defenders of God: The Fundamentalist Revolt Against the Modern Age* (New York: Harper & Row, 1989).
2. Kuhn, *Structure of Scientific Revolutions*, 2nd ed. enlarged (Chicago: University of Chicago Press, 1970).
3. Kuhn, *Structure of Scientific Revolutions*, p. viii.
4. Gareth Morgan, *Images of Organization* (Newbury Park, CA: Sage, 1986), pp. 339–344.
5. George Ritzer, in *Sociological Theory*, 2nd ed. (New York: Knopf, 1988), recognizes at least fourteen. Other schemes with fewer include Don Martindale, *The Nature and Types of Sociological Theory*, 2nd ed. (Boston: Houghton Mifflin, 1981), and Jonathan H. Turner, *The Structure of Sociological Theory*, 4th ed. (Belmont, CA: Wadsworth, 1986).
6. This section is indebted to William D. Perdue, *Sociological Theory: Explanation, Paradigm, and Ideology* (Palo Alto, CA: Mayfield Publishing, 1986).

Chapter 8

A CASE STUDY IN SOCIALIZATION

She used to say, "Be lazy, go crazy."

By the end of her life, she had left a trail of thirty-nine books, nearly fourteen hundred other publications, and ten films. She received twenty-eight honorary degrees and won forty awards. She spent extended parts of her life on fourteen field trips to study a variety of peoples in Polynesia. A section of Central Park in New York City is named in her honor.

Margaret Mead (1901–1978) was, by any account, one of the most remarkable social scientists of the twentieth century.[1] She seldom did or said the expected. If socialization were 100 percent effective, then her agnostic parents would never have faced an insistent eleven-year-old wanting baptism. She became a lifelong Episcopalian, much to the consternation of many of her professional colleagues. The well-known anthropologist Ashley Montagu once responded to a question from a religious college audience that the only anthropologist he knew who was a churchgoer was Margaret Mead. In fact, there are many others.

Churchgoer she might have been, but her social research rings with only a distant echo of her faith. This echo is heard in her deep concern with enhancing the neighborliness of all humans to one another through her lifework. She did move in some of the highest ecclesiastical circles, taking part in revisions of the Anglican Common Book of Prayer and in various ecumenical projects. At one committee meeting, they were discussing leaving out references to Noah's flood in the baptismal ritual. One bishop said, "Nobody believes *that* in this day and age." Mead retorted, "Bishops may not, but anthropologists do." She fought to include Satan in the modern Anglican rite of baptism as well. She wanted nothing to do with an insipid Church that no longer faced communicants with the question, "Do you renounce the devil and all his works?"[2]

Much of Mead's renowned abruptness took aim at what she felt was arrogance and snobbishness—on both sides of the aisle that often separates scientist from the people of the church. She felt that there was too much presumption on either side about having exclusive access to the knowledge of reality and the capacity to state the truth fully and finally. Yet the sheer energy and brightness of Mead sometimes misled her into the very presumptions she so thoroughly skewered in her colleagues. As she aged, she accepted the mantle of omniscience along with world fame. More and more she willingly and vociferously pronounced on virtually everything with complete surety.

Understanding Why People Are So Different

When Mead was an undergraduate at Barnard, the teacher whose presence most captured her imagination was a distinguished German, Franz Boas (1858–1942). He is known as the founder of modern American anthropology. Boas's goal was to document primitive cultures before they vanished under the onslaught of the modern world. He built anthropology on the conviction that firsthand contact with the "primitives" was the only way to understand them. His insistence on detailed and meticulous fieldwork transformed people's understanding of both primitive and modern societies.

Two popular ideas were important in the dominant social science paradigms at the turn of the century: evolutionism and racism. Evolutionism was used to rank all societies on a ladder of cultural superiority and inferiority. It ran from the hunting and gathering bands up to the horticultural communities, then through agrarian-based societies all the way to the pinnacle of modern industrialism. The assumption underlying this hierarchy is that the Western world is culturally superior to all other cultures.

According to another popular notion, certain races could claim to be the chief creators of the best in the West. This marked these races as superior. The military and technical capabilities of the West were superior. Its obvious economic dynamism, scientific expertise, and power to displace all other societal forms proved its superiority.

One explanation offered for this alleged superiority was biological. This explanation appealed to race, building on the equation that different races had different intelligences and thus different cultures; therefore, a superior culture represented a superior intelligence and thus a superior race. When combined, evolutionism and racism justified colonialism along with the harsh side effects of bringing civilization to the "savages." At the same time, it drew a clear boundary between white Europeans and people of color. Whites not only ruled but had the right to do so as a superior race. Social relations with the colonial natives acted to sustain and symbolize the prestige, privilege, and power of the Europeans.

This theory maintained itself through prejudice, armchair theorizing, and generous amounts of ignorance. Famous scholars, without ever leaving the library, wrote books using social evolutionary models. These include Émile Durkheim's *The Division of Labor* and *Elementary Forms of the Religious Life* (based on Australian aborigines), Herbert Spencer's evolutionary sociology, and Sir James Frazer's thirteen-volume work, *The Golden Bough*. Lewis Henry Morgan's *Ancient Society* includes some firsthand acquaintance with the Iroquois and a survey on kinship that included two hundred questions. Yet most of the book consists of secondhand information from the library. Marx and Engels based their theory of the evolution of early society on Morgan's work, not on field research.

Boas changed all that. He held that social science ideas that sound good and reasonable within a given communication pool may be completely wrongheaded. And the only way to know whether this is the case is by documenting those ideas in a variety of contexts with primary research. Boas set new, high standards for research, insisting that social scientists actually go to the people about whom they write. What they write is to grow out of explicit, carefully gathered information on the life ways and patterns of the people studied.

Margaret Mead was one of his most famous students. Extremely bright, graduating in the top six of her class, Mead was Phi Beta Kappa in economics and sociology (the two major fields of her academic parents). Her master's work followed in the footsteps of her mother's research on Italian immigrant families. Margaret Mead administered an intelligence test to 276 Italian-American children. Analysis showed a link between the degree to which parents used English at home and the child's score on intelligence tests. Intelligence tests, she said, are not universally valid measures. It is invalid to draw conclusions from them about relative differences in intelligence between various racial or nationality groups.

Mead had been admitted to Boas's graduate courses in anthropology while still an undergraduate. Inspired by him, she decided to become part of his grand scheme to reform anthropology. Settling on Polynesia as the arena in which to do field research for a doctorate, she took adolescence as her problem. It was a timely and important topic. It initiated her lifelong interests in psychology and human development as part of anthropology. Her questions were simple enough to ask but extraordinarily difficult to answer. Which mattered more: nature or nurture? Heredity or environment? Culture or biological destiny? How could anthropology and psychology answer these age-old questions?

Boas had personal as well as professional interests in these questions. Psychologist G. Stanley Hall's book, *Adolescence: Its Psychology and Its Relations to Physiology, Anthropology, Sociology,*

Sex, Crime, Religion, and Education (1905), had invented the modern notion of adolescence. Hall portrayed adolescence as a conflicted, troubled time of idealism. Teen rebellion was a by-product of the biology of young adult development.

Boas had several bones to pick with Hall. In the 1890s, Boas had taught at Clark University, where G. Stanley Hall served as president. The two had a dispute over academic freedom, leading to Boas's resignation, an event he long remembered. Further, Boas felt that the difficulties and conflicts of adolescence might stem as much from culture as from biology. He considered Hall's emphasis on the dominant influence of biology unreasonable. To settle this conflict required careful inquiry into the relative strength of the biology of puberty and the effects of cultural shaping. What Boas hoped for was a study that might help disprove Hall's theory. Mead undertook that research.

Paradise Found

The story begins in 1925 in eastern Samoa on the backwater island of Ta'u (population: 1,050). Then twenty-three years old, Mead arrived to carry out a five-month study of the passage to adulthood by adolescents, especially women. Her assignment was to test whether this universal biological event, marked by the onset of menses and other physical changes, is always accompanied by the sort of stress and conflict prevalent in the typical American teenager.

Gathering about her fifty girls and young women from ages nine to twenty, along with a control group of twelve, Mead interviewed them intensively and participated in their nightly dances. Napoleone Tuiteleleapaga served as her chief interpreter. The result was a stunning best-seller: *Coming of Age in Samoa: A Psychological Study of Primitive Youth for Western Civilization* (1928). In brief, it said that a period of storm and stress, guilt and identity crisis, rebellion and acting out is not a universal characteristic of adolescence. The biological changes could not be the inevitable creator of the distinctive characteristics associated with American adolescence because these characteristics are absent in this decisively negative case study. The biology is the same; the psychosocial results are dramatically different for Samoan youth.

The book came at a critical time in the nature-versus-nurture debate. At the time, the eugenics movement was seeking to engineer a superior race through selective breeding. If biology controls destiny, then science could create a new future for human beings. Charles Davenport, a leader in the eugenics movement, argued that personality traits such as shiftlessness, lawlessness, and even the behavior of prostitution were determined genetically. Social problems come from the "lower and inferior" classes. He claimed that the national destiny is squandered when the biologically inferior are allowed to multiply like rabbits while the superior upper classes (the "Nordics") use birth control. Davenport ran extensive research facilities funded by wealthy backers, including the Kelloggs, the Harrimans, and the Carnegies. Using one version of a sociological paradigm, Davenport was out to prove through science what Adolf Hitler would later try to impose through a world war.

Those in the eugenics movement wanted to pass legislation requiring sterilization of the "inferior" population. This, they thought, would improve the racial stock. One of Davenport's colleagues, Madison Grant, was a notorious racist. He attempted to gain control of the Committee on Anthropology (then part of the National Research Council). Through it, he wanted to eliminate government funding of cultural anthropology, diverting the funds to eugenics and physical anthropology. Grant, along with some well-known sociologists, lobbied for and won the most racist legislation in U.S. immigration history. The Immigration Restrictive Act of 1924 set strict quotas barring the "racially undesirable." Mead's research could hardly have been more timely.

Her book fell like a bomb on the playground of the racist biological determinists. It said biology could be made into whatever culture determined that it wanted or needed. Her powerful argument, phrased in lucid prose, was that people become what the cultural needs of a given society dictate. Genetic influences are unimportant. In America, young people need to become independent, future-oriented, self-guided, stress-tolerating, mobile adults. Mead said that they develop these traits by going through the extended identity crisis called adolescence. During this period, they have to break with their parents, choose their own vocational direction and future mate, and survive an extremely stressful time. Stress and rebellion are functional for the desired personality results. The cultural and social arrangements of this society induce these experiences.

On the other hand, Mead argued, Samoan society has different needs. Continuity and tradition are much more important. Violence is rare and the pace of life tranquil. There is no need for autonomous, mobile, high-powered, stress-tolerating personalities. Consequently, there is no need for the psychosocial transition of adolescence, stimulating conflict and social upheaval between older and younger generations. The results in Samoa are social arrangements allowing for a smoother transition into adulthood. In short, a painful identity struggle is not part of teenage life among the Samoans.

So persuasive was the case study that it led to nearly fifty years of consensus in anthropology about nature versus nurture. Nature may build a platform for human life, said most anthropologists after Mead, but the important parts of an individual's personality come from nurture. Human nature is extraordinarily malleable. The reason that people are different is because they are socialized by and into different cultures.

Paradise Lost

Enter Derek Freeman, an Australian anthropologist born in New Zealand. Since 1940 he has spent six years studying Samoa, mostly in the western part, 130 miles from Mead's island. His book *Margaret Mead and Samoa: The Making and Unmaking of an Anthropological Myth* is a thundering critique of Mead.[3]

His claims are simple: Margaret Mead was almost completely wrong in all her basic observations about the nature of tranquil, peaceful, sexually free Samoa. She was deluded by teenagers who made up most of what they told her. Samoan adolescence isn't a smooth transition, as Mead supposed. Instead, it follows something more like the American pattern. Samoa is not a South Pacific Eden. It is a place where wife beating, rape, murder, and other crimes occur. Yet Mead turned a blind eye to these elements, claims Freeman. The paradigm she adopted from Boas just would not let her see what was going on.

Mead's methods and results, according to Freeman, were bad science. She did not go to Samoa seeking truth but seeking a decisive argument for the importance of culture over biology. Her teacher, Franz Boas, sent her to Samoa to find proof for his own cultural paradigm. She did just that. Her work was a political tract against the eugenicists, biological determinists, and racists. In passing, Mead also struck a blow against G. Stanley Hall.

Freeman cites official statistics and results from his own years of studying western Samoa as well as from a short visit to Ta'u. He paints a radically different portrait of Samoan life. He calls up other anthropological studies of Samoa in his service (though his use of their information is not always careful). This is a classic case of a relatively unknown scholar seeking to slay a giant (after she was dead!). The sales of the book have been gigantic. Freeman has made a name for himself. The furor has created the most excitement that anthropology has seen in a long time.

Critics of social science have been prone to take Freeman's book as gospel.[4] It offers delightfully juicy proof that paradigms lead social scientists too frequently to make up their minds before they perform their research. Then they weave the data to fit the perspectives and points they wanted to make all along.

Where's the Beef?

Anthropologists, including most of those Freeman quotes in his own favor, do not see the matter quite as he does.[5] What they say in support of both Mead and Freeman is very revealing about the limits of sociology, as well as anthropology, as a social science. Their response underlines the pluralism that exists within social science, even on comparatively factual matters.

The Problem of Restudy and Replication

Almost never is the work of a social scientist redone. An anthropologist traditionally considers the group or village she studies to be "her own" and others are to keep out. Margaret Mead was miffed when Melville Herskovits (a colleague with whom she had several run-ins) assigned one of his students to restudy Mead's Ta'u. He had long suspected that Samoa was more complicated than Mead had portrayed it. Herskovits's student, Lowell D. Holmes, was to do a methodological restudy in order to test the validity of Mead's earlier work. This he did in 1954.[6]

Mead gave Holmes's 1958 book, *Ta'u: Stability and Change in a Samoan Village*, an unfavorable review. She cornered him at an American Anthropologist Association meeting in 1960 and blistered his ears with her unqualified displeasure. Holmes found Ta'u more competitive than Mead had. Where she had found no notions of romantic love, he found the mythology full of romantic folklore. Her opening chapter portrayed a beehive of activity. He found Ta'u so quiet that most days "you could have shot a cannon down the equivalent of Main Street without hitting a soul." They portrayed two rather different Ta'us.

Why the discrepancies? Holmes concludes that some of the differences in their views were due to Mead's interpreter-informant, Napoleone Tuiteleleapaga. Tuiteleleapaga was a Rosicrucian (a member of an esoteric, occult society that claims to have existed since the ancient Egyptians)—not a very typical Samoan. Nonetheless, Holmes's overall assessment was that Mead was not so much wrong as incomplete. He agreed with Mead's main conclusion that adolescence was immensely less stressful and traumatic for Samoans than for American teenagers in 1925. He also agreed that culture has an overwhelmingly strong influence on adolescence.

There are problems with restudies in social science. If the society studied is far away and exotic, it is often too difficult to duplicate the work. There still are so many other places yet to be studied for the first time. Then, if a research project takes several years and is large scale (such as Gunnar Myrdal's study of race in America), it is unlikely that resources or careers will be reinvested to cover the same ground. Some current sociological projects have budgets in the millions of dollars. Once completed, they are unlikely ever to be redone.

Yet in a discipline with multiple perspectives and paradigms, in which preconceptions and assumptions have powerful effects, restudy and replication seem crucial to achieve even a weak degree of objectivity. Such restudies are conducted on occasion. In sociology, for example, there are three studies of Muncie, Indiana. These restudies raise interesting issues about what counts as good data and how assumptions influence the social scientist's decision about what is worth studying.[7] In anthropology, there are classic, contrasting studies of Tepoztlán, Mexico: Robert Redfield saw light and harmony, while Oscar Lewis saw a darker side of conflict and struggle in the community.[8] Mead (stressing tranquillity and harmony), Holmes (underlining competitiveness and romantic love), and Freeman (focusing on conflict and crime) see Samoa in contrasting ways. There is some indication that Mead in later years saw her first Samoan experience as an "apprenticeship." She also admitted that her tendency was to treat the societies she studied kindly.

How should these sorts of differences be treated? Which constitute real differences in the society studied? Freeman's data come mainly from the more urban, western part of Samoa as well as from a different time period.[9] Do the contrasts between Mead's and Freeman's conclusions represent a right and wrong account of the same reality? Or do they reflect differences between two contrasting parts of Samoan life?

Can it be that neither the one-sided portrait painted by Mead nor the equally one-sided portrait from Freeman represents the full truth about Samoan society? Is a society a uniform reality, with all its members holding the same values, displaying the same personality traits, and exhibiting the same behavior patterns? Is it not more reasonable to think that social arrangements are multidimensional? Certainly they are often contested within a single social group. What one finds may depend on what one is looking for. Does Holmes give a more balanced picture than Mead or Freeman? These are persistent questions in social research.

The Problems of Comparison

Ensuring that the same things are compared and interpreting the data about them fairly are knotty problems. Mead set out to compare Samoan adolescence on what was the country's most remote and least changed island village with typical adolescence in America in the 1920s. Freeman set out to compare Mead's information on Samoan life with his own data from a part of Samoa that was much more changed by Western contact than Mead's village had been.

One of Mead's problems is the way she simplifies both Samoan and American teenage patterns, heightening the contrast between them. Freeman simplifies his own more urban, western Samoan data to heighten the differences between his account and that of Mead. Readers are left wondering whether these studies represent different conclusions about the same reality or differing realities that led to different conclusions.

This problem of comparison is central to sociology. Great minds like that of Alexis de Tocqueville, Karl Marx, Émile Durkheim, and Max Weber wrestled with the nature and characteristics of the new industrial society. Their conclusions and characterizations are very different. This is partly due to their having lived at different points in the industrialization and democratization process in European countries. Each saw the modernization process and the resulting condition of modernity differently, even though they were all supposedly looking at the same "reality." Even today, contemporary sociologists offer widely varying understandings of the differences and similarities between democratic capitalism and authoritarian socialism. How does the reader determine which differences are due to the qualities of the research object and which are due to the ideas and paradigms that researchers bring to their work?

Researcher Effects

Here's an obvious influence on the differences between Mead's and Freeman's outlooks: Mead was a young woman interviewing young women about delicate matters of sexuality. Freeman was an older man trying to determine the accuracy of Mead's information. Unfortunately, gender can create discrepancies in the sorts of information accessible to researchers (and even differences in its interpretation). Rapport between the researcher and informants is a paramount consideration in gaining sensitive information about people and their social arrangements. Research proves that people reveal very different things in differing social contexts. Researchers of differing age, gender, race, ethnicity, or perceived political-religious affiliation can receive very different answers to the same questions from the same people.

Freeman claims that Mead was systematically misinformed. Her informants deliberately lied, engaging in a common cultural game. In the practice of *tua fa'ase'e*, a Samoan tries to dupe a person and laughs behind his or her back if the bait is taken.[10] One wonders how Freeman, an older male who spent even less time at Ta'u than Mead did, established such effective rapport that he was able to determine that these adept liars were not lying to him. In other words, social science has to contend with a level and extent of researcher effects not experienced in the physical sciences. There are clear interactive effects between social observer and those observed.

This chapter has already suggested that the bias of perspective and paradigm can affect research results. Mead went to Samoa as a student of Boas when the issue of nature versus nurture was a hot topic. She went with a conviction that the eugenicists and racists were wrong. Her Samoan experience confirmed that. This is not to say that Mead was careless, deliberately obtuse, saw only what she wanted to see, or made up what she reported. But one cannot deny that she saw Samoa *through her own lenses*.

Becoming a scientist is not a matter of receiving a vaccine against bias. Being scientific means becoming aware of bias and developing procedures with a community of fellow scientists that expand one's openness to the reality he or she studies. Part of the Freeman-Mead flap is over bias and how to use it to get closer to the real Samoa. The ins and outs of this controversy are instructive for all social scientists. The goal of these researchers is to describe and understand social arrangements "as they are" and not as one's own paradigm would like them to be.

Insider and Outsider Interpretations

One other interesting facet of the Freeman-Mead flap is the Samoans' own response. Many Samoans have read what Mead, Freeman, and others have said about them. Some have been very vocal in disowning significant elements of the ways in which Mead and Freeman describe them. Social scientists are part of a distinct community of discourse that has its own culture and social structure, its own categories and ways of communicating. Social scientific communication pools create their own jargon and in-group lingo. They often write their "scientific descriptions" for an audience of other professionals. Yet professional categories and questions do not necessarily coincide with the distinctions and interpretations of reality held by the members of the social group studied.

Insiders reading a social science work describing their own group often feel that they have been mishandled by science. Their way of life, how it works, and its meanings disappear behind a distorted, one-dimensional book or paper. They experience such reports as having more to do with boosting the author's career or with firing salvos in a paradigm war than with the realities of their social ways. Yet it is difficult to settle the question of whose version is correct. The well-informed insider may be blinded due to the social group's own biases and illusions. The outsider may not have sufficient rapport or enough history with a group to see it "as it is." Or there may be many "as it ises," and somehow all accounts describe a bit of the truth.

In this case, Mead's interpreter and informant, Napoleone Tuiteleleapaga, wrote his own book, *Samoa Yesterday and Today and Tomorrow*.[11] What can be said about his portrait of Samoa? The introduction, he claims, was written by Margaret Mead herself in her New York office *shortly after her death!* A nice trick, that. And the style matches Mead's almost perfectly. With such a beginning, one wonders about the rest of the book.

None of these difficulties is distinctive to anthropology. All apply equally to sociology. None of them is new. Yet they do mean that no study can be taken at face value. Every "assured result" on which "all sociologists agree" must be closely examined. In evaluating the findings of sociology, the careful reader looks for restudies that reinforce a finding, fair comparisons, controls on researcher effects, and a sensitive handling of insider-outsider interpretations. When social research has these qualities, the reader can have confidence in it as a well-established body of findings. Neither readers nor researchers may be able to overcome all the ways in which paradigms affect how they look at the social world and what they see. Yet they can weigh the relative weight of different paradigms once they are sensitive to their presence.

Nurture Versus Nature

One postscript on Margaret Mead and her lifelong interest in children growing into adulthood: Mead concluded that human nature is extremely malleable, that it can become very different things in different cultures. Her work suggests that language, race, and culture vary independently of each other.

Today, researchers are reasserting that biology is far more powerful in shaping social arrangements than Mead and her followers ever imagined.[12] Sociobiology and biological anthropology stress the factors that Boas and Mead minimized. The genetic makeup and other biological givens of human beings create universal conditions that place limits on cultural variation. Sociobiology and other recent approaches seek to underline biological facts as foundations for social facts.

At present, the vote is still not in on Margaret Mead's Samoan work. Nature and nurture both contribute to what people become as individuals and as groups. The paradigm one adopts influences the balance given to biology and culture in creating socialized adults. Certainly, it can be said that in Margaret Mead, biology and culture conspired to shape a wonderfully vigorous and creative individual.

The difficulty of grasping a single issue such as the relative importance of culture and nature is simple in contrast to the difficulty of grasping the nature of the total modern world. The various sociological paradigms and analyses point in a variety of directions. Different social researchers see differing features of the modern world as important in understanding and explaining it. The next chapter portrays the variety of ways in which classic sociologists thought about the modern world. The disagreements over Mead and Samoa are small potatoes compared with disagreements over the nature of the modern world.

NOTES

1. Jane Howard, *Margaret Mead: A Life* (New York: Simon & Schuster, 1984); Robert Cassidy, *Margaret Mead: A Voice for the Century* (New York: Universe Books, 1982); Edward Rice, *Margaret Mead: A Portrait* (New York: Harper & Row, 1979); Margaret Mead, *Blackberry Winter: My Earlier Years* (New York: Morrow, 1972).
2. Howard, *Margaret Mead: A Life*, pp. 347–348.

3. Derek Freeman, *Margaret Mead and Samoa: The Making and Unmaking of an Anthropological Myth* (Cambridge, MA: Harvard University Press, 1983).
4. Anthony Flew's *Thinking About Social Thinking* (Oxford, England: Blackwell, 1985), pp. 7–9, is a good example of this sort of bad behavior, taking the charges against Mead at face value.
5. See Ivan Brady, ed., "Special Section: Speaking in the Name of the Real: Freeman and Mead on Samoa," *American Anthropologist* 85, no. 4 (December 1983): 908–947; also, Richard Goodman, *Mead's Coming of Age in Samoa: A Dissenting View* (Pepperdine Press, 1983), and Bradd Shore, *Sala'ilua: A Samoan Mystery* (New York: Columbia University Press, 1982). See also Derek Freeman, "Fa'apua'a Fa'amu and Margaret Mead," *American Anthropologist* 91, no. 4 (December 1989): 1017–1022; P. A. Cox, "Margaret Mead and Samoa," *American Scientist* 71 (1983): 407.
6. Howard, *Margaret Mead: A Life*, pp. 321–322.
7. Robert S. Lynd and Helen M. Lynd, *Middletown: A Study in Contemporary American Culture* (New York: Harcourt, 1929) and *Middletown in Transition* (New York: Harcourt, 1937); Theodore Caplow et al., *Middletown Families* (Minneapolis: University of Minnesota Press, 1982). Theodore Caplow et al., in *All Faithful People: Change and Continuity in Middletown's Religion* (Minneapolis: University of Minnesota Press, 1983), notes the Lynds' assumptions about the declining significance of religion. Robert Lynd himself attended Union Seminary in preparation for the ministry before giving up his faith. The early Middletown studies reflect a biographical and sociological conclusion that religion is dying and is relatively insignificant in modern life. The data from Caplow and other studies challenge this, demonstrating both that religious beliefs and practices have not declined and that secularizing changes postulated by the Lynds were fewer and less profound than they hypothesized.
8. Robert Redfield, *Tepoztlán: A Mexican Village* (Chicago: University of Chicago Press, 1930); Oscar Lewis, *Life in a Mexican Village: Tepoztlán Restudied* (Urbana, IL: University of Illinois Press, 1951).
9. Lowell Holmes's comments in *American Anthropologist* 85, no. 4 (December 1983), pp. 931–933, are devastating to the way Freeman compares apples and oranges in his critique of Mead.
10. Freeman claims that Mead's informants resorted to *tau fa'ase'e* or *tau fa'alili*, which means to tease or dupe someone. This is a form of recreational lying in which Samoans put a tall story over on the ignorant and then chuckle at them. Freeman, "Fa'apua'a Fa'amu," p. 1017.
11. Napoleone Tuiteleleapaga, *Samoa Yesterday and Today and Tomorrow* (Great Neck, NY: Todd & Honeywell, 1980).
12. Carl N. Degler, *In Search of Human Nature: The Decline and Revival of Darwinism in American Social Thought* (New York: Oxford University Press, 1991).

Chapter 9

THE RISE OF THE MODERN WORLD

Imagine doing geology and geography in a world where the continents move twenty to thirty miles every year (instead of every million years). Maps would continually be out of date. Planning your ski trip would be frustrating when you arrived to find the Alps replaced by a large lake. You wouldn't want to fly to Hawaii in case changes while the flight was in the air put the airport twenty feet beneath the Pacific Ocean.

Actually, if the world changed this way, people would want to map it carefully and monitor its movements. Only then could they understand where and when such rapid change takes place. Sociology came into being because the social world was changing so rapidly that all the stable landmarks were vanishing. "All that is solid melts into the air," as Marx put it.[1] Sociology is a child of this changing world. The central tradition of sociology deals with the historical transition from agrarian feudalism to modern democratic capitalism.

Marx, Weber, and Durkheim, major founders of sociology, have this change at the center of their interest. Each handles the relationships between individuals and the structures that emerge in the modern world. Many other classic and contemporary thinkers also seek to paint a picture of modernity, with its precursors and its likely future. Sociology offers a diversity of analyses and value judgments about what is happening. These various answers show how difficult it is to decide what the beast is that inhabits sociology's courtyard. Here's a sketch of some of the important answers that the creators of modern sociology give.[2]

Mapping the Modern World

Democratization

Alexis de Tocqueville (1805–1859) compared France, the United States, and Britain during their formative years. North Americans know him best for his analysis of democracy in the United States. This French journalist and political scientist said that the world is moving from hierarchy and rank to an equalization of conditions among people. He called this process "democratization." Everywhere he saw kingdoms and aristocracies melting down into democratic mass societies characterized by social equality.

In his view, ascribed status (that is, the rank one has due to birth) and status based on the social class to which one belongs are dissolving as modernity increases its hold. While wealth and intellectual differences remain, new status concerns preoccupy people. Moderns seek to be recognized as important, but they do so in ways different from those of people in the rigid classes of the past. In the modern scene, individuals are increasingly mobile, autonomous, and diverse. At the same time, they are more dependent on public opinion for ideas, direction, and recognition. In such a world, people cannot easily know how important or powerful others are.

Much modern status is based on money. Yet people are unsure how much of it others have or even how much they themselves must have to merit greater respect than their peers. Thus, visible symbols of status differences take on a new importance. More and more such symbols become matters of *personal* identity. Ethnicity, race, gender, personal adornment, the mode and expense of one's transportation all take on increased importance in modern life. In the absence of traditional markers, the conspicuous display of consumer choices becomes a common language used to signal one's importance.

Centralization of power is another trend that Tocqueville noted. Large bureaucratic structures capable of manipulating public opinion dominate government. The individual becomes lost in such bureaucracies and is weaker than ever before these power structures. For that reason, secondary or intermediate structures (churches, labor unions, political parties, voluntary institutions) increase their prominence in moderating centralized powers. Also, with class no longer as important as it was in the past, ethnicity and gender become consequential indicators of social distinction.

Religion's importance is another thing that impressed Tocqueville. He saw religion as an ultimate source of people's conceptions of physical and social reality. It provides a framework that brings intellectual order to the diversity in the world. At its heart is dogma (officially established and prescribed doctrines). However, democratization can hurt religion. It can dissolve dogma as it challenges all traditional authority. Tocqueville's analysis suggests that the modern individual takes public opinion as a new sacred dogma. Thus, official religion finds it difficult to maintain its traditions.

Yet democracy also has positive relations with religion. Tocqueville noted that political freedom encourages religious institutions and people's passion for religion. The United States is his key example. Here there are higher levels of participation and identification with religious groups than in countries where politics are totalitarian. In turn, vigorous religious groups foster attitudes about and relations of equality that are essential to freedom. The religious "habits of the heart" provide an essential nurturing climate for the practices of political freedom. Liberal political structures and vigorous religious life go hand in hand.

Secularization

Alexis de Tocqueville's fellow Frenchman, Auguste Comte (1798–1857), took intellectual rather than social change as the heart of modernization. What's crucial in modernization is a new mind-set. His "law of three stages" conceives of modern society as one increasingly governed by positive scientific ideas and worldviews. Religious ways of thinking control less and less of the modern mind. This transition from the theological through the metaphysical to the positive stage of thought is what modernization means. According to Comte, the present time is a period of crisis and transition. The conflict of diverse beliefs and worldviews in the modern world offers no unity of civilization. That is why this era is warlike and subject to poverty. This period, however, will pass. Someday people will not be divided by differing mindsets, with some thinking like scientists and others like bigoted, close-minded religious fanatics. All human thought and outlook will be scientific. Culture will be unified.

He also believed that the theological-feudal order is gone forever. The business class is replacing the landed aristocracy; science is supplanting religion; republican political forms are eroding monarchies. A new moral community is being created with the aid of sociologists. A new society, built on new ways of thinking, is being born. It will be a hierarchical society, with ritual and liturgy. There will even be a new "religion" with worship of Society as the supreme being.

Eventually modern society will be as stable as the medieval one was. What will unite and stabilize it is the new "spiritual power"—the power of science. Science will provide the stability of incontrovertible, clear ideas. Sociologists, scientists, and the captains of industry together will create a technical elite of experts who will solve problems as human civilization progresses. Humans are well on their way to achieving this peaceful, prosperous scientific-industrial society, according to Comte. The remaining problems are technical ones, solvable in principle by science as its powers increase. Comte was optimistic about the future, to say the least.

The Bourgeois Revolution

Karl Marx (1818–1883), a seminal thinker in sociology despite what one may think of his politics, makes modernization a matter of the bourgeois revolution. Modernization, he says, is a shift from a feudal society dominated by rural landowning aristocrats to the new, urban, property-owning bourgeoisie. Since a *bourg* is a town, the bourgeoisie is in fact a class of "city dwellers."

People in the Western world lived for centuries in a feudal order dominated by aristocratic landowners. This order originated when Rome fell and the power of the empire no longer held people together. Localities became isolated from each other. Local lords offered peasants in their region protection from outside raiders. In exchange, the peasants accepted a relationship that was virtual slavery: they became serfs. These local hierarchies and dependencies turned into a pyramid of stratification and domination.

In the eleventh century the transformation of modernity took its first quiet footsteps with the growth of cities. Seasonal fairs held outside the city walls became year-round activities, crystallizing into permanent marketplaces. The city proper annexed these *faubourgs* or medieval suburbs, inhabited by merchants. From them came the *bourgeoisie*, the traders, merchants, and manufacturers, who brought modern capitalism into being. At this point, the capitalist entrepreneurs took the front seat of history.

Modern social problems and conflicts, according to Marx, reflect the struggle over the wealth and property created by this new capitalist, market-dominated society. The democratic revolution (epitomized in the French Revolution) refers to political changes that the bourgeois brought about in order to cement their hold on productive power. Democratic politics are the politics of the bourgeoisie. They also developed science. They use science constantly to help cut the costs of their operations and increase their profit margins. Science also strengthens the means of social control (such as the military) that reinforce the dominance of the bourgeoisie.

Marx argues that one is either part of the problem (on the side of the bourgeoisie) or part of the solution (on the side of the workers, the proletariat). The poverty, suffering, injustice, racism, and sexism seen in today's world will end, he asserts, only with the revolutionary overthrow of the bourgeoisie by the proletariat. The central problem is the way in which private property allows the wealthy to control the poor and to take much more than can be considered their fair share of the goods of this world. Sociology helps people see the laws of history as they move toward revolution so that all can cast off the chains of oppression.

Marx claims that religion is an expression of and protest against human alienation. God, says Marx, is nothing more than a symbolic projection of real human powers. The attributes assigned to God are, in fact, the ideal attributes of the human race. Marx asserts that people make God in their own image. The structure and organization of religion reflect nothing more and nothing less than the powers of the ruling class. The elite control the training of clergy, the publishing of books, and the salaries of religious functionaries. So religion in the modern world (as in the ancient world) serves the goals and interests of this class of people. Only when society is rid of the bourgeoisie will alienation be overcome. Someday a perfect society of communism will appear, and then religion will vanish.

From this viewpoint, sociology is a scientific protest against the alienation of the modern world. It reveals that humans are alienated from their true nature in four ways. First, people do not control their *physical laboring activity*. Someone else sets the hours, the pace of the work, the movements of one's limbs. In short, a person's job description is written and enforced to exploit him or her. Second, the *products* of labor are like aliens to the workers. They do not own these products. Workers make them, but the company that employs the workers controls their disposal. Third, people are alienated from their *fellow human beings*. They compete for the same jobs and become enemies of one another. They are divided from management and often from people in the next work area.

In the end, human life is in some ways worse than that of animals. Humans are alienated from their *"species-being."* As a species, the distinctive human qualities mean that people should be free, intelligent creators through a satisfying work activity. Yet they become pitiful stomachs and muscles who work to live. Work stultifies and stunts people, dulling their minds and destroying their health. The human is no more than a commodity in the modern world. Sociology's purpose is to understand and free humanity from that world.

Eclipse of Community

Ferdinand Tönnies (1855–1936) takes modernization to be the displacement of natural, communal, intimate relations by artificial, impersonal relations based on rational calculation. In modernity, noncommunal connections tie people together in organizations. The mass society in which most people now live is held together by economic arrangements and secured by concentrated political power. Law and politics take commanding places in human lives, reducing the potency of traditional customs and warm networks of cooperative ties. Relationships in the modern urban center exemplify what Tönnies called the *Gesellschaft* (associational society). Tönnies found the *Gesellschaft* inferior to its alternative, the *Gemeinschaft*.

Gemeinschaft (communal society), found in towns and villages, builds on the strong relational ties of kinship, neighborhood, and friendship. This society has much healthier effects on human well-being. The family provides the first experiences of typically *Gemeinschaft* relational characteristics. Strong personal ties bind the family together, and such human connectedness becomes the model for other social relations in the community.

In contrast, fragile ties of the contract organize *Gesellschaft*. Here even the strongest relational bonds weaken. One initially experiences strong relational ties in one's family of origin. Yet in a *Gesellschaft* a major task of parenting is to teach children how to be independent and autonomous from the family. Because contractual ties overshadow social relationships, the *Gesellschaft* requires a strong state to enforce the voluntary agreements.

Otherwise, people would constantly break their agreements (even within the family) when it was advantageous for them to do so. Monetary values motivate and dominate city life. People violate social agreements and rules to enhance their income. Contrary to Marx, single social classes are not internally unified. Fellow members of the same class battle with each other, seeking monetary advancement. So classes are not groups unified politically, socially, culturally, or even monetarily. There is conflict within classes as well as between them. The state is essential for restraining such conflicts. The effect is that the state takes increasing amounts of power into its hands in order to preserve peace. The strength that such a state requires to hold society together is dysfunctional for the long-term health of a society. It becomes so strong eventually that it tears the associational society apart, creating the basis for the reorganization of a communal society.

Personally, Tönnies was strongly antireligious and anticlerical. He did little to develop a clear analysis of the place of religion in the modern world. One of his late writings indicates that he longed for a purely secular realization of the social values of the Christianity he so strongly rejected. In an autobiographical work of 1922, he spoke of a "creed of the holy spirit" that preserves what he considered valuable in Christianity. This unpublished, utopian essay, "The New Gospel," looked forward to the coming of the third age of history described by Joachim Fiore as an "age of the Spirit."

The Rise of a Diverse, Secular, Organic Society

Émile Durkheim (1858–1917) rather liked the modern world (in contrast to Tönnies). For him, modernization represents a shift to moral and social diversity, to a solidarity based on the division of occupational labor. The major shift is from what he called mechanical solidarity (with its moral and social homogeneity) to organic solidarity (characterized by moral and social diversity). Actually, many of his ideas about these two types of solidarity came from Tönnies. A society with mechanical solidarity is similar to the *Gemeinschaft*, while a society with organic solidarity matches the *Gesellschaft*. As one might guess from the names he gives to the two, Durkheim feels strongly positive about the *Gesellschaft*-like organic solidarity. Modernization is a progressive emancipation from traditional restraints of kinship, class, localism, and general social conscience. The heterogeneity and individualism of the organic society is a liberation from the homogeneity of the mechanical society.

Despite its diversity, this new form of society does not lose authority over the individual. According to Durkheim, organic society does not need the powerful state envisioned by Tönnies to enforce contracts on individualists with no moral sensibilities. The essence of any society's authority appears in the ways it constrains the individual. Some constraints are indirect, found in the society's collective consciousness as contained in traditions, values, and rules. Other societal controls (such as walls, fences, and police) act directly to restrain individuals. The modern world has both types of constraint, only they differ in form from those of the traditional mechanical society.

Pluralism and heterogeneity constitute modern life. Different kinds of people with different sorts of values have to learn to live together. This diversity is prone to dissolve the authority of society over the individual. It can lead to chaotic communities. Therefore, corporate, intermediate structures are essential for healthy moral life. In intermediate-sized groups, a communal and moral authority is developed that is effective with individuals. Unfortunately, the state increasingly absorbs the old functions of traditional local groups, considering the authority of secondary groups larger than the family a threat to its own power.

For Durkheim, the tendency of the modern state is to undermine the very conditions vital to healthy social and moral life. It is true that the state creates private rights that protect individuals from the abuses of secondary groups and intermediate structures. Yet it also undermines the authority of the intermediate groups that strengthen the moral life of individuals. In this Tönnies is correct: too strong a state is bad for the health of society.

Interestingly, Durkheim almost completely neglects social class in his writings. He simply does not see class groups as important in the modern world. At the end of *The Division of Labor in Society* (1893), he claims that modern social developments sterilize classes and remove social inequalities. The division of labor will gradually overcome all the tensions and conflicts of the transition to modernity. Individuals are all being tightly woven into an organic society, becoming mutually interdependent. Rather than producing conflicting class groups with different interests, modernization creates a living, organic, cooperative society.

For an ardent secularist, Durkheim held rather dramatic ideas about religion. Religion, he argued, is the origin of human thought as well as its basic framework. It divides the world into clearly distinct realms of the sacred and profane. Clear, distinct ideas originated in religious patterns of thinking. Rituals are the means by which one passes from the profane to the sacred. Rituals mark the boundaries of human lives and solemnize their most significant relationships, even in modern secular life.

The content or substance of religion, however, is not supernatural beings or God. Religion is no more than a symbolic expression of people's dependence on society. The essence of religion is the sacred community of believers. "God" is a symbolic way of representing the authority and nurturing power of all the social ties that bring humans into being and structure their lives. Periods of communal excitement or effervescence shape the specific content of what people take to be sacred. These may be times of collective mourning and tragedy (such as the Civil War) or of collective triumph and joy (such as the victory of the American Revolution). In Durkheim's estimation, people in all religions worship society as the supreme being, though they are normally unaware of what they are doing.

The eminent danger of the modern world, according to Durkheim, is the isolation of the individual and resulting anomie.

Anomie occurs when people have no sense of guidance, regulation, or restraint set by clear, strong norms. Disorganization threatens modern life, not misorganization (Marx's diagnosis). The individual is a bundle of powerful desires, willing and wanting. If there are no clear restraints on the individual, then society collapses into a heap of clamoring humans, each seeking to fulfill his or her own infinite desires. The unrestrained individual, nurtured by the disorganization and normlessness of modern society, is an unhappy and troubled creature. Pessimism and anxiety accompany periods of great striving and release. In those periods, individuals do not sense clear boundaries and goals. Suicide rates skyrocket. Crime and punishment multiply.

The solution for modern ills is to find ways of constraining the individual that are appropriate to the nature of the modern world. For Durkheim, there can be no return to traditional cultural forms. Ancient legal means utilizing draconian punishment will not work in modern society. Traditional religion can no longer provide the means to restrain the individual or unify the civilization. Mechanical solidarity (a unity based on the sameness of people) is now impossible. Intermediate institutions and groups where the individual has an identity are Durkheim's solution. In these groups, communally shared values and rules are created, applied, and made effective. With individuals embedded in intermediate groups, there can be both extraordinary societal diversity and societally effective restraints on heterogeneous individuals.

The Increasing Rationalization of All Spheres of Life

For Max Weber (1864–1920), modernization meant the penetration of "instrumental rationality" (*Zweckrationalität*) into all spheres of life. "Instrumental rationality" is a mind-set that invariably raises the question of the best means to achieve the goals of human life. By use of science, observation, and careful reasoning, it seeks the instruments or tools and techniques to achieve practically desired results. If something "works," then it is instrumentally rational. Its single value is efficiency.

This rationality expresses itself in the rise of formal law and complex bureaucratic organizations. It engenders an "occupational asceticism" in the majority of the population. This means that one approaches one's work as a "calling." People work hard and try to do their jobs to the best of their ability. They sacrifice time, family, and leisure in a constant striving to achieve in their vocation. They do this even when they have more than enough money to be comfortable. Inexorably, modernization encloses more and more of life into the master process of rationalization. Once rationalization penetrates key sectors of the modern world, it is powerful enough to force people and organizations to obey its imperative of efficiency.

Reason, not feelings, determines what people do and how they do it under the conditions of modernity. However, the basis of communal relations in a group is the subjective feeling that they are mutually involved in each other's lives. Such emotional ties come from shared traditions, values, or the mysterious powers of charisma. By contrast, modern associational relations exist when people connect with each other due to rational calculations of interest or consciously taken choices. Ancient cities and communities were communally organized groupings of closed populations (tightly knit kin or ethnic groups) bound together by emotional identifications. In comparison, medieval cities were associations of individuals. Out of them grew the modern city with its paramount ordering principle of rationalization.

Rationalization creates new groups and new dynamics between groups. The way in which wealth, prestige (or respect), and power no longer overlap as they did in the premodern world illustrates how complex the modern world is. In Weber's view, status groups dominate the traditional world. Such groups as aristocratic nobles or religious castes like the Brahmans of India are status groups. Their claim to respect and honor was based on a cultural style of life. Historically, the distribution of prestige was crucial to human social dynamics, even more important than the distribution of wealth and power. Those who had social prestige also had political power and even wealth. This contrasts with the modern world, where it is possible to have wealth without honor (for instance, in a crime family) or power without great wealth (for instance, President Harry Truman).

For Weber, the group of people called the social class really exists only in the modern world. It is oriented to relative positions in modern markets—that is, a category of people based on the control of wealth, jobs, and productive skills. Furthermore, unlike traditional societies with unified and powerful status groups, classes are internally divided. They are seldom able to crystallize and become powerful cultural actors. They cannot set the agenda for the whole of society as traditional status groups did. As a result, conflict in the modern world is very fragmented, and it cuts across groups.

Rationalization, according to Weber, also means the secularizing of social experience and institutions. What people consider sacred shrinks. Rationalization strips mystery from nature. Yet just when everything appears solidified into rational patterns, the "charismatic personality" strides onto center stage and disrupts everything. The sacred breaks into people's lives in the form of charisma.

In its pristine state, charisma undermines traditions. The charismatic leader is relatively antiutilitarian and is not concerned with pragmatic success or efficiency. Followers gather about charismatic figures (such as the Ayatollah Khomeini in Iran or Martin Luther King, Jr., in the United States) and create large social movements. Inevitably, however, charisma fades. When the movement grows too large for a single, dynamic leader to control it, it reorganizes. The bureaucrats take charge. A once-dynamic movement turns gradually into a boring but increasingly efficient organization. In a word, the charisma of the leader is "routinized." His or her vision is made practical. An effective, day-by-day, instrumentally rational leadership takes over. It translates charisma into utilitarian techniques and efficient systems that ensure the continuance of the movement.

Luther and Calvin were great charismatic figures in the West. Their original ideas and the social groups that carried their ideas generated a grammar of motives that oriented people practically to this world. Their routinized charisma provided powerful forces for social action among entire social strata. The ethos of the Protestant ethic, when spread into a new group, had power to transform an entire economy. The modern world rode into existence on the backs of ascetic Protestants (Calvinists, Puritans, Methodists, Baptists). In time, rationality penetrated religion. It too was made less emotional as the world became gradually disenchanted.

The history of the Methodists is a good example of the routinization of charisma. John and Charles Wesley brought a dynamic, Sect-type movement into being. Methodism expressed rebellion against the dead formalism of the Church of England. It met in plain buildings. Enthusiastic worship and lay leadership characterized the early days. Today the Methodist movement looks very much like a middle-class, comfortable, restrained religious organization, not much different from the Church of England. Stone church buildings, carpeted, well-appointed sanctuaries, formal services led by highly educated, robed ministers are characteristic. The dynamic movement has become a routine large organization.

Rationalization converts all of life into large, impersonal, bureaucratized structures. A monolithic, utilitarian, secular mentality and bureaucracy subordinates all values and relationships. The patriarchal, communal, and enchanted diminish along with the irrational, the personally exploitative, and the superstitious. All that remains is the rationally controllable. The problem of modernity is not *dis*organization (as Durkheim feared), but *over*organization. Rationalization squeezes the life out of people, leveling them before the great idol of efficiency. Organizations run according to administrative meritocracy, and schools seek to generate a universal education where all fit the mold of instrumental rationality.

Weber was pessimistic about the future prospects of the modern world. He saw it as doomed to serve the god of rationality at all costs, becoming increasingly bureaucratic and secular. The supernatural vanishes as more and more of life comes under the aegis of systematic reason. The world is something to manipulate and control, to master and exploit. Such an outlook becomes the passion shaping modern civilization.

The Many Faces of Modernity

If you are not frustrated by now, then you have probably been sleep-reading (a technique highly developed at American universities by second-semester freshmen). These are powerful portraits of the modern world. Their ideas not only differ but many of them conflict in ways that mean they cannot all be true. Yet there is truth in each of them.

When faced with a conflict in interpretations, the tendency is to credit the ideas that reinforce one's own sociopolitical and religious background. But Christians and sociologists are committed to seeking the truth about social arrangements, regardless of how uncomfortable that truth might be. Seeking the truth involves an arduous and costly process of putting one's current social conceptions at risk. One needs to test not only one's own ideas but also those of great social thinkers, using the expanding resources of research and information.

How does one do that? What contribution does a Christian perspective make in figuring out what is the truth about society? What are the critical questions that must be asked and that need at least provisional answers? What criteria can be used to weigh various versions of the modern world and of humans' place in it?

These are the questions for the next chapter and Part III. There is far more in sociology than a small book like this one can begin to explore. The following chapter looks at just a few of these significant issues. It reviews some questions that are useful for Christians who wish to increase social insight through a conversation between sociology and faith. Part III then plumbs the resources that are available as these critical questions are addressed from Christian perspectives.

NOTES

1. "Alles Ständische und Stehende verdampft, alles Heilige wird entweiht, und die Menschen sind endlich gezwungen." *Marx, Die Früschriften*, herausgegeben von Siegfried Landshut [*Marx, The Early Writings*, edited by Siegfried Landshut] (Stuttgart, 1971), p. 529.
2. This is indebted to Robert Nisbet's insightful work, *The Sociological Tradition* (New York: Basic Books, 1966).

Chapter 10

THE PERENNIAL QUESTS
OF SOCIAL INSIGHT

The desire for progress motivated the move into the modern world. Heightened freedoms for the individual, release from centuries of dead tradition, the triumph of rationality, technology—these were goals sought and achieved. The ills and restrictions of the past, the imbecilities of agrarian and urban poverty, the insults of status hierarchies, the immobilities of irrational customs, the ignorance of superstitions were all happily overthrown.

Yet with triumphs came bitter by-products. Individualism degenerated into morbid isolation. Rationality brought sterile disenchantment. The loss of tradition produced the loss of meaning. The triumph of technology gave birth to machinelike people. The destruction of the tyranny of aristocracy brought the tyranny of the masses. As the nineteenth century progressed, something went gravely wrong. The new industrial order, like the old order, had ways of diminishing human life, and sometimes these ways were more profound than the old ones. Furthermore, the ticket for the trip to modernity was one way. There was no return and no exit.

Sociology represents a wish to fulfill the promises of modernity. It attempts to gain more perspective and control over the processes of the change from the old to the new. Its classic practitioners constantly tried to figure out the processes and social products of modernization and how they might be turned to the benefit of all people. Many still consider one of sociology's important goals to be to minimize alienation and guarantee social and moral progress in measures equal to the obvious technological progress.

Sociological analysis of this process is even more urgent in the present. Not only do the most industrialized societies struggle with the social disruptions of industrialism but now technological progress threatens the global ecosystem with permanent damage and collapse. A few nations enjoy unprecedented levels of wealth while most people of this century face increasingly desperate levels of poverty and marginal existence.

Asking the Right Questions

The last chapter offered a glimpse of some of the classical analyses of modernization. Despite diversity in their portraits and language, each offers answers to a common set of questions that form the architecture of sociology.[1] These questions are summarized here:

1. What is going on here?
2. Why is it happening?
3. What is it like for actors living in it?
4. How good or bad is it for humans?

For any social arrangement and set of interactions, these are the primary and perennial questions for social analysis. Each of them contributes important direction and substance to a complete sociological understanding.

Minimal Description: What Is Going on Here?

Before sociologists can make sense of a social arrangement or a social interaction, they must know what is going on. This description is understanding in the primary sense. Before other types of understanding are possible, one must "get the facts straight."

Consider a person engaged in the various physical activities of pointing a gun, riding a bike, setting a plate of food down, raising a hand. People understand what is going on when they can label or classify the action appropriately and accurately. They cannot explain a social reality if they have misunderstood what that reality *is* in this primary sense. The person pointing the gun may be target shooting, robbing a bank, engaging in warfare, or hunting an animal. Frequently the context provides clues as to what is going on so that target shooting is not likely to be confused with robbing a bank. But there are many times, especially when observing actions and customs different from one's native culture, when one must ask actors what they are doing.

What looks like robbing a bank may actually be a training session for tellers in how to act when such an event happens. The bike rider may be testing a model in hopes of purchase, seeking to win the Tour de France, on her way to work, or simply getting exercise. The physical act of setting a plate down has many meanings. It matters whether it is a waiter serving a customer or a child feeding a cat—or whether it is a dutiful son bringing food to ancestral tablets to show respect to dead parents or an advertiser setting up for a photo shoot. To understand the physical act is to locate it within its appropriate action-meaning sequence—be it a restaurant transaction, care for a pet, the religious care of ancestors, or commercial advertising.

The simple physical acts one sees, such as raising the hand, tell very little about what is happening socioculturally. Perhaps a vote is being taken. Or questions are being accepted at the end of a lecture. Or it may be the raised hand that professional bike racers use to signal the need for a tire change. Only when one knows the social script of roles in a culturally defined setting can one begin to say what's going on.

Understanding in the primary sense means that one knows the category or type of social action involved. This usually entails labeling social action according to the commonly accepted, socially defined conventions of the actor's group. Looking into a church building and seeing a group of people sitting in pews tells us little until someone says, "wedding," "funeral," "prayer meeting," "organ concert," or "tour group." The initial foundation of facts is built through gathering observations of human actions. This happens through direct inspection of people's activity, through survey questions, intensive interviews, the analysis of written records — or all of these, plus other methods, put together.

Minimal description (one name for this primary understanding) stays as close to the data of human activity and interaction as possible. To misunderstand here means that all the other quests of sociology fail. To mislocate action patterns by mislabeling or misidentifying them means that one does not have an authentic case of social behavior to explain or evaluate. This happens, for example, when one looks at the American Revolution (its common nomenclature) as a social revolution when actually it is better classified as a war of liberation. What one needs to understand and explain is not a revolution at all but an instance of a national war of liberation.

Explanation: Why Is It Happening?

Social understanding is more than gathering facts, labeling, and classifying them. What is happening leads to the issue of why social worlds happen the way they do. Explanation relates the various social events, processes, and structures so as to put causes and effects together in valid ways. To say why something happens is to state what underlying forces and factors bring it about. To be more precise, explanation deals both with origins (what brought something into being) and continuations (why it is sustained in existence and what its variations are through time).

Minimal description provides fact-filled accounts of the hundreds of wars that have happened and continue to happen. Explanation aims at displaying the causes of various sorts of war. An explanation would include a description of the sociocultural factors involved in the outbreak of war and an analysis of what makes a particular war bloody or lengthy, what brings it to an end, and what leads to the bundle of its observed effects.

It is notable that some types of society are far more prone than others to engage in warfare. Hunting and gathering societies have little warfare, but warfare is endemic in horticultural and agricultural societies. The short history of industrial orders indicates no lessening in the frequency of wars. Indeed, dramatically greater casualties accompany twentieth-century warfare. Why should this be so? What is it about differing social arrangements that favors endemic warfare in some societies while warfare is virtually absent in others? What effects in social and cultural affairs appear when society engages in war or when warfare becomes endemic?

Explanation is a process of building theories and models so as to answer systematically questions about human experience. Hypotheses are tentative explanations of relationships between the facts of certain phenomena. Good theories are a whole set or system of validated hypotheses that systematically explain a given reality.

A major goal of sociology is "the grounding of precise and plausible hypotheses in strong and surprising theories."[2] Encompassing patterns of crime and suicide, revolution and romance, education and politics in powerful explanatory schemes fulfills what many sociologists consider the primary goal of sociology. An explanatory understanding of social facts is the most desirable and difficult sort of understanding to reach. Sociologists who answer this question well will have their names on plaques along the hallowed halls of sociology. Yet there are two other sorts of understanding that are neglected at one's peril.

Maximal Description: What's Life Like in This Social Arrangement?

Novelists are often better than sociologists at catching the inner feeling of a social world (*Verstehen*). The statistics and tables of sociology can say much about social worlds, but what they often fail to do is give an empathetic sense of what living in a given social world is like for its human actors.

Take the French Revolution. It is one thing to boil down historical information to a simple theory of revolution, as Tocqueville does. It is another to get a feel for what various French subjects thought and felt as they undertook and lived (or died) through the Revolution of 1789. Maximal or depth description goes deeply into the life world of the actors in a particular social arrangement. What were the motives and outlook of the small shopkeepers manning the barricades or marching on the Bastille? What were the typical social relationships and interchanges in the court and among the aristocrats? Why might they have miscalculated the mood of the country so badly? To answer these questions, one needs an in-depth description that includes small as well as large details. One needs to feel the confusions and passions of the various actors as they faced specific social structures and cultural patterns.

Similarly, the numbers in sociological tables speak of the enormity and dimensions of slavery. They do not say what it was like to be either a slave or a master in Georgia in the 1820s. One has authentically reproduced the sense of a particular way of life when the actual actors would respond to the description with recognition: "That's the way it was! Were you there?" To be sure, one can no longer talk to the Georgian slave of the 1820s. That makes validating such an account more difficult than if a sociologist were to investigate contemporary settings of slavery. Though illegal by international convention, slavery is still a contemporary if covert practice. Yet the principle of verifying the depth description as authentic is the same.

Minimal description is analytic, reports only critical observations, and tells the main story of a social institution or set of actions. Depth description is more synthetic. It sets forth enough of the total setting and culture so that an outsider can get a feel for what it might be like to live those experiences.

Evaluation: How Good or Bad Is This for Human Life?

Many sociologists attempt to avoid this fourth question. They have done so on the basis that sociology *as a science* ought to be value free (note that value judgment!). Sociology ought to deal only with facts.

There are several responses to this point of view. Answering the first three questions well, a sociologist often has enough information to assess a social pattern's typical impact on the people involved. This assessment may portray the sociocultural system only in terms of whether the actors themselves see it as good or bad for them. For example, a multiyear investigation of the family and voluntary associational structure of Soweto, South Africa, under the conditions of apartheid will uncover pervasive opinions by the residents of Soweto about their conditions and why they are so bad, plus opinions by white power holders about how good the blacks have it. Those opinions can be articulated in a sociological study. But sociologists frequently do more than that.

It is hard to imagine that a sociologist could be devoid of feelings once faced with objectively documented conditions and in the midst of suggesting how good or bad life is for Soweto's residents. In fact, many readers would feel a study that was "purely objective" was artificial, unenlightened, and devoid of wisdom, despite all its technical and sociological prowess. In practice, it is often not difficult to guess the evaluative conclusions of the sociologist, even when they are not directly stated. Actually, such studies often state conclusions with clear value judgments. The very nature of the reality being studied cries out for such comment.

W. G. Runcimann argues that all humans (including sociologists) operate with an idea of general benevolence as we investigate human affairs. If we did not do so, we would not be human. To be human is to care deeply for some of the basic goods sought by all humans. Beyond representing the evaluations of the subjects investigated, sociologists have their own evaluations. The major social thinkers reviewed in Chapter Nine expressed general evaluations of the modern world. Such evaluations are not all correct. What they show is the way in which factual descriptions and explanations of the modern world entail evaluations. There is coherence between what they take to be the facts of modernity and the evaluations they make of modernity.

Other intellectual practices also reason in this way. A doctor describes the major physical characteristics of a patient in order to get at the symptoms of ill health. The facts of the physical condition are what suggest health or illness to the doctor and set him or her searching for a possible treatment. So, too, the description of a society's major features is a step in the direction of diagnosing its ills. Once a society has been described, sociologists can say a bit about what needs to be done to make it a better place for all its members. Here is a summary of the classical figures from Chapter Nine, indicating their major evaluations of how good or bad modernity is for humankind:

1. Tocqueville: modernization is the equalization of conditions and the enhancement of political centralization. It leads to the diminution of the individual, who ends up feeling like a mere cog in a mass society of equals.

2. Comte: modernization is an intellectual and spiritual transformation to a society dominated by positive science and run by a triumvirate of technical elites—sociologists, industrialists, and scientists. After a time of transition, modernity will be a wondrous world of progress and order.

3. Tönnies: modernization is the switch from the warmly supportive *Gemeinschaft* to the impersonal, alienating *Gesellschaft*. It leads to fleeting, fragile relationships, a powerfully repressive state, and finally to the breakdown of modern society.

4. Marx: modernization is the by-product of the class struggle and triumph of the bourgeoisie. It leads to pervasive alienation, the making of all life into a commodity, class conflict,

and finally a transforming revolution. It is a society of massive injustice (misorganization).

5. Durkheim: modernization is the shift from a restrictive mechanical solidarity to a liberating organic solidarity. The by-products are isolation and anomie (the unrestrained individual and disorganization). Eventually science will correct the disorganization and injustice of modern society.

6. Weber: modernization is the increasing dominance of instrumental rationality. This leads to large, impersonal, bureaucratized structures (overorganization) and a utilitarian, secularized culture that brings lifelessness and drudgery.

Christians come to social arrangements with more than simply a notion of general benevolence. They have well-developed traditions of ethical and moral discourse. There are norms of justice, fairness, equity, and the welfare of the other that structure Christian evaluations of human connections and interaction. The Christian sociologist cannot pretend to be operating as a Christian without eventually engaging in the quest of evaluating social arrangements.

In sum, in any investigation of social reality, sociologists want answers to four basic questions. Minimal description seeks an accurate account, giving the basic facts by reporting observations and telling the story of the enterprise and type of interaction occurring. Explanation seeks hypotheses, models, and theories that make sense of the social facts and observations reported. Sociologists put causes and effects together to create models of a particular social reality. They wish to show how and why certain social formations and interactions occur when and where they do. Depth description succeeds when readers come away with a sense of the wholeness of meaning, action, and life in the context and time of an investigated social reality. Evaluation engages both the sociologist's and the reader's notions of human nature and their vision of the good society. Social arrangements provide advantages to some and disadvantages to others. What are the benefits and the costs of a given social formation and set of interactions?

In this case, readers are looking for a coherent account, showing how observations (the facts) fit into a larger moral assessment of the social reality. The sociologist's worldview and ethical tradition strongly shape the judgments he or she makes here.

The table below summarizes these foundational sociological questions:

The Perennial Questions of Social Insight

QUESTION:	TERM:	TASK:	CRITERIA:
What's going on? (Grasping)	Minimal description	"Fact" finding; reporting observations; telling the story	Accuracy
Why?	Explanation	"Theory building"; making sense; putting causes and effects together	Validity
What's this like? (Elucidating)	Depth description (*Verstehen*)	Getting a feel for the ethos, movement, feelings, and attitudes of people in the setting; what it was like for the agents to be a part of the social action; filling in the details of the setting and human actions	Authenticity
How good or bad?	Evaluation	Giving a judgment as to the effect of these phenomena and this arrangement on matters that make human life good or bad	Coherency

Seeking Christian Answers

Surprisingly, some think the Bible and Christian faith should act as a data bank. The Bible should provide all the information needed to make sense of all social orders. However, this is not the case here any more than the Bible offers all one needs to know about automobiles, genetic engineering, or history. It does provide Christians with a way of looking at sociology and social facts that, at times, suggests rather surprising and different answers to the questions asked by sociologists. Consider each of these areas of sociological activity.

Minimal and Depth Description and the Christian Story

Christians take the biblical story of creation, fall, reconciliation, and redemption as the largest frame of meaning. When Christians seek an answer to what is going on in social arrangements, they are not content with many of the answers they encounter. A Christian description cannot remain tied to the accounts of the actors involved or to the cultural scripts and the meaning that these scripts give to social worlds. To the Christian, all of these things are part of the larger story of a world made by and belonging to God, a world now in rebellion and alienated from God.

This is not to say that a Christian account denies the labeling and meaning that actors and cultures give to their social worlds. These meanings and stories are very real. Any account of social processes that ignores them necessarily distorts and falsifies reality. *What Christianity adds is the larger plot of history.* This gives a different spin to the reading of a variety of events and structures in a sociological account.

Two things in particular orient Christian social thought. These are the issues of idolatry (false spirituality) and injustice (distorted sociality). Christians understand human life and experience genuinely when they see it through these two lenses. The first concerns who the Creator, Sustainer, and Master of this world really is. The second has to do with who the human being is as the fallen image of that God.

What goes on behind and through all human affairs is an encounter with the living and true God. People's social affairs and meanings may well hide that reality and even contest it. Yet that is what is going on, even when human actors are oblivious to it.

Never to say that this is what is going on or to point out what is at stake for the God-human relationship in social affairs is to falsify the universe that humans objectively live in. Never to say that humans were created with the ability to be cultural creatures and to forge an immense array of social orders is not to tell the whole story about reality.

Explaining Why Things Happen as They Do

Science seeks close-range explanations. The eye of the needle it seeks to thread is very narrow. Science states that explanations are to negotiate a proper path between the ideal, suggested by the standard of "Occam's razor," and its primary danger. Occam's razor represents the principle that explanations must be as simple as possible without being trivial. Occam's razor gets rid of superfluous, irrelevant, unrelated causes and presuppositions in an explanatory scheme. *The ideal is to subtract explanatory principles until only the essential ones remain.* In fact, the fewer the principles, the better the explanation.

The danger of Occam's razor is reductionism, the removal of essentials. A balancing ideal to Occam's razor states that explanations must be sufficiently complete to account for all the complexity present in the phenomena under analysis. Explanatory schemes are to specify *all* the causes necessary and sufficient to bring about a particular state of affairs, an event, or a social pattern, and no less. *The ideal in this case is to add all essential explanatory principles until there are enough to generate a complete explanation.*

Reductionism occurs when certain valid causes, presuppositions, or principles are excluded from an explanatory scheme. Underlying the term *reductionism* is the concept of higher and lower matters. To reduce something is to claim that there is a more basic (lower) level that encompasses all the principles and laws essential for explaining the higher. Thus, sociology may be "reduced to" psychology, which in turn is reduced to biology, which is reduced to organic chemistry, and so on. The thorough reductionist would say that behind every twisted mind is a twisted molecule.

Reductionism is also known as "nothing-buttery": sociology is *nothing but* psychology operating among many people. Psychology is nothing but the sophisticated effects and operations of biological processes. Biology is nothing but the structure and operation of organic molecules. The claim is that if one knows enough about the more basic reality, one can explain without remainder all the states, processes, and events of the higher level of reality.

In part, this is a border dispute between disciplines. For example, most sociological paradigms resist psychological explanations for society because they are reductionistic. They are seen as too simple, as subtracting some necessary sociological principles. They neglect giving an adequate model and set of theories for the full range of complexity in social reality. Psychology can give only partial or pseudo-explanations of *social* realities. This does not disparage psychological explanations. It simply recognizes that they are limited. Their application is primarily to *psychological* realities.

This is also partly a dispute within sociology as to what features of human life are essential to explaining it. Some sociological paradigms (such as that of the structuralists) exclude the mental constructs and purposes of human actors from their explanations of society. In their view, societal processes and structures take place very much like the autonomous movements of natural law. What humans think or aim to achieve has little effect on the operating of societal laws. Explanations that include in their models the meaning systems of typical actors are seen as too complex, as including some extra explanatory baggage not really necessary. So the wielders of Occam's razor reduce this complexity in the explanation by removing the (in their view) unnecessary references to human feelings and ideas.

The rule for explanations is that they must be as simple as possible yet explain the full complexity and variation of the phenomena of interest. One of the differences between Christian social thought and secularist sociology appears here. Since Christians see human life as embedded in the cosmic drama of creation, fall, reconciliation, and redemption, the full complexity of human life cannot be fully accounted for simply by sociological (or psychological) explanations. Without reference to God, such explanations are finally reductionistic and incomplete. Christian faith sees a complexity in human affairs that secular sociology chooses to ignore. A complete explanation must include references to God. Christian sociologists refuse to reduce social reality to something less than it is under God.

From secular sociology's point of view, this is a case where Occam's razor validly cuts off irrelevant and extraneous matters that it does not credit as factual. The eyes of faith see that this is a case of reductionism motivated by the secular symbolic universe of modernity. In other words, these two conflicting worldviews disagree over what there is to explain in human affairs.

If this is God's world and humans are the fallen image of God, then secular sociology provides only partial (though valid) explanations. Such explanations are deficient because they lack the larger drama of the biblical story. If this is not God's world, then Christian explanations are unnecessarily complex, and Occam's razor needs to do its deed. As Christians, we think that in this case Occam's razor leads to reductionism.

Evaluating the Affairs of Human Social Experience

Christian faith brings with it a specific tradition of ethical and moral discourse. Its vision of the good for human life is far more concrete and comprehensive than general utilitarian notions or even notions of general benevolence. Consequently, its analysis creates a critical Christian social theory that goes far beyond what critical Enlightenment social theories offer.

Virtually all the great thinkers in sociology suggest that the modern world is in serious trouble. Modernity both solves old crises and creates new ones. Christian accounts of social arrangements radicalize most sociological diagnoses of social ills, rooting these ills ultimately in the problem of sinful alienation from God.

We do not spell this out in detail here because of the extensive literature in Christian social ethics. The various paradigms of Christian theology approach the matter of evaluating social formations in a variety of ways. Anyone who is curious can explore the various ways in which Christians spell out their evaluatory principles and categories. Social evaluation is one of the most important endeavors of Christian sociology because of the directness and extensiveness of overlap between faith and sociology in this arena. Yet such evaluation cannot be done without the material, models, and answers provided by the first three quests of sociology. Christian evaluation must be rooted in good descriptions and well-crafted explanations of social facts.

Part II ends with this keen awareness: sociology is made up of many voices and a variety of perspectives. What unifies the discipline are four crucial questions. If Christians wish to develop and deepen their social understandings, they will have to seek to answer those questions using the best of sociology combined with the perspectives, insights, concepts, and tools of Christian thought. What those resources are for thinking Christianly is the topic of Part III.

NOTES

1. W. G. Runcimann, *A Treatise on Social Theory*, Vol. 1: *The Methodology of Social Theory*; Vol. 2: *Substantive Social Theory* (Cambridge, England: Cambridge University Press, 1983, 1989).
2. Runcimann, *Treatise on Social Theory*, Vol. 1, p. 180.

PART III

Faith Seeking Social Understanding

Chapter 11

LEARNING TO SPEAK
WITH A BIBLICAL ACCENT

Now, you might say, we are in real trouble. Here we are as moderns, with our own distinctive social patterns and ways of understanding the world, our own vocabulary and rationality traditions, our own modern paradigms. How in the world can one bridge the yawning gap back to the worlds of meaning and social activity in the Bible? The Christian tradition of rationality takes Scripture as its authoritative voice. Yet the social and cultural worlds of the authors of the Bible are different from today's—so different that it is difficult to make sense of what is read in its pages.

This is no surprise to those who are veterans in studying the Scriptures. Scholars overhear biblical conversations on many strange and puzzling issues, discussed in foreign languages by people who lived in different communication pools than those of today. The gap between our cultural notions and those of the Bible are not always apparent, partly because there are excellent translations of the Bible into English that provide rough-and-ready equivalents in current cultural idioms.

Frequently, skillful preaching so reframes the text that the hearers are unaware of the gap. Reframing Scripture makes the Bible vivid for those with a modern set of concerns; it makes it sensible within modern worldviews. Since this country's culture is an individualistic one with acute psychological interests, stories from the Bible are often retold with the addition and elaboration of psychological details. Yet a close examination shows how little interest the authors of the Bible had in the internal feelings and personality traits of their characters. One can get into serious trouble when one confuses the reframing of Scripture with what the Scripture actually said within the cultural assumptions of its day and audiences.

An authentic encounter between sociology and Christian faith assumes a significant degree of mutual understanding. Because they are two different communication pools, that understanding takes place through learning each other's discourse as well as the language used to carry the central notions of each. Every tradition is embodied in a set of utterances and actions carried in some particular language and culture.

Sociology expresses itself primarily in the internationalized languages of modernity, especially English, German, and French. Anyone with facility in those languages, as well as discipline and time, can hack through the jargon and learn the practices of sociology. These people will understand the criteria by which some works are labeled exemplary sociology, and they can begin to judge the value of the differing paradigms that dissect the social aspects of human existence. The gap between an ordinary educated person and the texts of sociology is comparatively narrow, although, to be sure, some of the best sociology is expressed in highly technical writings that are difficult even for trained professionals to understand.

Christian faith expresses itself first in its originating texts in the Bible. Here are found the ancient languages of Hebrew, Aramaic, and Koiné Greek. Christian faith also expresses itself in the internationalized languages of modernity, articulating biblical understandings in terms that bear on modern life. The gap between the ordinary educated person and contemporary expositions of Christian faith is comparatively narrow. Learning the claims of contemporary Christian faith requires a reasonable expenditure of time and effort, but it is no more difficult than learning sociology.

The gap between any modern person and the biblical texts is significantly greater than one might imagine. What the texts of the

Bible say and how one interprets them within his or her contemporary religious, historical, and scientific paradigms are often very different things. The task of coming to terms with the Bible requires spanning a gap of more than two thousand years. One must cross several cultural boundaries and deal with texts where one cannot query the human authors about ambiguities. One reason for the variety of traditions and theological paradigms in Christian faith is that all these difficulties have resulted in different interpretations of the biblical material. Some of the interpretations are very different from what the Bible communicates. This chapter is the first of several considering issues involved in making sense of the Christian tradition so that it can converse with sociology.

The discussion begins with the Bible because all Christian churches consider it to be central to their beliefs and practices. The question in this chapter is whether the vocabulary and terminology of the Bible contain notions that overlap with those of sociology. Are the biblical writers self-conscious of culture and social structure? Does their discourse parallel that of modern social science?

Square Pegs and Round Holes

It should be said right off the bat that the concerns and concepts of sociology do not closely match those of Scripture and vice versa. This is because sociology is an intellectual enterprise that developed in and attempts to describe the internationalized world of modernity. Some questions it asks are new ones, never before asked. It uses concepts not found in the same sense in other places and times. If one asks what biblical authors say about sociological notions, he or she cannot normally expect to find the answers given in any direct fashion. This does not mean that answers cannot be found. But to find them, modern Christians must weigh the meanings and message of Scripture and then answer for the biblical authors.

The Bible is not a text in sociology, even though it treats many topics of significance to sociology. The Bible is misconstrued if it is taken as a primary sourcebook for sociological concepts and theories. Its primary subject matter is the living God in his relationships to the created world and to the history of humanity within that world. Sociology has as its primary subject matter human beings in all their multitudinous social arrangements, many of them as newly formed as the modern world. No one doubts the absurdity of asking what the Bible teaches about space satellites. It is just as absurd to ask that it have something to say about every modern social innovation.

Further, while the Bible talks about social arrangements, its principal interest is in how they bear on the *relationship of human beings to God* within the created and fallen order. It does not, because it could not, talk about all the sorts of social arrangements that humans have created of late or will create in the future. What it says in relation to the social arrangements of its day and cultures, however, provides clues as to the sorts of things it might say about contemporary societies. But these clues must be interpreted and converted into the intellectual currency and communication pools of the modern world.

This is not to deny the phenomena of prophecy. But prophecy's subject matter is not the details of future social structures and cultural patterns but the unfolding of God's redemptive purpose. To be sure, the Bible provides intimations of the divine community and the coming of God's city, the New Jerusalem, at the end of history. But none of this describes the centuries of intervening social history. Further, what is said about the final godly society is sketchy and full of symbolic language.

Sociology also talks about God. Yet it does so with an interest in how people's ideas of and actions toward what they believe is God create and reinforce certain sorts of *relationships among human beings*. What sociology says about how religion influences behavior in the modern world sheds light on some of the dynamics seen even in the biblical narratives. It illuminates what was going on back then. More to the point, where the sociology of religion is of significant aid is in identifying contemporary dynamics in religious movements and organizations. So, even with differences in interest between sociology and the Bible, definite connections can be drawn between sociological and biblical perspectives.

The Christian faith offers very concrete ideas about how an authentic Christian commitment and social arrangements ought to relate to one another. But Christians, like sociologists, have not agreed among themselves as to the best ways of thinking Christianly about social arrangements. The Christian faith is itself divided into several traditions. David Barrett documents seven major Christian traditions and some twenty-two thousand denominations.[1] Within those traditions, several theological paradigms shape influential Christian social philosophies. Some of these paradigms and their social philosophies provide natural points of contact between Christianity and sociology.

These next few chapters deal with Christian faith as a symbolic universe with several rationality traditions. Relating Christian faith to sociology involves relating several ways of doing sociology to several ways of interpreting Christian faith. The exploration begins with two questions. What does the Bible say about culture and social structure? And what is the grammar and vocabulary of the biblical worldview that is most directly relevant to sociological thought?

"The Bible Tells Me So"

Does the Bible speak directly and definitively about culture or social structure? One easy answer simply says yes—of course, it does. After all, the Bible is God's Word. The yeses want to underline and stress the value of the Bible for all of life. Some, known as reconstructionists, read the Bible as providing a detailed blueprint for a divinely willed society for all time and places. But this answer is fraught with difficulty once examined in detail.

Careful examination of this conclusion shows how selectively it uses the Bible. Its advocates choose only some of the cultural patterns and social arrangements found in the Bible and put them forward as "the biblical pattern." There will be more to say about the yes answer later on. It is more accurate to say that the Bible describes how to evaluate human relationships and connections *in all social orders* than to say it provides a blueprint for a single social world that is pleasing to God.

An equally important question for Christian sociology is how the Bible helps or doesn't help one to do sociology. To be really honest, we have to say that the Bible is not a manual for studying social arrangements. To be sure, it says many things about the social arrangements within which biblical peoples lived. But it says no more about random sampling, interviewer bias, symbolic interaction, or network theory than it does about quantum theory or electron microscopes. This is not to say that it offers nothing. But to say yes, the Bible speaks comprehensively and definitively about the subject matter and methods of sociology, misrepresents the richness and complexity of what the Bible actually offers to sociological thought.

So what is the answer to the question about the Bible's speaking directly and definitively about social structure and culture? We are convinced that the no answer to this question is more accurate. But to explain why this is a better answer is tricky. Readers will have to work hard to grasp this explanation, especially if they have never had an in-depth, cross-cultural experience. But stay with us. As we develop our own position in the next pages and chapters, we think it shows how the Bible fits in with doing Christian sociology.

The no answer builds on the fact that, as understood and used in social science, terms like *culture* and *social structure* are contemporary distinctions not clearly found in the Bible. They label modern experience in ways not done in biblical times. No one-to-one equivalent words in the Hebrew or the Greek cover the same range of meanings that the modern terms central to social analysis cover. This is a difficult notion for many beginning students of social life. Immersed in the modern world with its many taken-for-granted ideas about social relations, beginning students cannot imagine social worlds very different from their own. Nor do they see how earlier peoples might not even have conceived of their social world in the way that moderns do. Moderns have a tendency to read back into ancient worlds their own modern distinctions. Often people are not even aware that they are changing those worlds to fit into the modern mold, rather than understanding them on their own terms.

This does not mean that biblical peoples did not have cultures or social structures. A specific example of this will help spell out the problem. Consider the economic components of ancient Israel and the Roman world of the New Testament. Study very quickly reveals major differences between ancient economic activity and modern economies. Shocking as it may be, there is no concept of "an economy" in those worlds. M. I. Finley writes, "Marshall's title [*Principles of Economics*] cannot be translated into Greek or Latin. Neither can the basic terms, such as labor, production, capital, investment, income, circulation, demand, entrepreneur, utility—at least not in the abstract form required for economic analysis."[2]

This does not mean that the economic processes of the production and distribution of resources and supplies did not occur. These processes occur in all human societies. The many economic activities in the Hebrew and Roman worlds included growing and gathering foodstuffs, buying and selling, borrowing and lending, paying wages and offering gifts, taxing and carrying out public works, crafting and merchandising, inheriting and bequeathing. Information on all these economic processes enable the modern scholar to paint a picture of "the economy" of the ancient world. But the ancients would never themselves have put these elements together and thought about them in the way that a sociologist does. They did not have words that would be equivalent to modern scientific terms for discussing and analyzing economic arrangements.

This does not mean that no economy existed, any more than not having a word for malaria meant that they didn't die from the disease. Yet economic processes were embedded in the overall institutions of the societies. Tradition was decisive in deciding what to produce, how to produce it, and how to distribute it. To conceive of an "economic actor" making decisions on the basis of autonomous economic processes is not true to how people engaged in economic action then. Nor was there a world of interdependent markets within which economic action occurred. No such person and no such world existed until the industrial and capitalist revolution. Only in the modern world does economic analysis *as people today know it* become not only possible but important.

It is not illegitimate for the sociologist to reconstruct or reportray the ancient world in modern sociological terms. But such portraits can be anachronistic. They are illegitimate when sociologists (or biblical scholars) apply theoretical terms that misrepresent the processes going on. Understanding economic action in the Bible means at least understanding the choices people actually could have made. They were not moderns who happened to be traipsing about in sandals and communicating without telephones. Their social horizons and the choices they faced were very different from those faced today. To understand these ancients, one must enter and, as far as possible, dwell in their communication pools.

There are two delicate tasks here. First, one must see how people who lived in those ancient worlds thought and experienced their world, *in their own terms.* Then, one must create one's own systematic models of their world, *in modern terms.* But one must not confuse these two accounts.

There is another way of expressing this issue. Similar problems of translation occur between any culturally distant communication pools today. An anthropologist always struggles with how to understand cultures with very different ways of thinking and acting than his or her own and then with how to describe those cultures in the language of anthropology without distorting them. Once sensitized to this issue, one can sketch some of the connections that can be drawn between the language of the Bible and contemporary social thought.

Old Testament Ethnicity

The Old Testament has no specific words or terms conveying what modern social science means by culture or social structure. In Israel's everyday life-world, there was little need to develop explicit theories about either. Israel's existence presupposed a national life all of whose aspects were under the rule and law of God. Because the culture, nation, and people of God were overlapping realities, there was little room for modern types of cultural pluralism. The confrontation of one culture with another that raises issues leading to a self-conscious theory of culture and social structure does not occur until the modern world.

To be sure, early Israelites were keenly aware that people's ways of life and customs differed. But they did not create a social analysis for understanding those differences. Their concerns were existential and practical, not abstract and analytical. They saw their own culture (as regulated by God) as the only legitimate way to live. To be one of God's people, a person had to adopt their culture—that is, one had to become a Jew culturally. Every major change in Hebrew culture (from nomadic wandering in the wilderness to settled farming and city life; from a tribal confederacy to a centralized monarchy; from an independent nation to a dispersed, dependent people in exile) created crisis in Israel. There was no awareness of the cultural freedom evident in the social format of the New Testament church. And even that transition in cultural understanding created crisis among the Jewish followers of Jesus (Acts 15).

The focus of Old Testament Israelite life was on a uniformity of custom integrated around the worship of Yahweh. The paramount issue of its peoplehood was to ensure and enforce the strength of its customary patterns. Israel never considered its own customs nor those of other peoples objectively. An evaluative framework of ethnic distinctives filtered all information about customs and culture. Israel did not contemplate culture as such but only this or that custom and its conformity to or departure from the norms and values shaped by the covenant of God.

As the biblical story moves from Abraham to David, it recounts the building of this single nation with a uniform culture. This involved establishing a social structure governed by a genealogically validated tribal framework. Ethnically bounded Israel then settled in the land of Canaan where peoples with different customs, worldviews, and gods constantly threatened it. Israel's code of laws set boundaries that distinguished it from its neighbors and made it holy unto the Lord. A story such as that of Ruth shows how people thought about other cultures. When Ruth decides to accompany Naomi back to Israel, she assumes she will have to change her family, her religion, and her customs: "Where you go, I will go. Where you lodge, I will lodge; your people will be my people, and your God my God. Where you die, I will die—there will I be buried" (Ruth 1:16–17).

Over time, patterns of social oppression and false religion compromised Israel's corporate life, leading to the judgment of God. God carried the people into exile. At first they were a dispersed minority within a series of world empires. Then a tiny group of Jews returned to form a small, dependent nation in Palestine. Only in exile as a minority people and as a colonized dependent nation did the issues of culture and social structure become insistent. Yet even then, there was no development of abstract concepts of culture and social structure.

In the Old Testament, the prophets thundered against the twin sins of social oppression and idolatry with a conviction that the two are integrally linked. False religion, they said, leads to and legitimates social oppression. Social oppression generates the social conditions under which false religion is attractive. The prophets' analysis of the social dynamics of Israel is acute. Yet what they called for is not theoretical understandings of culture and social structure. What they seek is repentance and the renewal of life ways that are pleasing to God. It is noteworthy that they also condemn the social oppression and idolatry of other cultures.

Ezra and Nehemiah portray those who return from exile as undertaking a process of social reformation and spiritual restoration. These people rebuilt the physical walls around Jerusalem. They strengthened the law of God as a wall against idolatry and cultural contamination. They banished ways of life not enshrined in the law. One of their requirements was that Israelites who had married non-Israelites end their marriages. The desire for the purity of religion and culture set the stage for the development of the law-centered Judaism encountered in New Testament times.

In sum, there is no Old Testament grammar or vocabulary of social or cultural analysis corresponding to the concepts used by contemporary social science. One can tease out of Old Testament texts the symbolic universe standing behind its conception of life under the rule of God. It contains a moral and conceptual logic adequate to the issues and life-world of the ancient Near East. It speaks eloquently of the nature of the fallen human being, struggling to respond to God's love in a difficult and dangerous world. Its narratives draw the reader into situations as universal as the human condition. Nonetheless, there is no clear vocabulary encompassing human social life in a way that is similar to sociological analysis. The New Testament contains more overlap.

New Testament Pluralism

The New Testament displays two broad cultural worlds in confrontation with each other. The first is an internally divided Judaism encompassing subcultural diversity. Such groups as Pharisees, Sadducees, Essenes, Zealots, and "people of the land" jostled each other in Palestine. These Jewish groups espoused differing attitudes over how Jewish law and custom related to imperial Roman colonization and to the incursion of Hellenistic culture. The majority of the Jews, living scattered in the diaspora, spoke many languages. Greek was the common language of those in Roman provinces. Evidence indicates that diaspora Jews often accommodated their life-style to gentile customs. To the east of Palestine stood the Parthian Empire, with Jews present. Here Aramaic was the trade language. Jews spoke many of the local tongues (Acts 2).

Judaism confronted a broad, alternative cultural world labeled gentile, though gentiles were many different peoples. In the Roman Empire, there were the dominating Latin-speaking Romans as well as various local peoples submerged by Roman conquest. The Christian Church itself began as a Jewish movement largely made up of Palestinian Jews speaking Hebrew and Aramaic as their mother tongues. After Pentecost, it incorporated Hellenistic Jews (Greek-speaking diaspora Jews). Then Samaritans (half-Jews) and finally pagan gentiles entered the movement. Many passages of the New Testament deal with tensions due to differences of culture and social structure brought into the Church by these groups (for example, Romans 14; Acts 15).

Furthermore, Greek is the language of the New Testament. It was an internationalized language of world empire. Greek contains terms and concepts dealing with cultural and social matters at a more abstract level than does Hebrew. Greek spread under conquests initiated by Alexander the Great. Hellenistic culture interacted with a variety of languages and cultures brought under its influence. The Roman Empire was a beneficiary of this heritage. This is why the Greek language incorporates rudimentary elements that come to terms with pluralism.

The New Testament expresses its understanding of the message and mind of God in Greek. Here one finds terms that overlap in their meanings with major sociological concepts. This section looks at five words as examples of the vocabulary and perspective found in the New Testament that overlap with sociology. These are terms that refer to the "age" currently inhabited, the "world" or human life-world that orders human existence, the structuring "principles" that give form to human culture, and the "powers" and "principalities" that control crucial dimensions of social existence. Probing the vocabulary of the New Testament shows the way early Christians thought about their social world. It also reveals the fact that they did not yet think sociologically.

Aion: *Age*

The word *aion*[3] means "an age" — that is, an indefinitely long period, an epoch, a life span, or an eternity. God is the King of "the ages" (Revelation 15:3; 1 Timothy 1:17), one to be praised unto "the ages" (Romans 1:25; Jude 25), to whom be glory to the "ages of the ages" — that is, "forever" (Galatians 1:5). *Aion*, used with the Greek word for life, refers to life eternal, meaning the quality of the life of the age to come, received by those who enter the Kingdom of God through repentance and faith (Mark 10:30; John 3:36).

The New Testament frequently contrasts the present age with "the age to come." The Old Testament itself contains a contrast between the Day of the Lord, which was to usher in God's perfect reign, and the present imperfect order (Amos 9:13–15; Isaiah 65:17). The "age to come" is often used interchangeably with the "Kingdom of God." The present age opposes the age to come. During the present age, human existence is characterized by weakness and neediness, disease and mortality, sin and death. The ruler of this age is the Evil One, the god of this age who blinds the minds of unbelievers (2 Corinthians 4:4). The powers and princes rule with a wisdom characteristic of this age. They do not recognize God's presence in Christ. That explains why they put him to death (Colossians 2:15; 1 Corinthians 2:6). Christians should not conform to this age (Romans 12:2; Titus 2:12).

The present age stretches from the fall to the visible return of Jesus Christ to set up the Kingdom of God on earth. Already the age to come has broken into this age in hidden form with the first coming of Jesus Christ. His miracles and transforming power were expressions of the power of the coming age. Signs and wonders point to the hidden and quiet reality of the presence of the Holy Spirit, which is the power of the coming age. The gift of eternal life that people receive now is the quality of life of the age to come.

Aion portrays human existence as one of a succession of days and epochs limited by time. The current life-world is transitory and changing. Its length is indefinitely long. Its beginning is the creative act of God before the ages. Its boundary in the future is the ending of this age by the "coming age" of God's Kingdom. The finality and eternity of the coming age limits and relativizes all contemporary human experience and institutions, all knowledge and wisdom. All social institutions are profoundly temporal. Human institutions can only be understood by setting them within temporal boundaries and processes. The Bible does not view eternity as "timelessness" but as "ages upon ages."

Kosmos: *World*

"World" or universe is the normal translation for the word *kosmos*.[4] Its central meaning suggests a patterned order in reality. *Kosmos* is an interrelated structure producing a meaningful whole with the sort of orderliness that can be readily grasped. It is the opposite of chaos. The word has both a negative use (the world as an ordered reality opposing God) and a comparatively neutral one (the world as put into order out of chaos by God's power).

Kosmos has several denotations. It refers to the totality of the seen and unseen creation, the heavens and the earth within which God's eternal plan unfolds (Matthew 24:21; Romans 1:20; Luke 11:50; Acts 17:24; Hebrews 4:3). So Jesus Christ "was chosen before the creation of the *kosmos* but was revealed in these times for your sake" (1 Peter 1:20). Here the notion of *kosmos* is quite positive.

Kosmos also carries the meaning of the humanly inhabited world. This sense conveys either a neutral or negative connotation. Children are born into "the world." Satan tempts Jesus with "all the kingdoms of the world" (Matthew 4:8). It is a world ordered by political connections, structures, and authorities under God. Evil powers that motivate arrangements contrary to the will of God can pervert the order.

Kosmos approaches what sociologists mean by culture in the third of its meanings. Here it is the total world of human, earthly experience. It is the socioethical order in which human responsibility expresses itself. George Ladd defines *kosmos* as "the whole complex of human earthly relationships in which marriage, joy and sorrow, buying and selling, i.e., the totality of human activities are included . . . not merely the world of men but the world system and complex relationships that have been created by men . . . structures that are transitory and destined to pass away."[5] So there are elements in this Greek word as used in the New Testament that are very close to sociological ideas. But even in this use, it frequently has a connotation very different from what sociologists mean by social structures.

Normally, this third sense designates the world as a place of opposition to God. It is a humanly ordered reality substituted for the order God originally intended as indicated by life in Eden. So John says, "Do not love the world or anything in the world. The love of the Father is not in those who love the world. For everything in the world—the cravings of sinful humanity, the lust of the eyes, and the boasting of what one has and does—comes not from the Father but from the world. The world and its desires pass away, but those who do the will of God live forever [unto the ages]" (1 John 2:15–17). Paul reminds the Ephesians (2:1–2) that "you were dead in your trespasses and sins in which you once lived, following the course [the age] of this world."

God intended humans to live in time in an ordered and orderly world whose web of interconnections reflected his goodness and blessing. Instead, the order humans have created brings suffering, want, and curse. The dominant forces of the human world engender desires and create structures that alienate people from God and from each other. The human world is one of social oppression and false religion, a world into which Jesus Christ came to rescue and redeem sinners. An intrinsic part of that salvation is bringing into being a redeemed and redemptive community, living in the power of the age to come (Romans 8:18–25).

Stoicheion: *Principles*

The word *stoicheion* denotes elements, principles, or rudiments.[6] It occurs only seven times in the New Testament. What is known of its origins indicates that it referred first to the letters of an alphabet and then to the ABCs or rudiments of something. These elements are the fundamental principles of any art, science, or discipline. In 2 Peter 3:10–13, this word designates the "elemental substances" that structure the physical world. In the Day of the Lord, the physical elements dissolve or melt in a fiery cataclysm. In Hebrews 5:12, the *stoicheia* are the "basic elements" of the teachings of God.

The use of the word is somewhat obscure elsewhere in the New Testament (Galatians 3:3, 9; Colossians 2:8, 20). Here translations pick either "elemental principles" or "elementary spirits." It refers either to the elemental principles or to spirits that are basic forces and laws within the experience of the human as a cultural being. These elemental principles (spirits) shape or determine human behavior.

Some interpretations see the *stoicheia* as working within the fundamental laws or norms of a culture. In this understanding, *stoicheia* operate in traditions, public opinion, and accepted standards of behavior and belief (Colossians 2:22, "the prescriptions and doctrines of humanity"). Others take these elements to be spiritual forces that can capture the energy and outlook of human beings. When this happens, people's behavior springs from a spiritual orientation contrary to the freedom and life of God's Spirit. The traditions of the culture are infused by spiritual energy and force that push people away from God. By either interpretation, the "elements of the world" summarizes the structuring principles of life outside the fullness offered in Jesus Christ. People are seen as conforming to the ordering action of these *stoicheia*, whether they are normative elements of culture or spiritual forces behind them. This is similar to the common sociological idea that people are socialized into cultural structures and normative patterns to which they then conform. These make up the substance and orderliness of the common life within a culture.

Exousiai *and* Archai: *Powers and Principalities*

Most translations use the words *powers* or authorities and rulers or *principalities* as English glosses on *exousiai*[7] and *archai*.[8] In many contexts, these Greek words are interchangeable in meaning. Some uses describe political authorities (Luke 12:11; Titus 3:3; Romans 13:1). The other major use refers to authentic spiritual powers (perhaps angelic beings) that exist independently of human agency and decision. These creatures originally functioned in the ordering of a good creation (Romans 8:38; Colossians 1:16). Now in alliance with evil, they energize the disorderly rebellion of the world. Their opposition to God's Kingdom is part of what the cross triumphed over. This victory is part of the meaning of reconciliation with God (Colossians 1:20, 2:14–15; Ephesians 6:12; 1 Peter 3:22).

These beings are superior in power to humans and are capable of compelling people to behave and believe in certain ways. This is not a matter of the "demonic possession" of human personalities as portrayed in a movie like *The Exorcist*. Rather, through these spirits' active connection with social formations, elements of society are transformed into force, activity, and seduction. Principalities and powers do this by acting in cooperation with human agency. Social realities and enterprises can become aligned with these fallen powers. These human institutions become more than merely natural or semiautonomous social processes. They become spiritually potent realities with the capability of driving people away from God. They can induce disobedience and behavior destructive of the good.

Examples of powers in the New Testament are money and the state. Jesus describes money ("mammon") as a power alternative to God. Money as a power seduces people to sacrifice relationships, family, health, reason, and justice to secure more of it (Matthew 6:24; Luke 16:9, 11). Instead of trusting in God, people put their trust in money. Economics and sociology normally do not do a good job of explaining how a neutral social utility like money can have such power over people, institutions, and nations (though some of Marx's and even Weber's analyses of the power of money in human life suggest this perspective).

Likewise, the state as part of the total societal system of Rome is portrayed as a beast in Revelation 13. This underlines the state's potential to subvert its God-given purpose of serving righteousness by rewarding the good and punishing the evil (Romans 13). Here, as an antistate, it persecutes the righteous and aids the wicked. Its civil order is the disorder of tyranny and injustice. Nazi Germany is an example of the sort of state that becomes a power of evil and sweeps many good people into evil doings.

Thus, institutions that appear in the social science communication pool to be comparatively neutral social instruments furthering human interests turn out to be Jekylls and Hydes. Although meant for good, they are equally capable of driving people to lie, cheat, steal, kill, and sacrifice their lives. Money and power are extraordinary powers of human experience that the New Testament connects to suprahuman agencies in their evil expressions.

In sum, several specific New Testament terms provide a grammar or language of discourse with resemblances to some central concepts of sociology. Because these Greek words are part of a very different symbolic universe, they have meanings and applications different from those of sociological concepts. They paint a picture of human beings and their social worlds now existing in a fallen world, a world still orderly. Often the principles that structure the human life-world are corrupted and empowered by spiritual forces that alienate people from God and each other. The life-world of this age is one of human weakness, neediness, sin, death, and transitoriness. One day another age, brought by the coming of the Kingdom of God, will replace this one. In the meantime, people are being redeemed and brought into a redemptive community that already lives by the power of that coming age. Christians continue to live in the present age and world, but they are no longer to ally themselves with its spiritual forces and its principles.

Putting It All Together

Having words to talk about a given reality is important. Without words, humans would find it difficult to communicate or clarify what is going on and what these events might mean. The Bible provides a few words that overlap with sociological concepts. But words are not enough. And there is much more in the Bible besides the vocabulary used in its discourse. There is a narrative that moves from creation through the fall to a history of redemption. It culminates in the life, death, and resurrection of Jesus Christ as the Savior of the whole world. There is a redemptive community, commissioned to do God's will here on earth. It is to witness to the power and reality of the coming Kingdom in the midst of the kingdoms of this age.

Christian thinkers have combined these elements into theological models in order to develop social philosophies. Because there are overlaps between the vocabularies of the Bible and of sociology, one must ask how they interrelate. Bridges between these vocabularies are needed—bridges useful for a Christian approach to sociology.

The next two chapters travel further on this quest. Chapter Twelve considers how the narrative stories and legal prescriptions of the Bible suggest a coherent approach to culture and social structure. Then, Chapter Thirteen looks at some of the general theological paradigms that synthesize biblical material and contemporary issues. These paradigms offer models that Christians can use in thinking about social reality.

NOTES

1. Barrett, *World Christian Encyclopedia* (Oxford, NY: Oxford University Press, 1982).
2. Finley, *The Ancient Economy* (Berkeley, CA: University of California Press, 1973), p. 21; W. G. Runcimann, *A Treatise on Social Theory*, Vol. 1: *The Methodology of Social Theory* (Cambridge, England: Cambridge University Press, 1983), p. 13.
3. G. Kittel and G. Friedrich, eds., *Theological Dictionary of the New Testament* (TDNT), ten volumes (Grand Rapids, MI: Eerdmans, 1964–1976), Vol. 1, pp. 197–208; C. Brown, ed., *The New International Dictionary of New Testament Theology* (NIDNTT), three volumes (Grand Rapids, MI: Zondervan, 1975–1978), Vol. 3, pp. 826–833; G. Bromiley, *The International Standard Bible Encyclopedia* (ISBE), four volumes (Grand Rapids, MI: Eerdmans, 1979–1988), Vol. 1, pp. 67–68; Vol. 4, pp. 852–853.
4. TDNT, Vol. 3, pp. 868–895; NIDNTT, Vol. 1, pp. 521–526; ISBE, Vol. 4, pp. 1112–1116.
5. Ladd, *A Theology of the New Testament* (Grand Rapids, MI: Eerdmans, 1974), p. 399.
6. TDNT, Vol. 7, pp. 670–687; NIDNTT, Vol. 2, pp. 451–453; ISBE, Vol. 2, pp. 57–58; Vol. 3, p. 973.
7. TDNT, Vol. 2, pp. 562–574; NIDNTT, Vol. 2, pp. 606–611, 615ff; ISBE, Vol. 3, pp. 971–973, 926–928.
8. TDNT, Vol. 1, pp. 478–479; NIDNTT, Vol. 1, pp. 168–169.

Chapter 12

GOD AND CULTURE

Two lines have grown dramatically longer in recent days. The first is the line of nostalgics, whose most famous member is Jean-Jacques Rousseau. These folk suppose we have left something behind that is far superior to what exists now. Above all, they say, we must go backward as quickly as possible.

The second are the progressives. Their diagnosis is that we haven't gone forward quickly enough. The solution to problems created by our most recent gadgets is a new generation of gadgets. Having pulled ourselves out of the muck of backwardness, the last thing we need to do is to recreate the disaster called the past.

The error that Rousseau and his contemporary incarnations make is more than naive romanticism about the past (which always looks better the farther one is from it). It is the unsociological notion that there was a time this side of Eden when a "state of nature" existed. Humans lived in this "natural state" uncorrupted, uncomplicated by technology, commerce, civilization, or book learning. Close to nature, these simple and virtuous people loved spontaneously and unselfishly, enjoyed clean air and water and the abundant fertility of the earth, and lived in harmony with fellow humans. By this account, it is civilized society with its division of labor, its institutions of private property, and its artificial conventions that creates evil. As Rousseau put it in his most memorable line, "humans were born free, and everywhere they are in chains."

The major tendency of Christian social thought, with some sharp disagreements with Rousseau, has been to line up with the nostalgics and look to the past. This is understandable. The Christian rationality tradition makes the Bible the normative source for settling disputes over basic beliefs and life practices. The Bible is from the past. It is about past interactions between God and various groups of people seeking to understand and do the will of God. Christians believe that the clue to the meaning of the universe is in the texts of the Bible. How humans are to live is also encoded in its pages. They reject the modern prejudice that ideas are better simply because their copyright says twentieth century.

Even more significantly, Christian leadership and ideas were formative for Western civilization. For centuries, a vision of life drawn from the Scriptures animated European life. The fabric of everyday life was interwoven with Christian symbols, ritual, moral understandings, and stories. Then came modernization, industrialization, and secularization. Where Rousseau looks back to a mythical "state of nature," conservative Christians tend to look back to a mythical "Christian" state of society.

For some (like Louis de Bonald, 1754–1840) this means the hierarchical, authoritarian High Middle Ages. Others point to the founding era of American society. They find there a society shaped by explicit Christian laws, minimal government, patriarchal family structures, and unregulated economic activity. Much of the agenda and energy of the Moral Majority has fed off a romanticized idea of a lost Christian era of American history. However, some of those who look back see good only in Eden. For them, everything has been downhill since and will continue to get worse and worse. These are the profoundly radical conservatives, hanging onto the little good passed on from the past in the face of inevitable corruption.

Alongside them are Christians whose gaze is primarily to the future. In the optimistic nineteenth century, many of these Christians were convinced of the evolutionary, unlimited power of the gospel.[1] Things were getting better and better. Inevitably and gradually the whole of the human condition and history would change, bringing in a thousand years of worldwide peace, prosperity, and justice. At the end of that time, Christ would return, ending the regular run of history to set up his Kingdom. This point of view has few contemporary advocates. Along with the surrounding evolutionary optimism that energized it, this view sustained mortal blows from World War I and subsequent dismal history.

More common today is the forward-looking radical or revolutionary. Christian expectations of the imminent arrival of the Kingdom of God stir these believers. Even those whose pessimism concludes that the story line of history has gone completely downhill since Eden can easily become radicals. It is a short distance from quietly hanging on until Christ returns to fervently transforming a community into the Kingdom of God so that Christ will return. What utopians like Thomas Müntzer (1489–1525), Tommaso Campanella (1568–1639), and others seek is the instituting of the principles and values of the coming Kingdom of God in the here and now. The pattern of perfection is not in the past; it is in the future, but it comes to earth by revolutionizing contemporary life.

Whether performed by Christians or not, looking backward or forward is an act of societal diagnosis. Both groups declare contemporary social arrangements inadequate as measured by some past or future yardstick. Such insight demands societies or communities with greater degrees of justice, fairness, equity, fraternity, peace, prosperity, self-determination, and so on.

What does Christian faith bring to modern diagnoses of society? Do these forward or backward looking Christians bring a clear view of what society should be? Is there in the Bible a Christian or God-willed culture and social pattern? If so, should it serve as an absolute yardstick for measuring all cultures and social structures?

For a fair answer to this question, one must raise a prior issue. What value and meaning does the Bible give to the amazing diversity of languages, cultures, ethnic groups, and social structures that characterize the human condition? Are any of them closer to God's standards? What about the societal patterns of Israel as mandated, described, and institutionalized in the Old Testament? Is Israel a divine societalization of a single people? Are its patterns meant forever to be clues concerning what God wishes all other peoples and societies to be like?

Like No Other Nation on Earth

Israel—Called and Chosen

The discussion can begin at a point of agreement among Christians. Ancient Israel was a people called and chosen by God. "For you are a people holy to the Lord your God. The Lord your God has chosen you out of all the peoples on the face of the earth to be his people, his treasured possession" (Deuteronomy 7:6).

This special relationship began with the calling of Abraham from Haran (Genesis 12:1; Nehemiah 9:7). The liberation of Israel from Egyptian slavery affirmed God's covenant with the patriarchs. Mount Sinai formalized the unique bond between God and the people of Israel. God would be identified with Israel. To the people of Israel, the revelation of God would be given in a special way (Romans 9:5).

Yet this special connectedness placed covenant responsibilities on Israel and gave it a worldwide mission. Israel was to purify itself of all false religion. No other gods were to be worshiped alongside Yahweh. Israel was also to purify itself of socially oppressive and unjust patterns. Neighbors were to be loved, not neglected, ignored, or exploited. Justice and righteousness were to be clearly visible in the architecture of all social, economic, and political life. God associated God's name with this people above all other peoples. In turn, they were to associate their ways of living and thinking with the character of the God they served.[2]

Yahweh is a God of all the earth, not just Israel (Exodus 19:5-6). In choosing Israel, Yahweh's purpose was to display the glory and spread the knowledge of God to all peoples through this one people (Isaiah 11:9–10). Isaiah 44 is an oracle concerning Israel as Yahweh's chosen (verses 1 and 21), unveiling the claim to be the one true God. Israel is called as a nation for the sake of the whole earth. Isaiah 45, with its profound argument for monotheism, gives the theological reasons for that calling:

> There is no God apart from me,
>   a righteous God and a Savior;
>   there is none but me.
> Turn to me and be saved,
>   all you ends of the earth;
>   for I am God, and there is no other.
> By myself I have sworn . . .
> Before me every knee will bow;
>   by me every tongue will swear.
> They will say of me,
>   "In the Lord alone are righteousness and strength."
> (Isaiah 45:21–24)

Thus, Israel's worldwide task was to serve as a missionary people to the other peoples of the earth. It was to give the knowledge and blessings of Yahweh to all other nations. The Israelite priests and Levites mediated that knowledge to the chosen people of God. The chosen people of God were in turn to do the same for the world. They were to reflect the glory of God by exhibiting appropriate connectedness to God, to fellow Israelites, to strangers and resident aliens, and to the land. When the people of Israel refuse to fulfill this missionary calling, God places them under judgment. The book of Jonah has this message at its heart. It is the story of Jonah's refusal to recognize the true God as a God who loves all peoples.

This special calling did not come to the Israelites on the basis of race, culture, social structure, population size, or preexistent righteousness. It was an instance of free grace, redeeming grace. This calling and choosing did not mean that every Israelite trusted in Yahweh or properly served God. Disobedience is a persistent thread that runs through the history of Israel. Moses and the prophets issued clear warnings about the consequences of false religion and socially oppressive patterns. Disobedience to the ways of Yahweh led again and again to judgment (Amos 3:2). Yet always there was a faithful remnant.

The active element in the relationship was not ethnicity or genealogical purity. It was faith. Even individuals (such as Melchizedek, Rahab, Ruth, and Naaman) and peoples (such as the Ninevites in Jonah) not within the kinship web of Israel could enter into the blessings of Yahweh. In fact, the Old Testament foreshadows the incorporation of all non-Jewish peoples into the covenant and blessings of Abraham and Israel (Psalm 87). Yet the primary focus of the Old Testament is on establishing a people separated unto Yahweh and righteous in their social patterns, ready for the coming messiah.

Israel—A Holy People

Close examination of Israel's existence reveals a civilization snugly fitting its historical and cultural context. God did not create a culture for the Israelites any more than God gave them a divine language in which to converse with him and each other. God chose a people who already possessed patterns of family life, techniques for producing and distributing goods, language, kinship, and even religious ideas and ritual.[3]

Careful study suggests that the normative framework given by God in the narratives and law codes (the Torah) regularized and regulated the preexisting cultural substratum. Its most stringent and penetrating regulation was in the arena of religious ideas and practices with their implications for connections between human beings. The giving of the law at Mount Sinai came in the wake of the exodus, liberating Israel from slavery. The law incorporated forms of life reflecting the character of that deliverance and enabling Israel to remember it (Exodus 12). The law allowed

Israelites to respond to God's covenant. It dictated acknowledgment that all of their life, including social arrangements, was under the commanding presence of the God who had delivered them (Deuteronomy 6:5).

In the Torah's regulation of horizontal social relationships, the pattern appears to involve softening the harshness of the customary practices of the day.[4] Examples of this include giving rights to slaves and restricting the power of masters[5] and taking some first steps toward acknowledging women's dignity.[6] The Mosaic law resisted the contemporary severity of punishments by insisting that these punishments not exceed but fit the gravity of the crime. This is the meaning of "an eye for an eye" (Exodus 21:24; Leviticus 24:20). In general, the law protected the "small ones" whose position in society made them vulnerable or helpless (Deuteronomy 10:17–18; 15:7–11). It also provided conventions that appear oriented toward keeping Israel culturally distinct from its neighbors (for example, Leviticus 19:19).

Certain social structures ensured the cyclic leveling of differences in wealth and power in an agrarian-based civilization. The sabbatical year (every seventh year) rested the land and the worker. What the land produced naturally that year was for the poor and for the wild animals.[7] It also provided for slave release, debt forgiveness, and the special reading of the Torah (Leviticus 25:1–7; Deuteronomy 15:1–18, 31:10ff). The year of jubilee, the fiftieth year in a cycle of seven sabbaticals, was to be a year of liberty throughout the land (Leviticus 25:8–55). Real property sold during that half-century reverted to the original family (clan). Those whose poverty led them to sell themselves into indentured service were then released without qualifications.

These patterns indicate that God met the Israelites as and where they existed. God did not completely revolutionize their cultural patterns. Rather, God commanded patterns for living that would reform preexisting cultural patterns. The new norms connected their culture with God's character, purpose, and liberating deliverance from the social oppression of Egypt. As Yahweh cared for them in slavery in Egypt, they were to care for the "least of these" (Matthew 25:45). The legitimacy of their shared social patterns hung on the degree to which they mirrored and institutionalized relational patterns intrinsic to God's covenant relationship with the covenant partners.

A New People of God with Many Cultural Expressions

The New Testament provides the definitive clue that the cultural and social specifics of Israelite existence are not mandates required for all peoples and cultures. In the New Testament, the sociological structure of the people of God shifts from a single national group with ethnic boundaries to a church encompassing many peoples and ethnic groups. When this shift occurred, it generated many tensions. The early Church had sharp debates over whether Christians from non-Jewish backgrounds must conform to the customs of the Old Testament culture followed by Jewish people. The answer was a decisive no (Galatians; Acts 15).

Paul focused sharply on the "indifference" of religion to culture and social status where the people of God are concerned. No cultural or social distinctive prevents any person from being fully a part of the Body of Christ. "There is neither Jew nor Greek, slave nor free, male nor female, for you are all one in Christ Jesus. If you belong to Christ, then you are Abraham's seed and heirs according to the promise" (Galatians 3:28–29; see also 1 Corinthians 9; Romans 14).

Regulation of Culture in the New Testament

God's Torah was not fundamentally destructive or creative of culture. Rather, it regulated the ancient cultural patterns brought by Abraham's family and the Israelites when called and chosen for covenant connectedness. The New Testament displays a similar relationship between God's revelation and action, and human culture. The Mosaic laws, given to regulate Israelite culture, were not forced on gentile Christians. Gentile peoples brought their own cultural biases and patterns with them into the Church. Yet gentile customs came under the same sort of regulation. The gospel challenged and modified them in directions that reflected the implications of the liberating redemption provided by Jesus Christ. The New Testament never required a single, uniform culture among Christians, only life-styles congruent with the nature and meaning of Christ within *all* cultures containing Christians.

The "household codes" of the apostolic letters are good examples of regulations of preexisting gentile cultural patterns (Colossians 3:18–4:1; Ephesians 5:21–6:9; 1 Peter 2:13–3:7). These codes, modeled on Stoic and Jewish patterns, were Christian standards for relationships that preexisted faith. Such codes typically involved lists of vices and virtues. They appealed to the various actors of the Roman extended household to fulfill the duties of their role relationships in a particular manner. Peter and Paul Christianize the codes by connecting them to a Christian symbolic universe.

In Ephesians 5:21–6:9, Paul is not instituting a "Christian culture" for the Ephesians. When the Ephesians came to faith, they already lived in households with the power one-sidedly vested in the "paterfamilias" (the husband-father-master). It was a patriarchal structure with rights of throwing unwanted infants out to be killed by exposure to the elements, maiming and even killing slaves, and abusing wives. The weaker members of the household had little recourse when mistreated by the paterfamilias. Paul takes the three central family role-sets and connects each to Christ. In every case, he places limits on the powerful member and requires that the roles be played out with Christ as the motivating image and presence.

The paterfamilias no longer can see himself as absolute master of his house. The key theme of the Ephesian household code is submission. Its broadest note is reciprocity: "Submit to one another out of reverence for Christ" (verse 21).[8] In relationship to the wife, the paterfamilias is to enact his role in a manner that imitates the way Christ connects himself to the Church. He is to love her as his own body and give himself sacrificially for her. Her readiness to renounce her own preferences encounter a husband equally ready to deny his own interests and comfort for her.

The one-sidedness of parental authority in the Roman household that is connected to the Lord is handled similarly. Children are to obey parents "in the Lord." Fathers are not to exasperate and provoke the anger of their children. They are to do whatever will train them to obey the Lord and understand his instructions for life. The limits of a child's obedience are set by what the Lord requires. It is the life in submission to Christ that provides justifiable restrictions on the control of the paterfamilias. Christ's love and blessing of children, if taken as a role model, would transform the harshness that could contaminate this role set.

Most startling are the words on slavery. The Christian slave is instructed to serve as though the master were Christ himself: no hypocrisy, no slacking off, no resentment. The Christian master is to treat the slave with the same respect that he expects to receive from the slave. No threats are permitted. The reality is that both slave and master are enslaved to Christ. Both will receive rewards from him as their Master, without favoritism.

Without directly challenging the actual gentile Roman social structure, Paul connects its role enactment with Christ. He insists that Christians cannot simply continue life as if their faith commitment makes no difference in their attitudes and behavior. Paul is not saying to Christians that slavery is a good idea and that one ought to institute it. Nor is he saying that patriarchal family structures are God's patterns, so one should get on with buttressing the authority and power of the husband and father. Rather, Christians living in a social structure with slave holding and patriarchy as integral institutions have new role prescriptions as they enter into those social responsibilities. Living *in Christ* transforms how one lives *in culture*.

For first-century Roman culture, being in Christ meant placing sharp limits on the power and authority of the paterfamilias. Following Paul's household code would curb the abuses of the paterfamilias (as well as those of the weaker role partner). It would bring the actually enacted roles more into line with the liberating intentions and meanings of Jesus Christ. Culture and social status as such may be matters of indifference to religion, but the meanings and enactment of roles are not. Whether people are treated with the care, respect, and dignity due to bearers of the image of God is not a matter of indifference. Roles and structures that violate human dignity must be transformed and will be transformed when connected to the model and power of Christ. Other cultural contexts might require transformations of very different sorts. What is essential is connecting each to the person and character of Christ.

The Pilgrim and Missionary Principles

At work in this pattern of cultural regulation in both the Old and New Testaments are two complementary principles. On the one hand, the people of God are pilgrims in every cultural group. This age is not their home. No particular social or cultural context comprises the Kingdom of God. The political and economic order in which the people of God live is not God's order in any direct sense. Their citizenship is in heaven, in the age to come. So they are permanent strangers, "resident aliens" in their native societies. Thus, Christians are necessarily critical, necessarily half-hearted patriots, necessarily unable to give full allegiance to any particular social structure or cultural pattern. They can move across cultural and social boundaries without the loss of their essential identity.

Nevertheless, their calling requires them to live out the gospel within the culture and society in which they are set. Their task is missionary in whatever culture they find themselves. They are to contextualize the gospel, incarnating it within all peoples and all cultures. To contextualize is to transfer and translate an understanding or cultural trait to a new context. In this case, God's people are to take the meanings and messages of the biblical text and transfer them to social and cultural contexts with very different symbolic universes than those found in the Bible. Successful contextualization happens when, in the new context, the understandings and traits acquire meanings and functions roughly similar to those they had in their original context.

Christians must not compromise the gospel by accommodating it to the elements of any culture. When such compromise or domestication happens, the meanings of the gospel are distorted or lost. People then encounter a picture of Jesus and the Kingdom of God contrary to that given in the Bible. The controlling meanings become the culture's meanings in the very places where the culture needs to be challenged. Instead, the compromised gospel reinforces the cultural patterns. The culture transforms the gospel rather than the gospel transforming the culture.

While Christians are to avoid domesticating the gospel, they recognize that the gospel must be contextualized if it is to display its relevance to human life. Contextualization without domestication happens by carefully following the story of what God has done for God's people throughout history as recorded in Scripture. It also requires deep insight into the powerful forces of the culture into which the gospel is to be contextualized. Then, reciting the biblical story as a story for that context and identifying that society and its structures with the God who freed the Israelites from slavery and with Jesus Christ, the crucified redeemer, provide resources to connect that culture's own lifeways with the regulating and transforming effects of the gospel.

God's people are to dwell within both the plausibility structures and symbolic universes of their culture and of the Christian faith tradition. Together, with the help of the Holy Spirit, each Christian community is to develop its own "household codes," "organizational mandates," and "cultural ethos." Through these culturally specific patterns, they spell out ways to regulate and transform their culturally given roles. Through them, they explicitly connect culture to Christ. The result is not a single Christian culture. The vision is of tens of thousands of human cultures, purified and enriched by the gospel and by a redemptive community in the midst of each of those cultures.

The cultural freedom offered to Christian community is thus tied to a particular mission, a mission that continues the calling of Israel. The purpose of the cultural freedom of the Christian is to mediate the blessing of God in Jesus Christ to all peoples of the earth. There will be an authentically Chinese, Uzbeki, Bengali, Romanian, Mam, French, Cherokee, Iranian, and American Christianity. Contextualization means the gospel will speak within and to each culture through that culture's own communication pools. Yet it will not be a domesticated gospel, compromised and truncated by contextualization. God's own liberating voice will call elements of every culture into question. The Bible indicates that ethnic cultures from all corners of the globe will one day be purified of sinful elements and made to glorify God in the Kingdom.

The New Testament challenges many established Roman and Jewish practices and thought through looking both backward and forward. Some passages evaluate the contemporary institutions and social practices of the first century in terms of permanent, universal principles embedded in the Old Testament. When asked about the issue of divorce, Jesus recalls the creation account as a way of understanding the force of the Mosaic law (Matthew 19:1–12). He lifts up the inner spirit of that law, showing how many of the first-century Jewish applications of it are infringements of what God intended. He challenges contemporary practices in the light of the ancient will of God.

Other passages relativize a cultural practice by relating it to the coming age of the Kingdom of God. When asked a trick question about the resurrection, Jesus says that the whole institution of marriage will not be a part of social life in the coming Kingdom (Matthew 22:23–32). The New Testament even establishes a

different attitude toward singleness than that which was normative in Judaism. The Old Testament has no word for bachelor. An
unmarried or barren woman considered her life a disaster (it was
"cursed"). By contrast, in the New Testament Paul declares the
practical superiority of a single life (1 Corinthians 7:8–9, 27, 29,
32–35). No longer are marrying and having children the same
driving concerns that they were in Israel. The redemptive Child
has come. With the beginnings of the new age in him, marriage
and childbearing cease to have the cultural or religious significance they had in the Old Testament.

Still to be spelled out here is the theological basis for accepting
the variety of language groups and cultural zones as permissible
arenas for discipleship. How could Jesus and the New Testament
Church suddenly shift to a new pattern of relating to the many
cultures of the world? Is there anything in the Old Testament that
provides a basis for seeing monocultural Israel as a stepping-stone
to a later multicultural people of God? The next section looks at
where and why the various languages with their associated cultures got their start and what their fate is to be in the Kingdom
of God.

Languages and Peoples in Biblical Focus

Genesis 10:1–11:9 forms the heart of the Bible's account of
human dispersion and diversity.[9] It lays the foundation for accepting the validity and dignity of every language and culture. It
shows how biblical material, while overlapping with central concerns of sociology, handles them in a distinctly different fashion.
The passage can be divided into two distinct sections: a genealogy
and a judgment story.

All Nations Are Kin to Israel

Genesis 10 is known as the "Table of Nations." It is a verbal
map of the ancient peoples around Israel. Its literary form is an

alliance or segmented genealogy, setting forth the general roots and affiliations of various ethnic or tribal groups. This was important information for Israel in forging confederations, handling intermarriages, and setting boundaries. Kinship ordered the overwhelming majority of human connections in early Israel.[10] Kinship relatedness was crucial information for mobilizing social action and forging alliances. Moderns often find genealogies boring; the ancients did not.

This account is unique in ancient literature in its assertion of the common source of all peoples and nations. The genealogy lists seventy descendants of Noah's three sons, tying them to various lands, languages, and nations. The ultimate relationship of all humans to each other is that of brother and sister. All human beings are of common origin and thus of common dignity, whatever their differences. Any Israelite reciting this genealogy is forced to see surrounding peoples as distant kin. The genealogy offers no explanation why these groups dispersed, settled where they did, or developed different languages. That is elucidated in the complementary judgment story of Babel. The Table of Nations simply sketches the web of connectedness between the ancestors of Israel and those of the nations and lands surrounding it.

There is a pattern in the account. The genealogy circles in on Israel's own roots by first listing nations stemming from Japheth (Genesis 10:2–5). These are the peoples least involved in Israel's destiny, located farther away than the others (in what is now Cyprus, Greece, and Turkey). Next the genealogy lists nations descending from Ham (10:6–20). Here are Israel's chief rivals: the Egyptians, Canaanites, and Babylonians. Here is the story of the founding of Babel (Babylon) by the warrior and city builder, Nimrod. This is the beginning of the history of the city that is portrayed most consistently as anti-God in biblical narratives. Finally, it recounts Israel's own roots in Shem (10:21–32). Among these peoples are many of Israel's allies as well as the enemy, Assyria, and Elam (one of Babylon's close rivals).

None of the peoples listed are more than fifteen hundred miles from Canaan. They are all within the circumference of trade and travel of Israel. There is no indication that this list is meant to be comprehensive. Instead, there is literary significance in listing seventy names. This number corresponds to the seventy who went with Jacob into captivity in Egypt. Jesus' ministry includes sending seventy out to evangelize. This is a symbol of his intention that the good news of the Kingdom is for all peoples. The point of Genesis 10 is that all the nations in their lands with their distinct languages, including Canaanite groups and eastern powers who one day will carry Israel into captivity, are one in origin. Israel is close or distant kin *to them all*. The passage provides a basis for cross-cultural respect and affinity, even if Israel and her neighbors seldom lived out this possibility.

This genealogy gives no indication of the various histories, recorded later, of hostility between nations. If this were the end of the story, one might imagine that all these peoples existed in their diversity as one happy, extended family. But the story does not end here. The narrator goes on to tell a complementary tale. That the Table of Nations and the judgment story of Babel are set side by side signifies that they are complementary accounts of the diversity and dispersion of the peoples.

The Theological Meaning of Language Diversity

The story of Babel's judgment (Genesis 11:1–9) describes the intervention of God as the initiating cause of human linguistic divergence. That linguistic diversity underlies the scattering of the single human race into distinct peoples and nations. Several literary features give clues to the story's significance.

The story is arranged in a fashion that enhances memorization in a culture where the vast majority of people were not literate. It is a palistrophe or extended chiasmus—that is, each element of the front end of the story corresponds to a similar element in the second half of the story. The hinge on which the story turns is the

coming down of Yahweh to inspect the tower. If the corresponding parts are picked out, then the structure looks like this:

A All the *earth* had one *language* . . . (verse 1)
  B *There* they settled (2)
    C They *said* to one another (3)
      D *Come, let's* make bricks . . . (3)
        E Let's *build* for ourselves (4)
          F A *city* and a *tower* . . . (4)
            G *And the Lord came down to see* (5)
          F' the *city* and the *tower* (5)
        E' that the humans had *built* . . . (5)
      D' *Come, let's* go down and confuse . . . (7)
    C' They will not understand one another's *speech* (7)
  B' The Lord scattered them from *there* . . . (8)
A' the *language* of the whole *earth* confused (9)

Another way of highlighting the movement of the story is to
divide it into its two contrasting halves, separated by the coming
of Yahweh:

> Human deeds (A–F)
>   Inspection of the tower and city (G)
> Divine deeds (F'–A')

The major points stand out when the content and structure of
this story are set within the symbolic universe of Israel and the
ancient Middle East. This is the last in a series of primeval stories.
These stories deal with the whole of humanity and portray the
spread of sin followed by the judgment of God. This is the only
story in that series not followed by a sign of hope from God.
Instead, it moves quickly forward to relate another story: that of
the calling of Abraham and God's promise to bless all peoples
through the one people of God. This story says, in effect, that
there is hope for a world divided by language. God is calling one
people into being with a mission to mediate God's redemption and
blessing to all peoples.

The name *Babel* is also a clue that the story is polemical. For the Babylonians, Babel meant "the gate of God." By contrast, the Hebrew narrator associates the name with the meaning "mixed up, confused." The Mesopotamian cities built towerlike structures, called ziggurats, as gateways leading up to the heavens. Here is the original, towering skyscraper of the ancients. The human motivation behind it is social immortality ("making a name") and technical prowess, unifying the finest human talent. The inhabitants seek to bypass the command of the Creator to disperse and fill the earth.

The story ridicules this technical achievement. Meant to reach up to God, the tower is so small that Yahweh and the heavenly hosts must descend the heights of heaven in order to see it. Yahweh concludes that this tower is the prelude to more serious sin. God decides to place limits on human abilities to unite in sin. The judgment that falls on this effort initiates processes separating people into different language pools. Their single language is confused. Families move off into separate linguistic and communication pools. Yet this is not a hindrance to the worship of Yahweh. There is nothing here like Islam's insistence on Arabic as the divine language, essential for understanding God's word in the Koran. The Bible sees human linguistic diversity as rooted in the action and intentions of God.

One must be careful in interpreting this story. Its literary construction as well as its sparseness should not tempt the reader to speculate over details not presented. The narrative does not present the instantaneous formation of new languages but rather the confusion of the old. It is not offered as an alternative to synchronic studies of linguistic drift conducted by sociolinguists. (Such studies indicate the length of time and the processes by which once-related dialects of the same language become two "different" languages.) Nor does this story assert an instantaneous scattering of the families throughout the earth. What this narrative does is to connect linguistic diversity with the activity of God in human affairs. It describes the purpose behind God's action, which is to restrain the evil that can come from a total unity of humanity organized for its own glorification and arrogant accomplishments.

Walter Brueggemann suggests the sort of significance residing in this story.[11] There is a unity desired by the people as they resist God. They also fear scattering. Nonetheless, God scatters them as punishment for their use of unity in rebellion. On the other hand, there is a kind of human unity desired by God that is based on loyalty to God. This is the unity that will be seen at the end of human history, a unity completely opposed to the kind of unity portrayed in the tower of Babel story. This account says that a world ordered according to the goodness and joy intended by the Creator does not come into being through the actions of a self-securing homogeneous humanity, behaving as though God is not the Lord. But such a world also does not happen by the scattering of ethnic groups into autonomous parts. God's order does not envisage peoples who act as though the separate parts of humanity do not belong to each other. In both unity and scattering lurk the possibilities of obedience and blessing or disobedience and curse.

This world is one in which language is decisive. Speaking and listening are fundamental to true human community. The judgment of God is the historical cause of the very pluralization experienced by the modern world. The Church as a sociological body is a new language community incorporating the diversity of languages and their associated cultural groupings. In this new unity of peoples, diverse humans can come back together into a proper unity based on loyalty to the Creator and Redeemer of all peoples. The sign of tongues on the day of Pentecost (Acts 2) is an intimation that the Church is to be a multilinguistic, multicultural reality that, nevertheless, experiences a mystical unity and oneness in Christ. In looking forward, the New Testament envisions the coming Kingdom of God as incorporating this diversity:

After this I looked and there before me was a great multitude that no one could count, from every nation, tribe, people, and language, standing before the throne . . . and they cried out in a loud voice:

> "Salvation belongs to our God,
> who sits on the throne,
> and to the Lamb." (Revelation 7:9–10)

The Kingdom of God does not remove the diversity of culture and historical experience. The coming age does not wipe the slate clean. Rather "the kings of the earth will bring their splendor" into it and the "glory and honor of the nations will be brought into it" (Revelation 21:24, 26).

In sum, the Bible does not push any single culture or social structure forward as the "Christian culture." The linguistic and cultural diversity of the earth is an essential part of this fallen age. That diversity expresses both the judgment of God on sin and a fulfillment of the command for humans to fill the earth. In the final age, linguistic and national diversity will be represented and preserved. The final unity of humanity entails preserving the rich pluralization that has come about through history.

A Christian's evaluation of contemporary culture looks both backward and forward. On the one hand, the direction of cultural challenge and regulation seen in both the Torah and the New Testament is to characterize contemporary Christian codes of behavior. Christian advocacy and action encompass clear lines of orientation. The Christian code is passionate for the weak and helpless as well as for true religion and the ending of social oppression in all its forms. Proper connections to God, fellow humans, and nature mark its shape. Christian concern includes the earth as well as the animals that inhabit God's creation along with human beings. Christians act this very way because that is the pattern from the past.

On the other hand, none of Christians' contemporary institutional solutions can be taken as final in the light of the coming Kingdom of God. While Christians seek to have God's will done here on earth as it is in heaven, they patiently wait and pray for the coming Kingdom. God is creating a redemptive community in which there can already be anticipations and small expressions of the coming Kingdom. Christians seek to be good citizens of that Kingdom as well as of their earthly one.

If the argument of this chapter is correct, then the next question becomes: how can Christians think about and live in whatever society God places them? Are there any general principles or models that might guide the process of Christian thought and practice?

Chapter Thirteen displays the range of Christian thought about society and social institutions. As Christians interpret the Bible, they do not all come to the same conclusions about human culture and social arrangements. There is a diversity of Christian social paradigms similar to the diversity of sociological paradigms. Realizing this helps us see how complex the conversation is between Christian faith and modern sociology.

NOTES

1. Donald W. Dayton, *Discovering an Evangelical Heritage* (New York: Harper & Row, 1976).
2. John Bright, *The Kingdom of God* (Nashville, TN: Abingdon Press, 1956).
3. Israel's customs were placed within Yahweh's covenant Lordship and modified by his command. A. S. Van Der Woude, ed., *The World of the Bible* (Grand Rapids, MI: Eerdmans, 1986); J. A. Thompson, *Handbook of Life in Bible Times* (Leicester, England: Inter-Varsity Press, 1986). See also Roland de Vaux, *Ancient Israel: Its Life and Institutions* (New York: McGraw-Hill, 1961).
4. Willard M. Swartley's *Slavery, Sabbath, War, and Women* (Scottdale, PA: Herald Press, 1983) deals with the hermeneutics of some of these issues. A comparison of Old Testament law with the laws of Eshnunna (the Akkadian law code from 1800 B.C.) and the law code of Hammurabi (a Babylonian code dated at 1726 B.C.) shows significant advances. See Gordon D. Fee and Douglas Stuart, *How to Read the Bible for All Its Worth* (Grand Rapids, MI: Zondervan, 1982), pp. 143–144, and Christopher J. H. Wright, *An Eye for an Eye: The Place of Old Testament Ethics Today* (Downers Grove, IL: InterVarsity Press, 1983).
5. Leviticus 25:42ff, 46, 53; Exodus 12:44; 20:10; 21–23; Deuteronomy 15:13ff; 16:11–14; 23:15ff.

6. Genesis 2:23–24; Exodus 21:7–11; Deuteronomy 21:10–17; 22:28ff; 24:1–4; see also Proverbs 5:15–20; 18:22, 31:10–31; Malachi 2:13–16.

7. Exodus 23:10; see also Deuteronomy 25:4, Proverbs 12:10, Jonah 4:11, indicating humane concern for animals as a mark of a society pleasing to God.

8. The word *hypotásso* (to submit) in the middle or passive voice, as here, refers to the subordination of free agents. It denotes "a voluntary attitude of giving in, cooperating, assuming responsibility, and carrying a burden." Markus Barth, *Ephesians: Translation and Commentary on Chapters 4–6* (New York: Doubleday, 1974), p. 710. Contrary to common perceptions, the New Testament nowhere uses the terminology of obedience (*hypakouo*) for a wife's relationship to her husband, as it does for children and parents, slaves and masters, or for the Christian's obedience to Christ and the Christian faith.

9. The following is indebted to Gordon Wenham, *Word Biblical Commentary: Genesis 1–15* (Waco, TX: Word, 1987); Allen P. Ross, *Creation and Blessing: A Guide to the Study and Exposition of the Book of Genesis* (Grand Rapids, MI: Baker Book House, 1988); and Claus Westermann, *Genesis 1–11: A Commentary* (Minneapolis: Augsburg, 1984).

10. See Eric Wolf, *Europe and the People Without History* (Berkeley: University of California Press, 1982), pp. 88–100, for typical features of kin-ordered modes of production. See Norman Gottwald, *The Tribes of Yahweh: A Sociology of Religion of Liberated Israel, 1250–1050* B.C.E. (Mary Knoll, NY: Orbis, 1979), Part 4, for hypotheses about the social structural features of ancient Israel.

11. Walter Brueggemann, *Genesis* (Atlanta, GA: John Knox, 1982), pp. 98–104.

Chapter 13

THEOLOGICAL PARADIGMS

Christians always face a dilemma. On the one hand, they belong to a community subject to the authority of Christ: the Church. In that fellowship, Christ is the supreme pattern for faith and practice. He shapes Christians' character and conduct. They are disciples, learning to develop their views, attitudes, relationships, and actions according to his teachings and presence.

On the other hand, Christians grow up within a wider human community with its own culture and social practices, some of which are in opposition to those learned in the household of faith. In this wider human community, Jesus Christ is but one among many influences and outlooks. Many loyalties demand allegiance, some of which are indifferent or even hostile to Christ. Christians are inevitably part of their cultural worlds and invariably find themselves shaped by influences other than Christ.

This creates points of tension and conflict. What does Christ's authority mean in the midst of conflicting demands for allegiance? How are Christians and their redemptive community to differ from other people and other communities of the wider culture of which they are a part? How does the authority and influence of Christ relate to the authority and influence of the social structures created to give order and coherence to various societies?

Several penetrating and influential answers have been given to these questions. This chapter looks at a few of them as indicative of the diversity that exists within the Christian tradition.

If Christ Is the Answer, What's the Question?

Theology has not been unmindful of the dramatically changing world surrounding it. In the late nineteenth century, a German Lutheran at Heidelberg University became convinced that having only two ways of making sense of history was inadequate. The first way was Marxism, a quintessentially modern view, that said social history was controlled by economics. Change the economic structures (the infrastructure) and law, religion, ethics, philosophy, politics (the superstructure) would change. When people master the economic realm, they can master the full range of modern problems, ushering in a utopia. Economic arrangements yield single social results. Get the economics right and the social world will be right.

The other way of looking at history was a familiar one: Christian orthodoxy of the day. It simply reiterated an old answer that religious faith was the basis of human life. Secure religious faith in the population, and all modern problems would vanish. The idea behind this viewpoint was that Christian faith leads to a single set of social results.

The German Lutheran theologian, Ernst Troeltsch (1866–1923), felt that neither of these offered an adequate perspective. Marxism, he maintained, is wrong in making the superstructural elements a reflection of the economic. Specifically, it is wrong in claiming that religion is simply a reflection of social and economic organization. Religion has its own unique roots in human life. It acts with a degree of autonomy to shape and energize civilizations in quite different directions. Confucianism shaped China, Hinduism India, Islam the Arab world, Christianity the European cultures—all contributing to very different civilizations.

Furthermore, there exists a blatant embarrassment to Marx's analysis of religion as only a part of the superstructure. It is that Christianity was the religion of the later Roman Empire *and* of medieval Europe. Same religion but very different economic structures. Somehow superstructures should behave better and change along with changes in the economic arrangements. But in Marx's own backyard, this did not happen.

On the other hand, Troeltsch felt that many Christians were also wrong in thinking that obedience to Christian faith leads to one social result. Troeltsch learned to question this from the famous sociologist, Max Weber, who lived downstairs in the same Heidelberg house. There were at least three social results that grew out of Christian faith, three very different ways of relating faith to the social world. In a stunning thousand-page document, *The Social Teachings of the Christian Churches* (1911), Troeltsch nosed his way into dozens of dusty corners of Church history to document these three ways. In the process, he argued that all three grow out of emphases clearly found in the Bible.

The first response he called the "Church-type." In this case, faith relates Christians to the social world in a most affirmative manner. The Church-type seeks to create a universal community, to encompass within the doors of the Christian community the total population of an area. The Church-type considers itself the conservator of the well-being of the nation, protector of the moral fabric of human life. It legitimates the nation and seeks to create a Christian culture for the whole of the society. Its relationship to the social world surrounding it is most positive. It considers social structures of nations as natural or God-given preparations and contexts for the ministries and mysteries of the Church.

The Church-type deems itself the divine instrument embodying the miraculous power of God, even when individual priests or bishops may be corrupt. It acts as an objective institution that dispenses the sacramental grace of God. Even if individual leaders are corrupt, the Church is not. It is still able to throw its mantle over the full range of human institutions (from family to economic to political). By so doing, it seeks to make all of the life of society conform to objectively stated natural and moral laws. It adapts to the world in a reciprocal intertwining of Church and society that gives the Church a civilizational impact in structuring the societal culture.

Normally this means that the Church becomes the state religion. All within the boundaries of the state become members of the Church simply by the location of their birth. Troeltsch describes the medieval Roman Catholic church as the best historical example of this sort of community. The Church-type social outcome of the teachings of Christian faith appears where the Church becomes an overwhelmingly predominant faith and controls the state.

Troeltsch called the major alternative to the Church-type the "Sect-type." Its essential style is rejection of "the world." It is invariably a minority movement within a given society. Monastic orders and ascetic protest movements (such as the Amish or separatist, independent congregations) are examples of this type of community. Its organizational principle is voluntarism. This means that people become members of the Sect-type by conscious, adult conversion or decision, not by being born into the national or church community. It gathers true believers into strongly cohesive communities who regard themselves at war with the many surrounding societal and cultural patterns. Moral and doctrinal discipline are strict. Members are expected to conform to high standards. Those who do not are expelled from participating membership.

Sect-type Christians practice various forms of practical austerity, refraining from "worldly activities." These might include serving in the government, attending movies, drinking alcohol or using tobacco, and so on. The Sect requires that members detach themselves from the world, reduce worldly pleasures to a minimum, and cultivate Christian love within a tightly bonded fellowship of true believers. The Puritans and Anabaptist denominations of the sixteenth and seventeenth centuries are good examples of this social form. So too are the Benedictine monastics.

Troeltsch also developed the portrait of a third and increasingly more pervasive social form of Christianity. He called this form "Mysticism." The name is a bit misleading. He was not referring to the popular conception of mysticism (that is, an ineffable, ecstatic union with the divine). Rather, this is a form of religious involvement that is radically individualistic, personal, and contemplative. It is devoid of interest in either embracing the world or withdrawing from it. The burning issue is that of the individual soul's relationship to God. Being Christian becomes a very "personal" matter. Mysticism consists of a feeling about God and religious experience that does not have anything to do with joining ecclesiastical institutions or sectarian organizations.

The matters important to the Church-type (the objectivities of ritual, doctrine, history and tradition, and priestly ministration) are important only as a means to tie the soul to God. The relationship *between* individuals in a tightly knit fellowship of purified disciples, so important to the Sect-type, is also unimportant. Mysticism produces neither the all-encompassing sacramental Church-type nor the separated, disciplined Sect-type of organization. What issues from Mysticism is a loosely tied network of parallel religious personalities engaged in spontaneous religious experiences.

The first two social forms of Christianity have, in the past, been very potent in influencing the wider society and its cultural forms. The Church-type produced European civilizational unity in the High Middle Ages. The Sect-type was instrumental in creating some of the conditions that brought the modern world into being. It equipped individuals with character traits that enabled them to live in that world. Max Weber describes these Sect-type people as hardworking and thrifty, laboring in a worldly calling for the glory of God, accumulating wealth and bringing modern capitalism into being. Mysticism does not impact the larger social world very much because it is individualistic and indifferent to social structures. In practice, Mysticism fosters a profoundly personal religious experience that does not seek to change the world.

The modern charismatic movement arose after Troeltsch's time. It combines powerful elements of both Mysticism and the Sect-type. Some would see this as a potentially powerful form of Christianity for transforming modern society. As yet, it has not shown this capability. A more pertinent example of what Troeltsch meant by Mysticism is found among the loosely knit set of groups and cultural mood known as "New Age" religion.

Troeltsch agonized over the fate of the Christian faith in the modern world. He felt that neither the Church-type nor the Sect-type of Christian faith could muster the goods to influence or shape the modern world decisively. Modern problems seemed to him increasingly beyond whatever went on in Christian communities. If he was right that more and more people are adopting a radically individualistic style of being religious (Mysticism), the results are profound. Indeed, there is some evidence that more and more moderns are becoming radical religious individualists. This means there are fewer and fewer Church-type or Sect-type Christians actively relating their faith to the larger social world. Christ might be the answer, said Troeltsch, but the new world of modernity poses brand-new questions. New ways for Christian faith to be socially potent need to be invented. He died without uncovering what he considered a socially potent Christianity, suited to the modern world.

Christ Transforming Culture

The most famous work extending Troeltsch's ideas is H. Richard Niebuhr's *Christ and Culture*.[1] Niebuhr's extension creates a finer-grained model of the possibilities and actual styles of relating to the world. Its two opposites are similar in attitude to Troeltsch's Church and Sect. On the one end is what he calls the "Christ-of-culture" option. This stresses the idea that culture comes from the hand of God the Creator. The Christ-of-culture people believe that culture is a good and gracious gift of God. Sin has not changed its essential character. The culture may have flaws, but they can be corrected if people in the Church set to work on them. The best that the human spirit produces is identified with Christ. Christ has paramount authority in the Church.

However, Christ does not create a new morality or social structure for the Church or the larger society. Instead, Christ energizes and deepens the common, natural one present in all social groups.

On the other end of the continuum is the "Christ-against-culture" stance. Here culture is taken as something rooted in the revolt against God. Culture is part of the attempt of humans not to live under the authority of God. Culture by this account grows not so much out of some original culture in Eden that God gave to Adam and Eve. It presently expresses Adam and Eve's attempt to determine good and evil for themselves. Culture is an arena of evil powers, violence, oppression, greed, vanity, and so on. Culture is one way that humans determine for themselves, without reference to God, what is good and evil. The Evil One governs this age and world. To be faithful to God, people must reject it in favor of dramatically different alternative ways of living. Christ the Redeemer calls Christians out of an evil and adulterous world and into an alternative community ruled by the Sermon on the Mount. This world is regarded as a kind of sinking ship, while the Church is considered a lifeboat. The task of the Christ-against-culture Christian is to get as many people off the ship and into the lifeboat before the ship goes down. No attempt is made to save the ship (that is, the world itself). That would be a waste of time and effort. Saving souls is the only legitimate concern of Christians holding this position.

Niebuhr's significant additions to Troeltsch's ideas are the churches of "the center." These take culture and social arrangements to be a mixture, retaining the goodness intended by the Creator yet distorted and corrupted by sin's influence. Christ is not identified with the prevailing features of any concrete social order. Yet he cannot be separated from them either since he works with and through them. Christians need to build on what is good in society and yet challenge what is evil. There are disagreements between the churches of the center over how to do this.

The first of Niebuhr's churches of the center embraces the "Christ-above-culture" position, which sees all cultures as embodying a dim apprehension of God's will and way. Accordingly, something of God's goodness is expressed in every people and in every nation. Reason comprehends truth even apart from faith, and such truth is present in every culture. Supernaturally unaided reason discerns a "natural law" built into the social structures that are necessary for both physical and social life. Every society incorporates elements of God's natural law into its moral and socially authoritative values and norms.

Many of these societies train their members to exhibit prudence, courage, wisdom, and temperance in their behavior. These are natural virtues. Christian revelation adds a higher, more demanding way that complements these, building on the foundation yet going beyond natural reason and law. Christian faith brings the additional virtues of faith, hope, and love (charity). These supernatural virtues do not displace the natural. They affirm, deepen, and bring them to perfection. So Christ is "above" culture, completing it at the same time that he builds on it. This view is closest to the Christ-of-culture position.

Niebuhr's second church of the center takes the "Christ-and-culture-in-paradox" outlook, which stresses the dualism of the Christian who is both disciple and citizen. Christ's Kingdom differs dramatically from temporal kingdoms. Yet Christians must live in the kingdom of this world along with other humans. As citizens, they are subject to the laws and patterns of the temporal world. As disciples of Christ, they are subject to the higher law of the Sermon on the Mount. Hence, for Christians there is one "law" and set of arrangements *within* the Church and another "law" and set of arrangements *outside* the Church. Both are legitimate, though different. These two realms are not to be confused because God established both for the good of human life. However, the Christian exists in both kingdoms at the same time and is subject to both the law of Christ and the laws of the culture. At times, the Christian will feel tensions and paradoxes between the demands of church and the culture. Later this chapter will spell out this position in detail.

Niebuhr's third church of the center holds the "Christ-transforming-culture" position, seeing human cultures as corrupted by sin yet potentially subject to God's will. The various components of social arrangements and culture can be reoriented to God's glory, converting and transforming them so that they conform to the will of God. A proper ordering of the whole of community life according to God's standards is an essential part of the Church's mission. Christians are to penetrate the earthly kingdoms, transform them, and bring them more into accord with the will of God. Christ is taken to the world, not only to transform personal lives but to transform the social structures within which Christians live and move.

Niebuhr's ideas offered a very helpful extension of Troeltsch's. Niebuhr recognized that there is more than one issue at stake in the way Christian faith relates to social reality. One issue is the *basic orientation* (positive or negative) that a Christian community takes toward the prevailing culture surrounding it. Another is the *typical strategy* for carrying out that orientation (advocate a state religion, create a separate alternative community, compartmentalize church life and civic life, seek gradually to transform the social structure, and so on). This chapter builds on Niebuhr's and Troeltsch's scheme in order to provide additional insight into the patterns of Christian paradigms for relating faith and social reality.

A Road Map of Christian Social Thought

Clues from the work of Troeltsch and Niebuhr help to schematize typical paradigms of Christian social thought. These paradigms can be seen as existing on a continuum of attitude toward social institutions. Some approaches view social institutions as negative realities, functioning primarily as *restraints on evil*. Some view them as positive realities in human life, as *training grounds for community.* Within this continuum, the church community itself can be characterized in terms of different models of its role within the other social institutions:

Christian Approaches to Social Institutions

INSTITUTIONS AS TRAINING GROUND FOR COMMUNITY		INSTITUTIONS AS RESTRAINT ON EVIL
Church as integral to the social order	Church as one of a number of autonomous institutional arenas	Church as an alien movement: the coming of the Kingdom within the Old World
(1)	(2)	(3)	(4)
Christ of/ above culture	Christ and culture in paradox (strict autonomy, complementarity)	Christ transforming culture (church as a moral witness)	Christ against culture

Each of the four locations identified in the above table tends to develop a unique theological paradigm for thinking Christianly about the social institutions of the larger society and the Church itself as a social institution. The following paragraphs characterize each of these briefly:

1. *Christ is the fulfiller of the best in human culture.* The Church is to be coextensive with the social order, producing a unity of civilization. This is Troeltsch's Church-type of social doctrine and combines Niebuhr's Christ-of- and -above-culture since both seek to encompass the whole of social life under the Church.

2. *Religious and civil affairs are strictly separated.* This is the two-kingdom doctrine. In this paradigm, the strict counsels of the Sermon on the Mount apply when a person takes the role of Christian, acting within the sphere of the Church. If one is carrying out a role within public, civic institutions,

then a different set of rules applies. In one's role as Christian, one is nonviolent and turns the other cheek. If that same person fills the civil role of police officer or soldier, he or she will use force when necessary to protect public justice and order.

3. *Churches are oriented to transforming civil life.* This paradigm sees one of the Church's missions as involvement in all the normal arenas of the social life in their society. Yet there are several tactical differences over the means to follow in order to produce desired social changes.

   a. The *social gospel* advocates the use of voluntarism, public witness, and the democratic process. Walter Rauschenbusch and other American Christians at the turn of the century saw the task of the Church as "converting" social structures. They were optimistic that a Christianizing of the social structure was possible.

   b. *Christian realism* is a movement that grew up after World War I had dashed most of the hopes of the social gospel. It argues that the social gospel was naive about the power and persistence of sin in society. It also sees pacifist and nonviolent Christians as naive. In this world of conflict, self-interest, and sin, coercion and force are necessary means for bringing about greater degrees of righteousness and justice. Reinhold Niebuhr is the best-known theologian advocating Christian realism.

   c. *Militant, nonviolent, direct action* was the hallmark of Martin Luther King, Jr. Social structures change neither through private piety, violent revolution, or coercive might. Christians must follow the example of Christ himself. Confronting evil directly yet nonviolently allows one's enemies to be transformed into one's friends as their conscience is convicted. Perceiving the unrighteousness of given laws, social arrangements, and state practices, they will turn from following them and advocate their change. Gandhi showed the whole world the power of nonviolence combined with noncompliance with evil. King Christianized Gandhi's strategy.

    d. *Reconstructionism* is a recent movement built on the radical idea that God intends social structures to be completely transformed into a theocratic order. This borders on the Church-type. In the United States, reconstructionism has advocated constitutional amendments to name Jesus Christ as the head of American society. The legal and penal codes are to be reformed in the light of the Mosaic law. Social institutions are to mimic those distilled out of ancient Israel's ideal patterns. To the present, this tiny minority movement has had little impact on most Christian denominations, much less the larger society.

4. *Christians stand with Christ against culture.* Churches drawing the strongest boundaries between the Christian community and the prevailing culture feel that there are always cultural elements completely incompatible with Christian participation. These incompatible elements are best symbolized by the sword—the use of violence and coercion by the state. Christians can have nothing to do with the wider society's legitimation of un-Christian patterns of behavior. They cannot compromise by fulfilling roles that use force or coercion. Typically, the most articulate advocates of this approach are the Anabaptists (though a good case can be made for Fundamentalists as examples of this position). Anabaptist means "rebaptizer." This name was chosen because the reformers considered infant baptism invalid and insisted that adults who had been "baptized" as babies receive another and valid "believer's baptism." They have solved the problem of not participating in the evil of society in two typical ways. Some create *parallel social orders*. These withdraw into separated communities. In North America, the best-known groups are the Amish and the Hutterite Brethren; both these groups practice family farming. Many of the Amish completely

reject modern technology as well. The Hutterites and the more liberal among the Amish are technologically progressive and accept more modern innovations, such as electricity and tractors, as not incompatible with Christian life. The Amish live in separate family homesteads. In contrast, the Hutterites are a communal sect. All families live on the same homestead and eat all meals together.

Other Anabaptists such as the Mennonites and Brethren in Christ practice a *noncompliant participation* in modern life, living in the midst of the rest of society. They seek to change society by what John Howard Yoder calls "revolutionary subordinationism."[2] Culturally, they are similar to other citizens, but they refuse violence, military service, and patterns of injustice that mark the processes of the social structure. They "revolutionize" the structures by living within them. What they refuse to do is to compromise their role performance to fit demands that are incompatible with Christ's way of love and peace. Their church community also builds on the existence of an alternative social order, yet without creating a withdrawn parallel community.

The Social Teachings of Two Christian Churches

Each of these four approaches to thinking and living Christianly in relationship to the social structures of the modern world is worthy of careful consideration. This section looks in more detail at two of these approaches: the Lutheran paradigm of the "two kingdoms" (an example of position number 2 on the table) and the Anabaptist paradigm of "solidarity with Christ" (position number 4). Chapter Sixteen outlines the Calvinist paradigm of social transformation (position number 3) as an important approach to social change. The introduction in this section to how Christian paradigms work reveals some of the possibilities for relating Christian faith to sociological paradigms.

Be Sure You Know Which Side of the Street You're Driving On

Martin Luther (1483–1546) is the creator of the "two-kingdom" paradigm. He was a complex thinker with marked dualisms in his thought, most notably in his theological principle distinguishing the law from the gospel. Luther believed that there are two realms of existence (an idea that comes from Augustine's *City of Man and City of God*).[3] These are the dual realms of creation and redemption, of Adam and Christ, of law and gospel, of this age and the age to come. In the secular kingdom, the Creator rules a sinful world through the state and the law, establishing civil justice and obedience. God as Redeemer rules over the Kingdom of God, which is a spiritual kingdom of believers, governed by Christ and the gospel, that establishes personal faith and love.

Believer and nonbeliever alike participate in the realm of creation and fall. Both are subject to the law and the sword of the secular kingdom. But only those who are regenerate by God's grace participate in the realm of redemption and are subjects of the Kingdom of God. The Christian is simultaneously and wholly citizen both of the world and of the Kingdom of God. As Creator and Redeemer, God is the single ruler of both realms. So the two should never be divorced (as in various forms of secularism) or identified (as in a unity of church and state or church and society).

The secular kingdom belongs to God. No authentic kingdom rightfully belongs to Satan. It is God who brought this world into being and established the fundamental institutions that structure and enrich human life. These essential structures include the family, production and exchange, and the government. Everything that is temporal, physical, and "worldly" has its roots in God and is under God's control. Therefore, the Christian is properly involved in the world. Luther affirmed the "sacred secularity" of the ordinary affairs of everyday life. It matters not whether people engage in their occupations from motives rooted in Christian love (Christian righteousness) or based on reason alone because of compulsions imposed by the secular kingdom (civil righteousness). In both cases, people undertake tasks, including service in the police and the military, that serve the common human good to God's glory.

The realm that is distinctively Christian is rooted in the redemption by which God brings the Church into being. This is the realm of the believer's existence in Christ, the realm of the Church. The secular kingdom serves to preserve the earthly, the temporal, and the physical by establishing civil righteousness. The Kingdom of God helps people achieve true Christian righteousness. It operates according to a government of grace that frees people from sin, from the law that condemns, and from the wrath of God. The "compulsion of grace" affects lives through the preached Word of God, the sacraments, and Christian love. It is a government over the heart through the Spirit. There is no need for the force used outside the Church. Although all people are equal before God in the freedom given in the Church, the civil arena requires hierarchy and authority. Force is necessary in civil life because evil must be restrained in order for human life to go on.

Though the Church is not the secular kingdom, it is not to be artificially separated from it. Luther felt that the Anabaptist groups were too negative toward the temporal, civic culture. He fought to keep music, art, and sculpture in Church life and worship. The Roman Catholics also were too negative toward temporal, civic life. Luther saw this negative attitude in the elevation of "religious vocation" above all other vocations. Further, Catholics made monastic life the only place where one could find first-class citizens of the Kingdom of God. Instead, Luther advocated the opening of monasteries to release priests and nuns into ordinary civil life. He also asserted the right of all Christians to marry and to engage in secular vocations as callings from God that are equal in dignity to the priestly vocation.

In this world, the Christian accepts social structures for what they are: the Creator's gracious restraints against evil. They are "emergency orders" suited to an age of evil. Christian social responsibility is not so much to transform them as to be transformed people operating within all social structures. Regarding their secular occupations as religious callings, Christians bring love into those structures. Love thus infuses and gives content to the law operating in the civic arena, while the law gives love a specific social form through which to express itself. Love and the law in the form of social institutions provide a multitude of avenues to benefit fellow humans and foster goods all need for life.

This does not mean that the Christian is simply passive within the secular realm. Faith activated by love moves to correct the abuses of either the temporal authorities or those who submit to their rule. Against both the unruly mobs and the arbitrary rulers, Luther advocated civil obedience and political justice in a community of law and order. Against irresponsible parents and indifferent public officials, Luther sought community chests to reduce beggary and education funds to eradicate illiteracy. Greedy merchants bore the brunt of his criticism, and he called for economic justice and governmental restraints on unfair commercial and labor practices.

Yet there are limits to what Christian social responsibility can accomplish. God requires the secular orders to preserve their relative autonomy from the Church. These "emergency orders" are incapable of being so transformed that they operate according to principles prevailing in the Church. While the normative principles that structure the Church are faith and love, the normative principles of the secular realm are reason and justice. Complete or even substantial Christianizing of the orders of civic life is not possible. Nor can one say any particular set of secular orders (such as the American, medieval European, or Puritan New England) is "the Christian order." Christians are called to operate within different expressions of the emergency orders, which vary in their cultural and social particularities. Christian faith can illuminate reason. Love can temper justice. But these transforming virtues cannot create a Christian politics or Christian economics.

Christians are to obey both Creator and Redeemer as they live in this age. In response to the Redeemer, they live in the freedom of the gospel, exercising a faith active in love, saying yes to God's graciousness everywhere. In their obedience to the Creator, they live within the constraints of the law, exercising a love seeking social justice, saying no to sin in all its forms.

Sociology fits into Luther's scheme as a secular calling suitable for Christian service. Much of its reasoning and results serves to clarify the nature of the secular orders. Thus, sociology might provide a more informed basis on which to reform the social structure in directions consonant with the divine purpose for such institutions, which is to act as restraints against sin. Sociology, however, cannot serve as an instrument to bring in the Kingdom of God or to Christianize social structures. This would be a confusion of the two kingdoms.

Insofar as Christians become sociologists, they bring to their professional role the motivation of faith active in a love that seeks social justice. There is no necessity to create a distinctive Christian sociology. Sociology operates in the secular realm where reason and justice are the normative principles. Sociology can deal with the Church insofar as it is a purely human institution and a community with legal entailments in the secular order. Insofar as it is the realm of freedom, the realm of the gospel and the Spirit, sociology has no special access or insight. The things of the Spirit are known only by the spiritual. Sociology can document the outer activities and relationships of the Church as a social institution, but it cannot penetrate to its authentic essence as a realm of redemption.

In Luther's day, the Anabaptists in particular were most unhappy with this way of relating faith and society. Such modern denominations as the Amish, the Hutterites, the Mennonites, the Brethren, and the Brethren in Christ are descendants of the Anabaptists. Here is their counterproposal.

Be Sure You're Driving a Christian Car on Both Sides of the Street

Niebuhr categorized the Anabaptists under the "Christ-against-culture" approach. This, however, is a misleading way to label them. Anabaptists are not opponents of culture as such, for culture includes language, family, transportation and communication systems, education, and so on. What they reject are certain "ways of being cultural."[4]

Typically, they see the prevailing culture as identified with and controlled by principalities and powers opposed to God. Its institutions are not the "emergency orders" of God; rather, they are part of the kingdom of darkness. To the degree that cultural patterns conflict with the pattern of life and the demands of discipleship of the Lord, the Christian must be "against culture." Jesus offered a formative new definition of what it means to be human. His life showed how people are to live within the fallen order. They are to strive to be in their culture but only "as loyalists to the cause of Christ." So there can be no dual-track ethic such as that proposed by Luther. If Christ's will is love and peace, then it must be love and peace *everywhere*.

No single spokesperson stands for the Anabaptists in the way that Luther does for the Lutherans. So there is more variation within this paradigm. What it stresses is "solidarity with Christ" as the key to the relationship of Christians to culture. The story of Jesus and the way he lived constitutes a social strategy and political way of being in the world. He is the criterion of both personal and social life. Nothing is to cause people to live in a way that does not conform to his example.

Luther stressed the fact that the Christian must live in the surrounding cultural world in a mode of compromise. In the secular kingdom, Christians operate according to norms and patterns that differ from those that govern life in the Church. The Anabaptists insist that nothing in the world has an authority greater than that of Christ. There can be no compromise. There is only a single set of norms and patterns that must govern Christian life.

The story of Jesus Christ is what provides a distinctive moral vision and political strategy for Christians. Throughout his life he was an agent of social change, refusing to conform to the conventions of the reigning cultural and social arrangements. He refused the way of violence advocated by those who coalesced into the Zealot uprising of 66 A.D. He refused to take the role of a nationalistic Messiah, leading a messianic insurrection against the Romans. His social ethic was guided by the boundless love of God that expresses itself in servanthood.

Nonetheless, his was a political mission, and it evoked hostility and persecution. He proclaimed a coming Kingdom whose hallmark would be service. The disciples misunderstood what the new social order would be like. But Jesus never rebuked them for thinking that it would be a new social order. Its ethic is the ethic of the cross, the ethic of nonviolence. His example is to be followed by his disciples. This is not a general example, requiring that Christians mimic all the details of his particular historical life. Rather, the constantly reiterated feature of his life that the New Testament makes authoritative is the concrete social meaning of the cross in relationship to power and enmity. Servanthood replaces domination and power. Forgiveness and love replace enmity and hostility.

The Church is to be an alternative society that serves as a visible presence of the way of Christ. In many of its social forms, the Church historically has not been this. The downfall of Christ's intention for his community came when Constantine made Christianity a state religion. The Church then began to bless the present order, to embrace the state as a proper enforcer of justice and order by means of violence and coercion. It called on the state to defend the growing power and wealth of the Church. Its alliance with the state debased Christian truth and its central symbol of the cross. Compromise became the norm. The Church became deeply involved in nationalism. By identifying with the state and nation, un-Christian divisiveness entered the courts of Christ. Constantinianism blinded the Church's universal vision and enfeebled its prophetic consciousness in the midst of society.

The true church community is a voluntary fellowship of those who pledge loyalty to the way of Christ and share a common life together. It is a community of memory, fostering an alternative consciousness centered on the story of Jesus. It practices both physical and spiritual mutual aid and caring. Mutual discipline aims at reproving open sin. The Christian fellowship excludes unrepentant people from active social participation in its life, but not from love or the redemptive goals of the Church. Separation from the world is an essential mark of the Church. In all its relations with the prevailing culture, there is a certain guardedness. The Christian is to accept the role of outsider in every society.

This does not mean the refusal of responsibility to care for the larger civic and physical world. The Church is present in the world as a transforming community. The manner of that caring is crucial. Christians must care for the created world in ways that do not hide their basic loyalty to and solidarity with Christ. This manner is best seen in relation to the state where Christ's way is most risky and costly. Even though the state resorts to evil, it nonetheless carries out the providence of God. It provides those conditions necessary for human society in general and the work of the Church in particular. That in itself does not mean that God approves of all the means used by the state. Yet God does require that Christians be subject to the state. At times this requires disobeying the state because of obedience to Christ (for example, by refusing the military draft).

So Christians are *in* cultures but only *in loyalty to Christ*. This means a selective cultural involvement, marked by care not to compromise with the evil present in any particular social institution. As Scriven puts it:

We should all think it odd if someone claiming to be Christian tried to redeem human sexuality from within the brothel, as though this were a proper means of cultural transformation. The radical [Anabaptist] point is that we must be prepared to keep our distance from any number of social institutions, including some that are ordinarily considered honorable. Even if few of them resist the church's values as sharply as prostitution does, there are many from which we must at least withhold our *full* participation.[5]

The Church reaches beyond itself to care for the larger creation and culture in several ways. It engages in social critique, urging power holders to consider available alternatives that move the culture in the direction of the divine morality. Such critique will set forth the highest standards that are conceivable for a given society at a given time. The Church addresses the actual level of comprehension it finds. It seeks to prompt the larger society to reconsider its values and the means it uses.

The Church also is a transformative example as a small-scale model society. It is constantly to be a social pioneer, engineering new patterns of life and thought. In the past, it has laid foundations for modern conceptions of human rights. It created hospitals and schools when the larger society and state had no interest in doing so. The Church is to express a constantly inventive vision on behalf of society as social arrangements evolve and create new groups with new needs.

Finally, Christians will occupy many positions in organizations and institutions of the larger culture. They bring to those roles the way of Christ, the way of nonresistant love and forgiveness. The discipleship of Christ will be expressed and modeled even here in a transformative manner. Christians do all of these things because of the apocalyptic hope for a new society brought by God. The values and purposes of Christ will triumph in the end. Embodied in the Church, those values and means can make a difference even now, as Martin Luther King's example demonstrates.

Sociology fits into this paradigm in several ways. As a tool of social understanding, it serves the Christian role of social critic, assessing realistic alternatives that can be pressed on policymakers. Sociology can also serve as a partner to stimulate the constantly inventive vision of the Church. It helps identify those victimized in society and neglected by its various institutions. It can aid in discerning the consequences of pioneering efforts to create new avenues of life and service in the light of the coming Kingdom of God. In the midst of the complexities of modern life, sociology becomes an important tool in the political mission of the Christian community.

This is not to say that one needs a Christian sociology. Christians will always be wary of the role that sociology plays within the prevailing culture. Sociology is not free from the temptation to serve the power and purposes of the coercive state. It also can serve the need of mammon to create illusions that legitimize greed. Christian sociologists will be keenly aware that sociology is sometimes used as an ideology of liberal capitalism and state socialism. Neither capitalism nor socialism is the Kingdom of God, and neither can receive unqualified Christian legitimation. Sociology's history demonstrates its affinity for the prevailing values of its host societies. These are reflected in its research agenda and its interpretative models. So Christians must beware even here.

Christ Among Sociologists

We have picked two very contrasting paradigms of Christian social doctrine in order to illustrate some of the contemporary debate. Christians share broad agreements about the reality and supreme authority of Christ. They all read the Bible and accord it central importance in making sense of their character and identity. They all agree as well that the Church is to serve in some senses as an alternative community, set against the prevailing culture. The problem comes in spelling out how and why that which is genuinely Christian is to distinguish itself from the surrounding culture.

If Christ is supremely authoritative, how does that authority relate to all the other cultural authorities (family, economic, political, social, scientific, literary, philosophic)? This question was raised in several ways in the previous chapters. For Christian faith, it is the crucial question. It spells out what the scope of Christ's authority is in relationship to sociology as a disciplined means of understanding social worlds. Christians who understand the social doctrines of Christian faith differently, who belong to different theological paradigms, will answer that question in somewhat differing ways.

If one knows that there are several different theological accents, one will not expect to hear a single Christian voice in the conversation between faith and sociology. Because there are multiple voices on the side of sociology as well, one can expect a many-sided, pluralistic discussion. Seeing the variety and complexity that God seems to enjoy in other arenas of creation, one cannot but think that this diversity too may please God as a means to God's glory.

Beware those who start their sentences with "The Christians . . ." or "Christianity . . ." just as much as those who say, "Sociology indicates. . . ." Knowing that there are several brands of each enables the reader to ask, "Which Christians?" "Which sociologists?" "Which paradigm interprets matters that way?"

To say Christians are diverse in their thinking about theology and society is not to argue there is nothing that unifies them. There are a few fundamental elements that underlie all Christian social thought (or *ought* to). The next chapter highlights several of these.

NOTES

1. H. Richard Niebuhr, *Christ and Culture* (New York: Harper & Row, 1917).
2. See also Charles Scriven, *The Transformation of Culture: Christian Social Ethics After H. Richard Niebuhr* (Scottdale, PA: Herald Press, 1988).
3. Paul Althaus, *The Ethics of Martin Luther* (Philadelphia, PA: Fortress Press, 1972), pp. 43–82.
4. This account follows Scriven, *The Transformation of Culture*. See also John Howard Yoder, *The Politics of Jesus* (Grand Rapids, MI: Eerdmans, 1972), *What Would You Do?* (Scottdale, PA: Herald Press, 1983), *The Priestly Kingdom* (Notre Dame, IN: University of Notre Dame, 1984), and *When War Is Unjust* (Minneapolis: Augsburg, 1984).
5. Scriven, *Transformation of Culture*, p. 183.

Chapter 14

THE ELEMENTARY FORMS
OF THINKING CHRISTIANLY
ABOUT SOCIETY

On August 7, 1961, Major Gherman Titov of the Soviet Union became the second person safely to orbit the earth. He recounted his experience later at the World's Fair in Seattle, saying, "Some say God is living [up] there. I was looking round very attentively. But I did not see anyone there. I did not detect angels or gods. . . . I don't believe in God. I believe in man, his strength, his possibilities, and his reason."[1]

One person responded, "Had he stepped out of his space suit he would have!"

The monumental question at the end of the twentieth century is not communism versus individualism, East versus West, or even humans versus nature. It is whether humanity can succeed in living without God. The prophets made this issue clear long ago. Today's shattered world is due to the rupture in proper relationships to God and to one's fellow humans. Because people pursue life-styles contrary to God's creational will, their relationships to themselves and to nature are disorderly. Humans are designed to exist in an ensemble of proper relationships.

When the fifty-four-volume *Great Books of the Western World* (1952) came off the press, someone noted that the longest essay in the introductory survey of "102 Great Ideas" was on God. This person asked Mortimer Adler, the noted philosopher and coeditor, why "God" was the most extensive chapter. Adler responded, "It is because more consequences for life follow from that one issue than from any other."

Friedrich Nietzsche, the famous nineteenth-century nihilist, recognized the tremendous consequences that came from dismissing God in his parable, *The Madman*. A madman runs into the marketplace crying incessantly, "I'm looking for God, I'm looking for God."

"Whither is God?" he cried. "I shall tell you. We have killed him—you and I. All of us are his murderers. But how have we done this? How were we able to drink up the sea? Who gave us the sponge to wipe away the entire horizon? What did we do when we unchained this earth from its sun? Whither is it moving now? Whither are we moving now? Away from all suns? Are we not plunging continually? Backward, sideward, forward, in all directions? Is there any up or down left? Are we not straying as through an infinite nothing? Do we not feel the breath of empty space? Has it not become colder? Is not night and more night coming on all the time?"[2]

Knowing that this world belongs to God and longing for the coming of his Kingdom means seeing sociology differently than those who don't. But what is the difference? What are the elements of Christian faith that are particularly significant in thinking Christianly about society? This chapter highlights a few of these components. Note that we said, "A few." This chapter covers only a small circle of ideas within the many important elements in biblical literature and theological reflection. What we seek to do here is to provide two basic tools for such faithful thinking. There are many more. These are basic tools for all Christian thought, regardless of the theological paradigm one works in.

Thunder and Lightning in the Prophets

There are two interconnected tracks on which the message of Old Testament prophets run. The judgment made against the people of God and the peoples of the world boils down to two shortcomings: false spirituality and oppressive sociality. Idolatry and injustice are the chief sins condemned by the prophets. Listen to Amos:

> For three transgressions of Israel,
>   and for four, I will not revoke the punishment;
> because they sell the righteous for silver,
>   and the needy for a pair of sandals—
> they who trample the head of the poor into the dust of the earth,
>   and push the afflicted out of the way;
> father and son go in to the same girl,
>   so that my holy name is profaned. . . . (Amos 2:6–7)

> Come to Bethel—and transgress;
>   to Gilgal—and multiply transgression;
> bring your sacrifices every morning,
>   your tithes every three days . . .
> for so you love to do, O people of Israel!
>   says the Lord God. (Amos 4:4–5)

Bethel and Gilgal were centers of idolatrous worship for the northern kingdom of Israel. God invites them to continue their idolatrous piety at the expense of multiplying their transgression.

Other prophets display this dual vision. Hosea criticizes the infiltration of Israel by the Canaanite fertility cults. He issues God's judgment: "I will punish [Israel] for the festival days of the Baals, when she offered incense to them" (2:13). Hosea also notes the corruption of social relations accompanying the idolatry: "They deal falsely, the thief breaks in, and the bandits raid outside" (7:1); "they utter mere words; with empty oaths they make covenants; so litigation springs up like poisonous weeds" (10:4); "they multiply falsehood and violence" (12:1).

Micah 6:8 is an excellent summary of these two themes:

> He has told you, O mortal, what is good;
>   and what does he require of you
> but to do justice, and to love kindness,
>   and to walk humbly with your God.

These convictions run parallel to the great commandment of Jesus: to love God and to love one's neighbor. How humans exist in their social arrangements is a living commentary on how they understand and connect themselves to God.

One implication of the words of the prophets is that placing anything in the position or status that God is meant to occupy leads to the disruption of proper human relationships. Idolatry is a path leading to social injustice. Several Christian social analysts latch onto this biblical pattern and seek to show ways and times where this is true in the modern world.[3]

Consumerism and the Idolatry of Things

Stan D. Gaede, a contemporary Christian sociologist, portrays humans as relational creatures.[4] They are meant to live in a network of linkages with God, fellow humans, and nature. Yet they have rejected God's creational plan and gone their own way. This distorts and shatters the intimacy and totality of relationships that they were meant to experience. Sin estranges and alienates people from God, from fellow humans, and from nature. God created humans good. Now they are fallen. Their creational design and their sinful brokenness leave them with deep needs. They long for satisfying ensembles of social relations. Yet they experience a continuous inability to forge those very relationships. Gaede calls this the "relational dilemma."

Humans seek to solve the relational dilemma in several ways, one of which is to substitute one relationship for another. People can substitute a lesser reality for a higher or a higher for a lower. One can connect oneself to a relational partner by overestimating that partner's place in one's life. If people treat the less-than-divine as divine, they involve themselves in an idolatrous relationship. It is also possible to underestimate a relational partner's appropriate place in one's life. Gaede diagrams the relational possibilities in this way:

THE OBJECT TREATED AS:

		God	Humanity	Creation
T H E O B J E C T	Creation	a. creational idolatry	d. creational humanism	g. normative
	Humanity	b. humanistic idolatry	e. normative	h. humanistic utilitarianism
	God	c. normative	f. theological humanism	i. theological utilitarianism

On the chart, positions c, e, and g classify the appropriate relationships. Here one treats the object as God intended and as its inherent nature warrants. In these cases, one relates to the object according to God's normative will, treating humans *as humans* and created reality *as created reality*. If one treats God *as God*, then one gives God the status appropriate to God's being and God's actual place in the universe.

Idolatry occurs in two ways. People may treat humans as though they are the ultimate being in the universe (position b). Or they may treat creation as though it is divine in status and not just in origin (position a). People seek to secure in the less-than-divine the relational goods that can come only from the true and living God.

Overestimating creation as if it holds the status and importance of humans (position d) and underestimating God as if God were no greater than or no different from humans (position f) are forms of humanism. Putting humans (position h) and God (position i) on the same level as the nonhuman created world treats them as lower in status and different in kind than they are. It justifies using them in the same way that one uses nature to provide the goods of life.

Gaede offers several examples of how idolatry can affect modern social orders. One illustration is consumerism. Here people give such power and status to material goods that they create an idolatry of material things. The modern social order ranks people on the basis of their possessions. Culture is driven by a relentless pursuit to accumulate the most prestigious material goods, from cars to homes to clothes. The fashion and advertising industry reinforce this socialization by providing motives for and images of the good life. People then orient their energies around the conspicuous display and consumption of rare and expensive goods.

Christian social science explores the connections between this form of idolatry and the psychological, political, economic, and social conditions of society. The analysis of commodities, possessions, and money presses beyond observations of how repressed sexuality or market forces drive social interactions concerning them. Its explanations and evaluations include idolatry as a category for labeling and explaining the pervasive power that consumerism displays in distorting modern social orders.

The effects of a society taking material possessions as central powers and ends of life ramify into all sorts of social arrangements (perhaps better called "derangements"). These results include wide differences in wealth, environmentally wasteful products, wants redefined as needs, laws protecting property more rigorously than human life, and self-worth tied to relative material affluence. Even churches become stratified by wealth and cultural capital as a result of this idolatry. People mistreat the poor without compunction because on this scale of worth, the poor are the least worthy members of the social order. They demonstrate this by their lack of material possessions.

The idolatry of created things thus becomes a critical tool in the hands of Christian thinkers. It suggests that sociologists look for certain relationships and dynamics that they would otherwise overlook without this distinctively Christian category.

The Rise of the West and the Idolatry of Progress

Bob Goudzwaard, another social scientist with deep Christian commitments, also focuses on idolatry in modern society.[5] For Goudzwaard, the interesting dynamic in modernization is the powerful faith in progress. Here the overestimation is not of material things as such. The idolatry focuses on the future, the new and different, the processes of nature and history as leading inevitably upward and onward, and on human powers and perfectibility.

Goudzwaard identifies a number of crises that accompany the current level of modernization. These include the north-south divide, the conflict between rich and poor, nuclear proliferation, threats to the ecosystem, crowds of people turning to psychologists for help, and the use of drugs to bury problems. What is frightening is the pervasive sense that there are no good solutions. The noneconomic problems multiply, and people also face new economic problems that render traditional economic methods impotent. One major reason that these problems of modernity have not been solved is because people isolate economic and noneconomic problems and seek separate solutions. Yet these problems are intertwined, expressing the civilization's essential character. They are integral to the total inner spirit and movement of modern society.

According to Goudzwaard, two depth levels act as persistent and powerful underlying sources of the whole package of modern problems. One level has to do with the social architecture of Western society as a totality. There are common social structures in modern industrial orders that generate wealth and poverty. These structures enrich the Northern hemisphere at the expense of the Southern. They devour the landscape and poison the earth. These typical outcomes are the logical, natural consequences of the structures of current economic, political, and class systems. Sociologists who feel that anomie and conflict are aberrations, fleeting or marginal features of the transition to an industrial or even postindustrial order, are wrong.

Underneath these civilizational structures is another depth level. It consists of the animating cultural commitments or the habits of the heart of those who fill the positions of modern social structures. The problems humans face are due to more than just their structures of common life. The critical problems of the

West also exist in Russia and East European countries (sometimes in intensified form), even though they have social structures somewhat different from Western ones. This is because East and West share certain "religious motives" that are central to modern civilization. These religious motives spring from a profound faith in economic and technological progress, which is present in all modern societies regardless of differences in social structure. This modern faith acts as an all-embracing vision, shaping the thoughts, feelings, and actions of people in the modern world. It does this just as profoundly and powerfully as medieval Catholicism shaped much of the civilization of traditional European cultures.

This faith takes what is considered worthwhile and important (economic productivity, enhanced technical capabilities) and makes them something of ultimate worth. No other values or considerations can challenge this faith. Economic and technological factors take preeminence in industrial orders for the sake of progress. Considerations dealing with ethics or justice are secondary. The civilization allows only limited ethical corrections to the process and pattern of modernization. One effect is the diminishing of individual freedom in all sectors of life. The demands of the evolution of progress are all-encompassing, swallowing up people and countries one by one. This animating religious vision for life is currently forging a global system within which the marketplace becomes the sovereign totalitarian force.

Goudzwaard argues that progress no longer sparkles as it did thirty years ago. Three weaknesses are now glaringly evident. The earth's tolerance for dramatically heightened uses of energy and increased pollution is at its limit. Current structures of resource use and waste disposal are not sustainable or globally replicable without ecological collapse. Second, inflation and chronic structural unemployment are persistent realities in the modern world. Inflation is a by-product of the commitment to economic progress, while structural unemployment is related to technological progress (which constantly is making jobs obsolete). Unqualified commitment to these forms of progress has to be equally a commitment to live with these problems.

The third vulnerability manifests itself in all the ways the modern order stresses and does not support people. Moderns increasingly are more managed than managing. They must adjust to the imperatives of economic growth and technical change (and many people must adjust to monotonous, mindless jobs). They suffer from a shortage of time, a shallowness of relationships, the mindless hammering of advertising, and the manipulation of the mass media.

Western civilization patterns and adjusts itself to a comprehensive system for the promotion of economic and technological progress. This animating heart of the culture exerts permanent pressure on all aspects of human experience. The idolatry of progress closes off virtually all solutions that do not entail further progress, *regardless of the sacrifice of human or earthly goods*. One contemporary thinker compares the current human situation to riding a tiger. The tiger goes its own way regardless of its rider's intentions. The tiger of progress may well carry human beings to destruction. Yet to jump off would be even more dangerous. So humans continue the uncontrollable ride, wherever it might end.

Goudzwaard ends his book with an account of how Christian analysis and action might challenge this idolatry. He argues that people must reestablish progress as a worthwhile but not ultimate consideration. There are multiple, distinct, legitimate goods and norms for human life in this world. None should become the exclusive, ultimate norm or good at the expense of the others. To allow economic values to ride roughshod over religious, aesthetic, familial, and health considerations is to make a false god of economics. Equally, other values cannot be made ultimate. Humans cannot make aesthetic norms and goods decisive considerations for family life or business decisions. Each value or set of values has its own appropriate sphere of expression and prominence. What is needed is a balance and play among the various spheres of human life with their different norms and goods. Out of that balance will come a more abundant life for all.

Idolatry thus comes in many forms and can have a profound impact on human life and relationships. Looking for the presence of idolatry reveals a great deal about the dynamics of a social order. Christian social analysis will frequently reach for this tool in its kit. In addition, the Christian thinkers' tool kit includes notions about how to think appropriately about human beings.

The *Imago Dei* and Sociology

The nature of human nature is a fundamental part of the models in all social theories. Every social theory bases itself on an account of the sort of creature the human being is. Christian models take the human as the *imago dei,* the image of God. In modern social theory, these accounts include answering a range of crucial questions.

These include the following: What are the basic parts of the human being? What makes up the human "self"? Is the human in society free, an agent setting his or her own destiny by means of uncoerced choices? Or are humans objects whose action and destiny are set by external and internal forces? Is the human an active, free participant in society or a passive reflection of the molding powers and shaping structures of society? Which is more influential in the human individual and in society: the rational or the nonrational qualities of human nature? Are people most adequately understood as self-interested in thought and action? Or are they also other-oriented, caring for at least a few others, willing to sacrifice their pleasures and goals? Are people innately good, inherently evil, a mixture of good and evil, or a kind of moral blank slate?

What are the role and the significance of biological dimensions of an individual's being? How does the biological relate to the spiritual (the body to the soul)? Are people best understood by watching their outer behaviors (one is what one does)? Or is it better to pay attention to the inner meanings (motives, attitudes, beliefs) that infuse external action and behaviors? How are the basic components of adult human nature acquired? How far are individuals creatures of their biology and their genes (nature)? How much can the environmental influences (nurture) redirect and reshape people? Do humans even have a "nature" (that is, a set of inherent characteristics that express themselves regardless of the environment)?

These are critical questions. How social thinkers answer them changes their overall notion of human social arrangements. What are some of the contributions that Christians bring to this discussion?

The Human as a Holistic Duality

Christians say humans are more than the sum of their material parts. That's an implication of the statement that humans are "body and soul" (or, as some put it, "body, soul, and spirit"). The heart of this contention is that the human is, in some significant sense, at least a duality.

Dualism is currently out of intellectual favor. That is because of an unbiblical set of dualisms in which the body is contrasted with the soul, the brain with the mind, the social with the personal, the material with the spiritual, the secular with the sacred. Today's culture is riven by a series of dichotomies that denigrate one side or the other. The religious often highlight one side of a duality and downgrade the other. The secular highlight the opposite side and downgrade the side lifted up by the religious. Some have argued strongly that this has had devastating results in Western life.[6]

John W. Cooper recently examined in detail the issue of dualism in human nature.[7] He argues persuasively that the Bible justifies viewing the human as an embodied soul or a besouled body. The human being (speaking *ontologically*) is a duality of body and soul, brought into being and sustained by the creative activity of God. At death, body and soul are separated. The soul continues in a self-identical existence with Christ until the resurrection of the body. While humans have a soulish continuance apart from the body after death, they are not complete in God's purposes apart from their body. Only when they become transformed body-souls through the resurrection and reside in the divine society of the Kingdom of God are they complete.

Functionally, however, humans are a holistic unity. In life on earth, body and soul are so intertwined and embedded in each other that they function as a single totality. As living beings, humans are single entities. All individual capacities and functions interrelate and integrate into a systematic unity. It is impossible to pull the human apart into clearly separable elements. Nor can one part be identified as "the real human" and the other as the husk or inessential packaging of the real self.

Thus, under observation, humans appear in every way to be self-identical with their bodies. The qualities identified as spiritual operate with, in, and through the physical. The witness of Scripture and the resurrection of Christ demonstrate the dual makeup of human beings. In the end, Christians believe in the resurrection of the body more than in the immortality of the soul. The notion of a disembodied soul floating around somewhere or playing harps in the sky is contrary to Christian thought.

The implications of all this for sociology are profound. Christian sociologists cannot treat the embodiedness of humans as irrelevant or nonessential. That humans are male and female, that they come in various ethnic "packages," that they move through biosocial stages and phases of life are foundational to the Christian sociologist's understanding of the human being. The way in which a society manages and reshapes people's physical selves is an important clue to its inner spirit and cultural center.

Christian social analysts must be perceptive and notice the dualisms that social arrangements often create. They must fight the deleterious effects of these dualisms. Social injustice frequently seizes on the differing physical packaging of gender, race, and ethnicity and uses these differences against people. Even the

Church can fall into the false dichotomy of body against soul, treating persons primarily as souls or as bodies rather than as whole beings. That is why, during the days of slavery, there were churches that distorted the gospel. They believed that their duty was done when they had "freed the souls of African Americans from sin." To these churches, African Americans' bodily existence as slaves had nothing to do with the gospel.

The Three-Zone Model of the Human

What about a more comprehensive model of the human being? Can Christians say more than that the human is an embodied soul? Does the Bible offer a detailed account of humans, sufficient to answer the questions raised in sociology? The simple answer is no. No definitive psychological or sociological map of the human self, spelling out the elements for a *scientific model* of human nature, exists in the Bible. There is, however, a clear and adequate theological model of human nature. And the Bible offers a general psychosocial model of the human. Bruce Malina calls the latter model the "three-zone model of the self."[8] It uses various parts of the body to indicate central features of human beings as they relate to their various relational partners.

Modern psychology seeks to penetrate the inner self. Many of its models concentrate on interior aspects of the human psyche. The cultures within which biblical revelation came did not focus their models of the human on the inner person in the same way. Rather, they viewed persons primarily on the basis of externally observable behavior. For them, the social functions of human activity were crucial. In the Bible, various parts of the body symbolize the major ways humans function.

Three zones appear again and again. These are the zones of emotion-infused thought (the inner self), self-expressive speech, and purposive action. The human fits into its larger world by means of inmost reactions (the eyes and heart), which are expressed through language (the mouth and ears) and activity (the feet and hands). At times, a biblical text has only one of the zones in view. When it wishes to describe the whole person, all three zones appear, as in Proverbs 6:16–19:

> There are six things that the Lord hates,
>   seven that are an abomination to him:
> haughty eyes, a lying tongue, and hands that shed innocent blood,
> a heart that devises wicked plans, feet that hurry to run to evil,
> a lying witness who testifies falsely
>   and one who sows discord in a family.

In this passage, the three zones are repeated twice in differing orders. The punch line is the last line. The particular sin being scored is that of the person who, through inner attitudes, self-expressive words, and actions, destroys the unity of the family.

In this model, only God truly knows the human heart. Humans know it only by its expressions in speech and in action. That is why people judge by the outward appearance while God can judge by the heart (1 Samuel 16:7). The heart is the center of a person's being, out of which comes the motive force leading to his or her words and deeds. People's inmost reactions are hidden not only from their fellow humans but often from themselves. Eyes may give away one's inner thoughts and attitudes, but only God and his Word can penetrate to the center of one's being and transform it, giving him or her a new heart.

In addition, the Bible uses these three zones as a way of portraying the Trinity. God the Father is hidden, dwelling in light inaccessible. No one has seen the Father. God the Father is identified with transcendence. Yet God's eyes range throughout the entire earth seeking those who are righteous (2 Chronicles 16:9). God the Son is the Word of God spoken, the self-expression of the heart of God. God the Spirit is the finger of God, the active power doing the work of God on earth (Luke 11:20; see also Matthew 12:28). The typical functions of each member of the Trinity are mapped by identifying them with one of the zones of essential human functioning.

One advantage of this model of the human being is its relatively general nature. It is a model that moves with minimal difficulty across cultural boundaries and through time. The Bible was meant for all cultures and times. Were it to provide a precise, fixed, detailed model of the human being, it would not speak powerfully and directly to peoples with differing worldviews.

This biblical model gives Christian sociologists the freedom to explore the variety of alternative, more detailed models of the human suggested by scientific research. Models that do not obscure the vision of the human as a responsible creature, living from an inner center of being and expressing itself in speech and action, are viable candidates for inclusion in a Christian sociology.

The Imago Dei *as Relational*

Christian discourse on human beings does not answer many of the questions that exercise sociology. Rather, its interest is in the fundamental nature of the human being as the image of God (*imago dei*). Douglas Hall's survey of Christian thought draws a distinction between the substantialist and the relational concepts of the *imago dei*.[9]

Substantialists see humans as possessing a substance or built-in quality that is the image of God. Typically, this is taken to be human rationality (intelligence and language capability) or the moral ability to choose right and wrong (freedom). The image of God is something humans are or ought to be—that is, humans are or ought to be free and rational.

Alternatively, the relational concept of *imago dei* sees it more as something that humans do, something that happens. The human being is to be thought of as a "being-with"—being with God, with fellow humans, with the environment, and even with oneself. Humans image God when they relate properly in their interactions with each of these four realities of their world. The old substantialist tradition uses static models. Regardless of what one does, what interactions are happening, the image is simply there.

The relational model is dynamic. Only when proper relating is happening is the imaging of God occurring. It is an event, not a substance.

By singling out rationality and freedom as basic characteristics of the human being, the substantialists are not far off the mark. These are essential qualities, necessary for the image of God to appear. The problem is that these are not completely exclusive qualities of the human being. An earlier chapter mentioned the recent work on primate rationality as manifested by the language abilities of apes and chimpanzees. To be sure, the human may have these qualities in such a degree as to claim a qualitative difference from animals. By themselves, however, these abilities do not constitute the image of God.

Genesis implies that the image of God is the encounter of males and females in a community of loving relatedness:

Then God said, "Let us make humankind in our image, according to our likeness; and let them have dominion over the fish of the sea, and over the birds of the air, and over the cattle, and over all the wild animals of the earth, and over every creeping thing that creeps upon the earth."
So God created humankind in his image,
In the image of God he created them;
Male and female he created them. (Genesis 1:26–27)

Embedded in the physical world of nature, the male and female together are to be the image of God. Here can be seen a living, visible mirroring of the invisible, living God. The loving community of the Trinity's relatedness of Father, Son, and Holy Spirit is mirrored in human community. So too the human community's dominion over and stewardship of the earth represent the Godhead's connectedness to the created world.

So the image is not primarily a matter of *what humans are* (the substantialist notion) but of *how they live together*, connected with God, with each other, and with the natural world.

The encounter of persons who are distinct (male or female) and similar (male and female) and who make up the single humanity is to image God. This occurs when humans as males and females are *with* one another (coexistence), *for* one another (proexistence), and are *together* (in community, covenant, and communion). Sin in the social dimension is a violation of these ways of being related. Being *apart* (autonomy), being *against* (estrangement, alienation), and being *above* (prideful mastery) or *below* (slothful subservience and refusal of responsibility) express sinful brokenness in imaging God.

This is why issues of justice are so basic in the Bible. Injustice is a violation of the essential character of humanity. It prevents the highest calling of humanity—to portray at a human level the character and activity of God. Justice and love together constitute this imaging activity. Justice means "establishing the material and institutional relationships that best guarantee to every person the right to participate fully in the life of a community of love."[10]

The humans' essence as God's image extends to their relationship to nature as well. God's dominion commission to Adam and Eve positioned humanity to be the stewards of earthly bounty and goodness (Genesis 1:28–30). The natural world is there to sustain humanity physically. Humans are to be *with* nature, not *against* it. Human communities are not to engage in life-styles that ravage and destroy the earth. God's relationship to nature is not one of exploiting and polluting. Nature is not there to be fought over or to be used profligately to support a wealthy elite while a substantial minority or majority starve.

Imaging God means building and sustaining communities of justice, peace, and love that care for the earth while meeting the authentic needs of all human beings. The technological, high-consumptive societies that are the quintessence of modernization consistently violate social justice and environmental stewardship. This is not to say that Christians have technical blueprints for solving the various problems of modernity. Yet Christians do have a vision of justice, love, and environmental stewardship that is broad enough to sustain those committed to searching for and finding the appropriate answers.

Dual Vision

Thinking in a Christian manner about human societies requires raising at least two fundamental questions. The question of idolatry looks for whatever is given the accent of the sacred or the status of the divine in social affairs. It asks, "What comprehensive vision of history, humanity, and destiny animates the sociocultural system and drives people to their greatest heights of energy and sacrifice?" Locating points of idolatry within a sociocultural system provides clues as to its deepest motives and challenges.

The question of social injustice is tied to the conviction that humans are to image God in the ensemble of relationships within which they exist. Christian social thought has a long tradition of concern for tracing the outline of oppression and marginalization. Every social order stigmatizes certain people and provides advantages to others. The types of inequality and discrimination vary from society to society. The analysis and understanding of poverty, crime, discrimination, sexism, racism, war, and violence relate to Christian desires for more humane social arrangements.

Several other elements are useful in constructing a Christian perspective within sociology. The next chapter examines these.

NOTES

1. *Seattle Daily Times*, May 7, 1962, p. 2.
2. Walter Kaufman, ed., *The Portable Nietzsche* (New York: Viking, 1954), p. 125.
3. J. A. Walter, in *The Human Home: The Myth of the Sacred Environment* (Tring, Herts, England: Lion Publishing, 1982), deals with the sacralization of place. The modern world disenchants or desacralizes much of the world. This pervasive secularization is balanced by the re-enchantment of certain places, such as wilderness areas, historic buildings, national monuments, certain cemeteries.
4. Gaede, *Where Gods May Dwell: Understanding the Human Condition* (Grand Rapids, MI: Zondervan, 1985).
5. Goudzwaard, *Capitalism and Progress: A Diagnosis of Western Society* (Grand Rapids, MI: Eerdmans, 1979).
6. Brian J. Walsh and J. Richard Middleton, *The Transforming Vision* (Downers Grove, IL: InterVarsity Press, 1984), Part 3: "The Modern World View."

7. Cooper, *Body, Soul, and Life Everlasting: Biblical Anthropology and the Monism-Dualism Debate* (Grand Rapids, MI: Eerdmans, 1989).

8. Malina, *The New Testament World: Insights from Cultural Anthropology* (Atlanta, GA: John Knox, 1981), pp. 60–70.

9. Hall, *Imaging God: Dominion as Stewardship* (New York: Friendship Press, 1986).

10. J. Philip Wogaman, *Faith and Fragmentation: Christianity for a New Age* (Philadelphia, PA: Fortress Press, 1985), p. 185.

Chapter 15

WHAT CHRISTIANS WANT
IN SOCIETY

Someone once asked G. K. Chesterton what he thought of civilization. He replied, "It's a wonderful idea. Why doesn't someone start one?"

Christian social theory is a critical one because it includes ideas of what social arrangements ought to be. It has no blueprint for all the diverse sorts of societies and cultures of the earth. Yet it possesses several ethical norms that are transculturally valid. These can serve to develop a critique of the disorder in any social order.

Any critical social theory is interested in going beyond a simple description of social affairs. Evaluation and diagnosis of the rough edges of social relationships are an essential part of Christian thought. For these to be done well, there needs to be more than accurate, authentic description and valid explanation. Clear and coherent ethical norms are equally essential.

In one village, there was a man who went out of his way every day to walk by the clockmaker's store. He would carefully adjust his watch to match the time on the clock in the store window. One day the owner of the store asked him what he was doing. Sheepishly, he said, "I'm the timekeeper at the steelworks. My watch malfunctions, and I need to know each day what time it is so the whistles starting and ending work are as close to on time as possible."

Astonished, the clockmaker confessed, "I hate to tell you, but this window clock doesn't work properly either. I have been adjusting it every day before I go home—by the sound of the factory whistle in the afternoon!"

How can one be precise about time when one's only recourse is a malfunctioning watch adjusted to a faulty clock? Similarly, how can one be clear in thinking ethically about social issues? Christian faith claims that there are norms for human life that transcend the collection of standards set by faulty cultural notions of right and wrong. These norms are derivable from Scripture. They serve as a framework of directives useful for judging how good or bad given sociocultural arrangements are for humans.

These norms are not societal blueprints. The sociocultural systems that humans create are too numerous and diverse for one blueprint to fit all the contingencies and changes. Chapter Twelve argued that God's relationship to culture is one of regulating preexisting human arrangements. From the patterns of that regulation, humans can see ways in which God's character and commands are relevant for social critique. Yet it often takes much hard work and thought to show the connections between the norms coming from such analysis and contemporary social arrangements.[1]

Chapter Fourteen introduced the two major norms of idolatry and social injustice. False spirituality and oppressive sociality are destructive of the chief goods of human life. The acts of loving God and neighbor are the meaning and purpose of life. Cultural and social patterns often violate these standards. This chapter spells out in more detail some of the values and norms that orient Christian social practice and critique.

Christian Norms from the Microlevel to the Macrolevel

North American Christians normally start at the microlevel of the individual, the family, and the primary group when they think through ethical matters. This reflects the impact both of individualism and Protestantism on the culture. This is not a necessary way to begin. God most frequently addresses his covenant people jointly, rather than addressing specific individuals. The Bible certainly deals with individuals, but invariably it does so through the framework of the community of nations, the chosen people, and even humanity as a whole.

The overarching vision for human life is a social one. At the end of Scripture, the book of Revelation portrays the final events and arrangements. When the struggle against evil is finally triumphant, when human history ends with the return of Jesus Christ, God's City descends to earth (Revelation 21–22). The New Jerusalem is a complete social world, working according to God's design with God's very presence at its center.

The Old Testament image for this is contained in the Hebrew word *shalom*.[2] Shalom is the condition of people existing in perfected community within transformed nature. All relationships—with God, fellow humans, and nature—are harmonious and right. Justice and peace prevail in a righteous and responsible community. The word *shalom* conveys the idea of a holistic existence in which people are empowered, the environment flourishes, and God is gratefully acknowledged as Lord.

Normally translated by the word *peace*, shalom is not so much the opposite of war as of anything that disturbs the well-being of communal human existence. One of God's names is Yahweh-shalom: "Yahweh is shalom." Shalom refers to the full compass of goods that God gives to human life, including the gift of salvation for a broken and rebellious humanity. It includes all those things that bring hostility and tension in human relationships to an end. The New Testament describes shalom as present finally in the New Jerusalem.

Jack and Judith Balswick take shalom to be the widest perimeter of God's intention for human good.[3] It encompasses all the other norms for social relationships and structures. Within that large perimeter, they place the Christian norms of covenant, *koinonia*, and neighborliness. Each norm focuses on a different level of social organization without being exclusively limited to that level.

Covenant

As the imagers of God, humans can expect the governing principles for life to reflect the God who made them. Covenant refers to the unqualified commitment of love that God graciously offers his people. He makes a covenant with Noah (Genesis 6:22), with Abraham (Genesis 15:18, 17:7–9), with David (2 Samuel 7), and so on. Jesus inaugurates the New Covenant by the sacrifice of his life on the cross. His faithful loyalty is pledged without conditions (as there would be in a contract) placed on the fulfilling of certain stipulations and terms by the other partner.

The Balswicks see covenant as involving four elements. Together these provide a guiding framework for human community, especially in the family. At its heart, covenant means a committed, firm connectedness between people, be it husband and wife, parents and children, or wider ties of kinship and friendship. The initial commitments people make in human affairs may be partial, based on fantasies and illusions; they may be only conditional. Yet the ideal is that individuals come to the place where they are committed to those in their inner circles in the way that Jesus is committed to them—without reservation, without selfishness, without limits. This is the heart of relationship: loving and being loved.

Grace (unmerited favor) is the atmosphere for that committed relatedness. It means that people live with each other on the basis of forgiveness, not law. Law demands perfection if people are to retain the rights of relationship. Legalism chokes the spontaneity and freedom necessary for healthy relationships. Grace means people work out roles and relationships so that the order and regularity that give shape to shared humanity serve the needs of all. Humans process the shortcomings and events that damage or threaten the relationship by means of the severe mercy of authentic forgiveness.[4] Grace frees people for responsible, committed relationship.

Empowering is the third element in covenant. It refers to the actions and effects of interaction that create mature social relationships. Empowering "is the process of helping another recognize strengths and potentials within, as well as encouraging and guiding the development of those qualities."[5] This does not mean controlling or enforcing a certain way of doing things. It is a reciprocal, mutual recognition and enhancement of each other in a relationship. People are thereby enabled to serve and give themselves out of the strengths that God develops in them. This is not codependence but a healthy interdependence. It involves being loyal and supportive even when differences and adversity threaten to undermine the commitments that individuals have to each other.

Intimacy is the norm for communication in human social relationships and the final element in covenant. Humans possess a unique ability to know and be known, granted as part of their amazing linguistic capabilities. In the garden, Adam and Eve were fully transparent and open to each other and God. They were naked and unashamed (Genesis 2:25). In the fallen world, one experiences the effects of sin in one's masking of true feelings and the difficulty in knowing each other. People are fearful because their social relationships are not structured by the commitment and grace of covenant. So they hide from each other and from themselves. Love, forgiveness, and empowering foster the conditions for deep levels of communication and intimacy.

Jesus made these sorts of actions and commitments toward his disciples. He loved them to the very extent of giving his life for them. He accepted and forgave them when they deserted him in his hour of need. Grace infused his every touch and look at sinful human beings. His forgiveness and love were not manipulative. He set people free and empowered them to live without fear or shame. Regardless of their social origins or the stigma that society attached to them (as Palestinian society did to prostitutes, tax collectors, and lepers), Jesus' actions gave them new beginnings. He opened himself to them on the deepest levels, telling them all that the Father told him. This intimacy and communication were like none they had ever experienced before. Was it any wonder that his life changed all of human history?

The Balswicks see this covenant ideal as focused first on the family. Ideally, it is there that humans learn commitment, grace, empowerment, and intimacy. It is there that these actions can be practiced in their deepest forms. Christian social thought will measure family structures and role relationships in part by these Christian normative principles. Within the Christian Church, the norms of ideal role relatedness within the family extend also to those who are one's spiritual brothers and sisters.

Koinonia

Koinonia is a Greek word referring to the relationships of a group of people united by sharing a common identity and purpose. It points at the level of social organization that is larger than the exclusive, kinship-based family and smaller than the inclusive, territorially based nation-state. Such organizations include church congregations, labor unions, professional associations, clubs, recreational organizations, and fraternities or sororities.

The closest knit group at this level is the primary group. It is the small circle of people with whom one has face-to-face relationships involving personal disclosure and emotional identification. These sorts of groups shade off into the social network of weak connections often called a secondary group. Here members share a more specific common purpose and identity and may have face-to-face dealings without strong emotional bonds. Larger organizations are secondary groups, honeycombed with primary groups. Research indicates that most people are able to sustain strong primary ties with a maximum of twenty-five to thirty other individuals.

The New Testament portrays the *koinonia* ideal in terms of the church. Jesus says that people are to transcend the exclusivity of their family ties by considering all who belong to God as similar to their own kin. He says:

"Who is my mother, and who are my brothers?" And pointing to his disciples, he said, "Here are my mother and my brothers! For whoever does the will of my Father in heaven is my brother and sister and mother." (Matthew 12:48–50)

Both Peter and Paul indicate that the Church is the "household of God" within which humans are sons and daughters of God and hence spiritually kin with each other. Significantly, the chief social format for the early church was the house church. This was a small congregation of fifteen to forty people meeting in the home of a well-to-do member. This format maintained the group size most effective for creating strong ties among people.[6]

Koinonia was also at work in the larger Jerusalem church. It included many members from the Jewish diaspora, Galilean-derived disciples, and Jerusalem-based converts. This diverse membership developed a financial crisis. For many to stay in Jerusalem and be taught the witness about Jesus by the apostles meant they needed food and housing. Yet they were in a location where they were not employed or propertied. In response, local Palestinian Christians with property began selling their possessions and providing materially for those of their spiritual family without means. This became a fulfillment of the economic ideals articulated by Jesus.[7] It also served as a prototype (not a blueprint) for the sort of *koinonia* (sharing, fellowship) that Christians were to extend to each other elsewhere.

In the Christian vision, one's most intense and demanding obligations are to one's families of origin and orientation (1 Timothy 5:3). Yet Christians are also obligated beyond normal cultural expectations of how people are to care for others in their primary groups. The New Testament makes it clear that Christians have special obligations to those who with them are a part of the household of God (Galatians 6:10). Christians are also obligated to those, Christian or not, with whom they come to have strong connections.

Many of the problems of modernity stem from the weakening of primary group ties. Social evils like racial discrimination, substance abuse, addictive behavior, the neglect of the elderly, alienation, and delinquency flourish in mass societies where such ties are exceedingly weak. Part of the task of Christian community is to foster primary groups where caring flourishes. Here people can discover unconditional love and a sharing of the life journey that will help them cope with many of the deficiencies of modernity.

Neighborliness

The outer limits of secondary groups include people who are recognized as members of one's civic community (village, town, city, country) but with whom one has few dealings. One may relate to them casually, perhaps around an economic transaction. Yet being fair and efficient in such transactions does not exhaust the responsibility that one's connection to these people carries. One also acknowledges their common humanness when one comes to their aid in times of crisis or special need. This ideal is set out in Jesus' famous parable of the Good Samaritan (Luke 10:25–37).

If Christians' clearest obligations are to those with whom they stand connected by the strong ties of kinship (real or spiritual) and of common primary group membership, they cannot escape the obligation that comes from their general connectedness to all other humans. People are more willing to sacrifice resources, alternative commitments, and energy for their own family than for a stranger. Parents may well bankrupt themselves to save their child. They will not bankrupt themselves and their immediate family to help an anonymous child, though they may well give substantial, even sacrificial gifts to help. The degree of help may not be the same, but the principle of connectedness is.

Jesus says that people are obligated to the stranger (and hence also to future generations). Within their powers to help, Christians are to do to others as they would have others do to them. They cannot turn away from the starving or those pressed down by injustice. They are to love their neighbor as themselves (Matthew 19:19).[8] Jesus ties the sense of the proportion of help to a sympathetic principle. Christians are not to give each person what he or she deserves but what they creatively can imagine that they would need were they in the other person's shoes.

Further, Jesus ties that creative self-sacrifice to the concrete person who may (inconveniently) show up with a real need. The neighbor (Jesus' word is singular) is that person presented to the Christian here and now. Yet neighbor love for this individual may well involve Christians in group actions seeking better laws or institutions in the service of all individuals. While Jesus' command focuses on an individual, it is not individualistic. It seeks the common well-being of the whole world. Yet it does not do so abstractly. The neighbor ethic requires Christians to make every human being special. Christians cannot sacrifice this or that so-called expendable individual in the service of the masses, the proletariat, or progress. Jesus' transcendence of nationalism, gender, race, and ethnicity in this command makes it one of the most powerful engines of social justice in human history.

Balswick and Morland diagram these social ideals in this fashion:[9]

LEVELS OF SOCIAL STRUCTURE AND BIBLICALLY PRESCRIBED IDEALS

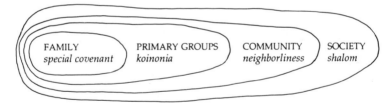

These are useful and helpful summary guidelines for the evaluative norms followed in Christian social evaluation. In practice, they need to be much more detailed in order to be applicable and fruitful for analysis and for strategies for change. Nonetheless, this description suggests starting points for thinking Christianly about various concrete social orders.

What is missing in this discussion so far is the larger nation-state and the global perspective. There is a very long tradition of political philosophy and legal discourse within Christian thought. Political theology is one of the fastest-growing areas of contemporary theological writings. Issues of liberation theology, Marxist-Christian dialogue, Third World theological reflection, massive global poverty, and the militarization and arming of the world's nations lie at the center of this development.

The remainder of this chapter focuses on the Kingdom of God as the central New Testament notion with clear political overtones and implications. For two millennia, the Kingdom of God has served as the central hope and image for the comprehensive conformity of collective existence to the will of God.

The Kingdom of God and Social Hopes

Matthew summarizes Jesus' preaching simply: "Repent, for the kingdom of heaven has come near" (4:17). Mark sketches the central message in similar words: "The time is fulfilled, and the kingdom of God has come near; repent, and believe in the good news" (1:15). Luke (and the book of Acts) repeatedly speaks of the Kingdom of God as the central theme of Jesus (Luke 4:43; 9:2, 11; 12:32; 22:29; Acts 8:12; 28:23).

This notion of Kingdom was familiar to first-century Jews. The Old Testament portrayed God as Israel's King.[10] The Hebrew word for kingdom (*malkuth*) refers to the abstract dynamic or idea of reign, rule, or dominion (Psalms 145:11, 13; 103:19). In Isaiah 52:7, the "good news" is defined as the announcement, "Your God reigns" (NIV, NRSV) or "Your God is King" (NEB).

The New Testament also sees the Kingdom (Greek, *basileia*) of God as God's reigning activity (Luke 19:12; 23:42; John 18:36; Revelation 17:12).[11] The Kingdom of God is God acting as king in the world. It means the active exercising of rule whereby God sustains creation and brings about God's goals and victory in human hearts and history.

This notion is what unites the Old and New Testaments. The single thread joining them is the anticipation of the coming

Kingdom in the Old Testament and the announcement of its arrival in the New. There are a variety of difficult issues that surround a proper understanding of God's Kingdom in its various aspects and ramifications. We agree with F. Dale Bruner's analysis and summary of that Kingdom in terms of the four aspects that define its chief implications.[12]

1. The Kingdom of *heaven* or Kingdom of God is the entirely future new world. When Christians pray, "Thy kingdom come," they pray for the new heavens and new earth. They pray for the end of history, the final vanquishing of evil, the second coming of Jesus Christ. This Kingdom represents the kingly activity of God most fully known in heaven come to be present in the same way on earth. When this Kingdom comes, it unleashes unearthly forces. It is beyond human reach or acquisition. Christians pray for it to come because it is something people cannot build or realize on the basis of their human efforts. In the fullest meaning, the Kingdom of God comes with the end of the current age.

2. The Kingdom of God advances with the increase of the unadulterated *Word of the Kingdom*. The Protestant Reformation stressed this element. The chief means by which God's Kingdom extends itself in this world is through the spoken Word of the gospel. The Word reaches people's hearts and elicits faith. The Word of God's kingship tells humans how to live and thus change history. That Word gives people hope in the final revelation of God's Kingdom when heaven comes to earth. The future coming Kingdom is present now in truth and power when the Spirit makes the good news effective in more and more hearts and arenas of life.

3. The Kingdom of God is God's rule in the *hearts* of men and women. Wherever Jesus rules in human hearts, the kingly activity of God is present. This is the sense of the Kingdom that pious and revivalist Christians have found most

congenial. It focuses not on the change of worlds (from this age to the eternal age) or on changes in this world (social reform or revolution). Rather, the relevant changes are those that take place in the inner person of the individual believer. In announcing the Kingdom, Jesus called for people to turn their inner thinking and life activity around (to repent). When they do, they enter the Kingdom by submitting to God's rule within their hearts.

4. The Kingdom of God is God's presence in *history*. Wherever God's presence is effective and active, peace and justice reign in human society. If the King is present in one's heart, God will activate one's hands and feet. The believer will not be passive. Rather, he or she will join with others to help God's will be done on *earth* (not just in his or her heart) as it is in heaven. The social gospel movement and liberation theology underline this side of the Kingdom of God.

So the Kingdom is not simply a gift that comes at the end of history. Nor is it just the effective Word of God's kingship, received by repentance and faith (as Christians do in their hearts). It is something to be lived out as Christians band together to bring increased peace and justice to the peoples of the earth. Human beings may not be able to build *God's* Kingdom, but they can bring their own kingdoms more in line with God's Kingdom. Today's social worlds can reflect in a limited way the social perfections of God's Kingdom.

In summary, "(1) the Kingdom in the full sense comes with the end of the age; (2) the major present agent of this kingdom is God's Word, which awakens (3) the obedient response to it; then this obedient response—faith issuing in love—(4) works in and through groups and structures for justice in the world."[13] Because Christians already participate in the Kingdom of God, they are able as believers to modify their behavior and involvement in the kingdoms of this world. Christians can evaluate those human kingdoms against the elements of God's kingly activity and rule that are described in Scripture.

Chapter Fourteen dealt with the two major structuring principles of God's Kingdom. In God's Kingdom, there is nothing superior to God. God's name is hallowed and God's will is obeyed. His loving care and covenant commitment render all evil null and void. No authority, power, or imperative structure can resist God's reign. The great illusion that anything is more loving, more powerful, more beneficial, or more important than God vanishes. To see the true and living God is to be done with all false spirituality and foolish idolatry.

Furthermore, in God's Kingdom humans are the object of God's perfect, loving, and preserving activity. God is the supreme Good Samaritan, who seeks all those wounded by the evil that entered this world with sin. God is the great Shepherd who seeks lost sheep. The Lord is the suffering Servant who takes on the sin and guilt of all in order to end them. None can draw on God's power to mistreat fellow humans. The Holy Spirit does not allow indifference or vengeance to control human behavior. God is the one who loves the neighbor as God's self. The heavenly Father gives his unique Son to save humankind from its inevitable destruction.

There are Christians who take all of this to mean that they are commissioned to establish or bring in the Kingdom by their own efforts (although inspired by the Spirit, to be sure). This attitude has had both an evangelical and a liberal phase. Many evangelical Protestants in the first half of the nineteenth century were postmillennialists. They believed that gradual social reforms brought on by the leavening effect of Christian conversion would perfect society. When social changes reached a certain level of justice and peace, a thousand years of continuous social and international harmony and prosperity would begin. At the end of this thousand years (*post*millennial), Christ would come, setting up his Kingdom. The major means to achieve this aim were the conversion of sinners and the joining together of likeminded Christians in movements to abolish such evils as slavery, prostitution, and alcohol.

By the late nineteenth and early twentieth century, the major North American Christian groups who still advocated a sort of postmillennial view were Protestant liberals and those in the Social Gospel movement. The liberal version identified the Kingdom of God with the abstract principles of love, peace, and justice. These they saw as coming inevitably through the workings of evolution, education, and Western civilization.

The Social Gospel movement was far more realistic and activist than that of the liberals. Those who embraced it did not simply wait for the Kingdom to evolve into being as the social Darwinists thought it might. They saw the massive, growing ills of the city. To solve them meant actively tackling them from many sides, using legal reforms, economic transformations, and the creation of new social structures and educational institutions. Concerted social action was essential to create new structures of justice, which the conversion of human hearts alone could not accomplish. The movement spoke of converting social structures as a parallel to converting individuals. Followers sought to do God's will on both the individual and social levels.

What all three of these groups share is the idea that humans can bring in the Kingdom by a series of appropriate collective activities. Unfortunately, this represents a one-sided understanding of the Kingdom. The common mistake is the idea that human activity can bring in or establish God's Kingdom. The Lord's prayer indicates that *God* is the one who brings and builds *God's* Kingdom. Christians can only wait for it, pray for its coming, seek it, and turn their lives about and enter it when it is near.

What these groups got right was the notion that God's coming Kingdom has profound implications for the sorts of social arrangements to be tolerated by citizens of the Kingdom. It also profoundly influences the kingdoms that human beings build. If

God's Kingdom is one of justice, of shalom-peace, and of righteousness, what should human kingdoms be like? How do the kingdoms of this world relate to the Kingdom of God? Our answer is given in the next chapter.

NOTES

1. Christopher J. H. Wright, *An Eye for an Eye: The Place of Old Testament Ethics Today* (Downers Grove, IL: InterVarsity Press, 1983); Alan Verhey, *The Great Reversal: Ethics and the New Testament* (Grand Rapids, MI: Eerdmans, 1984); and Stephen Charles Mott, *Biblical Ethics and Social Change* (New York: Oxford University Press, 1982) present the issues covered here.
2. See "Peace" in Colin Brown, ed., *The New International Dictionary of New Testament Theology*, Vol. 2 (Grand Rapids, MI: Zondervan, 1976) pp. 777–780.
3. Balswick and Balswick, *The Family: A Christian Perspective on the Contemporary Home* (Grand Rapids, MI: Baker, 1989); Jack Balswick and J. Kenneth Morland, *Social Problems: A Christian Understanding and Response* (Grand Rapids, MI: Baker, 1990), p. 49.
4. Lewis Smedes, *Forgive and Forget: Healing the Hurts We Don't Deserve* (New York: Harper & Row, 1984); Walter Wangerin, Jr., *As For Me and My House: Crafting Your Marriage to Last* (Nashville, TN: Thomas Nelson, 1987); David Augsburger, *Caring Enough to Forgive/Caring Enough Not to Forgive* (Ventura, CA: Regal Books, 1981).
5. Balswick and Morland, *Social Problems*, p. 53.
6. Robert Banks, *Paul's Idea of Community* (Grand Rapids, MI: Eerdmans, 1980).
7. Halvor Moxnes, *The Economy of the Kingdom: Social Conflict and Economic Relations in Luke's Gospel* (Philadelphia, PA: Fortress Press, 1988).
8. F. Dale Bruner, *Matthew: A Commentary*, Vol. 2: *The Churchbook: Matthew 13–28* (Waco, TX: Word Books, 1990), pp. 704–706.
9. Balswick and Morland, *Social Problems*, p. 55.
10. John Bright, *The Kingdom of God: The Biblical Concept and Its Meaning for the Church* (Nashville, TN: Abingdon Press, 1953).
11. George Ladd, *Jesus and the Kingdom* (Grand Rapids, MI: Eerdmans, 1964) and *A Theology of the New Testament* (Grand Rapids, MI: Eerdmans, 1974); Leonhard Goppelt, *Theology of the New Testament*, Vol. I (Grand Rapids, MI: Eerdmans, 1981), especially Chap. 2.
12. Bruner, *Matthew: A Commentary*, Vol. 1: *The Christbook: A Historical-Theological Commentary: Matthew 1–12* (Waco, TX: Word Books, 1987), pp. 119–125, 243–247.
13. Bruner, *Matthew*, Vol. 1, p. 125.

Chapter 16

THE KINGDOMS OF THIS WORLD
AND THE KINGDOM OF GOD

Few issues create more heat among Christians than how to be involved in the surrounding non-Christian world. Christian blood, shed by fellow Christians, shamefully inscribes parts of Church history because of this disagreement.

Chapter Thirteen outlined the broad spectrum of social teachings of Christian churches. Some theological paradigms seek a complete Christian civilization. The medieval European Catholic church is an example. Some seek only a tightly disciplined, minority movement of highly committed Christians. The Old Order Amish and the communitarian Hutterite Brethren are such movements. In addition, Chapter Thirteen looked at two theological paradigms of the relationship of Christianity to society: the Lutheran and the Anabaptist.

This chapter goes a step further. It outlines the position of the Reformed tradition (sometimes called the Calvinists) found among Presbyterians, Reformed churches, and other Christian denominations. These groups also seek to obey and follow Christ in the largest halls of societal life. But their theological paradigm is different from that of either the Anabaptist or the Lutheran. For them, the Christian movement can never appropriately exist simply as a small cell within the larger society, sealed off in its own attempt to be pure. If the Christian's influence is only inward and spiritual, it falls short in part of its obedience to Christ. Nor can the Christian community appropriately concede as much autonomy to a whole arena of life in the way that the Lutherans do with their two-kingdom doctrine.

For Reformed Christians, the basic doctrine is the Lordship of Christ, his right of rulership over all the affairs of the world he made. Whatever concerns Christ concerns the Christian community. There is a legitimate distinction between church and state. But there is no legitimate boundary separating a sacred realm solely of concern to the Church and a secular realm solely of concern to the state. In some ways, the Calvinists have been the most "secular" of all the saints. They constantly seek to transform the so-called secular realm in the light of the will and Word of God. This has made them more active and politically involved than most other Protestant movements. The originator of many of their ideas is John Calvin (1509–1564).[1]

The Kingdoms of This World Shall Be Christ's

W. Fred Graham calls Calvin the "constructive revolutionary." By this he means to suggest that Calvin laid foundations for many of the ideas leading to the modernization of Western civilization. His pastoral and political involvements in the life of Geneva, Switzerland, hammered out a new pattern for Christian involvement in social affairs. His theology and social ethic created styles of Christian living that Puritans and other reform movements adopted. Austere as some of these Christians might seem, they created an activist Christianity, trying to apply the principles of God's Kingdom to the affairs of this world. In fact, sociologists have seen fingerprints of the Calvinists all over modern economic, scientific, and political developments.

Max Weber's *The Protestant Ethic and Spirit of Capitalism* develops a detailed argument that much of the ethos and spirit of capitalism comes from Calvin's later followers. Robert Merton's *Science, Technology, and Society in Seventeenth-Century England* claims that Puritans were formative in the early development of modern science. Their intense scientific activity grew out of their sense of Christian vocation and their views of God's Kingdom. Others trace modern democratic forms of political life to the influence and ideas of Puritans and other activist Calvinism. Intense study and debate continue over the complex details of these hypotheses. Certainly these are not settled issues, nor was all of Calvin's influence simply positive. Nonetheless, it is impressive to see how much evidence there is for intimate connections between Calvinism and modern economic, scientific, and political arrangements.

Calvin himself would not be happy with all the developments that claim to come from him. His own ideas are not fully modern. Yet they are a beginning point that changed much of Christendom. They continue to provide resources for a dynamic view of the Kingdom of God and of human kingdoms. Furthermore, Calvin's own social identification with the poor and critique of the excesses of the wealthy have been forgotten by many of his modern-day followers. Successful "Calvinists" with money and power sometimes argue for social and economic positions completely opposite to those of Calvin—and they do so allegedly in his name. Calvin comes off sounding like a conservative defender of the status quo. He was far from that.[2]

Calvin's central ideas about society run something like this. God created humans as good, bound together in original connections of love and equality. Those links shattered at the fall. In Christ, God begins the full restoration of right relationships among humans. The Church of Christ is the visible society of those whose relational connections unite them to one another in Christ. The Church's own life is to be marked by this restoration. It is to have a corporate life exhibiting wholeness, justice, and love. Within and without its walls, the Church exhorts and disciplines Christians so that they will think and live Christianly in gratitude toward a loving God. This, at its best, is at the heart of the Calvinist vision. But the Church is also concerned with the social relationships of even non-Christians.

God's concern is with the whole human race. Even after the fall, humans are united by a sacred bond of fellowship. The Christian's neighbor is any and every person who shares this planet with him or her. Christians cannot be concerned simply to perfect Christian fellowship and neglect the fellowship that is God's will elsewhere. Yet the human solidarity God desires is not readily apparent in contemporary social orders. Rather than affirming solidarity with each other, humans spoil the order intended by God. God provides a rich bounty to bless and sustain humans, but they snatch God's rich provision, hoarding, monopolizing, and gouging others in order to enrich themselves. Some people take more than their fair share. Then they withhold the abundance they have acquired from those with nothing. This perverts the original order of nature by breaking the ties of connectedness that God designed humans to display.

The Church is the place where the restoration to good order begins. Calvin concludes that a restored human solidarity in Christ, however, does not eliminate all the inequalities of society. For one thing, the restoration God seeks is never complete in this age. The full restoration comes only with the Kingdom of God. So the Church cannot try to suppress the hierarchy that is necessary in the continuing civic and political order. Its functioning requires the order of leadership, command, and obedience. The normal order between male and female is equality. This was the original order in the garden of Eden. Yet now humans live in a provisional order. So human relationships often continue in structures of inequality in the provisional order.

When Christians teach equality, they do not eliminate differences that exist between parents and children, professors and students, husbands and wives, or surgeons and patients. Nonetheless, living in Christ provides the basis for exercising authority without oppression and for acceptance of that authority without servility or shame. Community in the Church is intended to model a new human solidarity and care. The civil order is also to experience some of God's restoring grace. Magistrates (judges, city councillors, mayors, presidents) and citizens are to experience a similar solidarity within the continuing hierarchy. What the Church advocates is mercy and mutual consideration in all the provisional relationships that continue to be marked by hierarchy.

Wealth and power differences often mark different strata within a given social order. Some of these are illegitimate because they express sinful exploitation. Even legitimate stratification in society is provisional. Such strata as exist are limited groupings that will be set aside by the new perfected human community inaugurated when Christ returns. Already in this age the Church is to respond to that coming new human community. The Church is to arrange its own life to match its new life in Christ. Its relationship to the larger civic community will also express an awareness of that new human community. It will seek not only to transform the inner communal relationships of Christians within the Church proper but to transform the social relations of the civic community as well.

The Church is commissioned by Christ with a freedom and authority to speak God's Word to sinful society. The larger civic society is subject to the lordship and rule of Christ. It may not know or acknowledge this to be the case. But that does not change the reality of Christ's kingly rulership over all human affairs. His Word is not a limited message, meant simply for true believers. It is a Word that speaks to the whole of human life and aims at claiming it back for God's Kingdom.

The persistent tendency of sinful society is to set up illegitimate social strata and to exploit legitimate strata. Society regularly is run in accord with the self-interest of those who benefit from its social and economic arrangements. Where this is happening, the Church must speak in no uncertain terms. Where human solidarity and compassion do not govern social relationships, there the Church will speak and act prophetically within society. How it performs this speaking and acting in society is what sets apart the Christ-transforming-culture position from the Lutheran and Anabaptist approaches.

There is an undeniable separation of church and state according to Calvin. Yet both exist under the single Lordship of Jesus Christ. So the Church cannot avoid being active in its relationship toward the state. On the other hand, the state cannot dictate to the Church. To allow civil rulers to rule the Church as well is a confusion that damages the mission and identity of the Church. The temporal cannot subordinate the spiritual. Yet the spiritual must seek to transform the temporal in the light of the eternal order of God's Kingdom.

For Calvin, the Church has four principal tasks in service to the state. It prays for political authorities, encourages them to defend the poor and weak against the rich and powerful, calls on their help in promoting true religion (even to enforce ecclesiastical discipline), and warns the authorities when they are at fault. Many non-Calvinist Christians would probably happily agree with the first two duties and with the last. Yet all sense a problem with the third task of asking political authorities to promote true religion. It is here, in fact, that Calvin displayed some of his most dramatic failures of Christian love and compassion. Nonconformists in Geneva were silenced, expelled, and, in a few cases, executed. To be fair to Calvin, his own efforts at insisting on mercy and compassion in civil affairs were often frustrated by political authorities.

By insisting that the Church could warn political authorities when they were at fault, Calvin laid the foundation for modern notions of free speech. He also went a step further than Luther as to what can appropriately be done when the political authorities stray far from civic righteousness. Luther was content to allow resistance to evil and obedient suffering. Calvin permitted revolt and rebellion at times. Calvin cared deeply for the poor and the refugee. He pressured the government and sought laws to protect the weak and curb the flagrant conspicuous consumption of the rich. Yet he did not advocate revolutions of the hungry and the poor on their own behalf.

If these people are to revolt, according to Calvin, they must first find allies among the lower government officials. Rebellion or revolution is legitimate only when led by the lower magistrates against higher corrupt ones. These legitimate political officials in the lower ranks must agree with the poor and oppressed that the government has subverted its God-given duties. Then, if the corruption will not be cut out, revolt may be the only recourse. Even violence can thus be a legitimate Christian act when it restores a corrupted state to its true functions.

For his day, Calvin advanced dramatically new ideas about wealth and poverty, as well as about commerce as a means to wealth. For Calvin, wealth is not a necessary sign of God's favor and election to heaven. Weber's portrait of the latter-day Calvinist and capitalist, viewing worldly commercial success as a sign of God's favor, represents a departure from Calvin's ideas. Such "Calvinists" forget and distort what Calvin himself said about wealth and poverty and their place in God's restored human community.

If wealth does not signal God's election, neither does poverty serve as a proof of God's displeasure and election to hell. Both in fact are spiritual opportunities and dangers. Both wealth and poverty are channels of grace from God. They are means by which people can demonstrate the human solidarity that comes from authentic faith. Yet the wealthy, for the most part, reject the grace that God bestows with their wealth. Instead, they idolize their possessions, making it virtually impossible for them to enter the Kingdom of God. God calls them to use their wealth for the benefit of the community, especially the poor.

The rich abundance that comes from God is to be used according to a rule of love, not a rule of asceticism. Asceticism is no more a proper response to wealth than is luxurious self-indulgence. If people keep too little and deny themselves too severely, they put themselves in bondage to their own untended appetites and eventual ill health. They must keep enough of what God gives them to live simply. But the poor are God's messengers in society, placed here to check on the faith and charity of those with means who claim to walk with God. The well-to-do are to give out of their plenty to these messengers of God. If instead they indulge in extravagances and conspicuous consumption, they put themselves in bondage to the passions of the sinful self and to mammon. The poor help free the rich from the idolatry of money by giving them the opportunity to break with its power.

The simple act of giving, however, is not enough. The charity that serves to boost the prestige and name of the giver is well known. So is the charity that reflects no more than giving a pittance off the top of a fortune. Giving is to be done on the basis of compassion (the rule of love), even when it might cut seriously into one's own comfort. Such giving must not demean the poor, for one is giving to one's brothers and sisters. Giving is not only to show but to foster a restored human solidarity in love and equality.

Overall, Calvin's economic ethic means that anything contributing to the impoverishment of a part of society is evil. He had particularly harsh words for those engaged in monopoly and speculation, making money off the misery of others. His ethic, however, does not undermine private property. Private property really is private. But what makes it legitimate are the uses to which it is put. Private property must be used for the common good of society. The modern notion that one has a right to do whatever one wishes with private property is foreign to Calvin's vision. He affirms the individual and individual rights without falling into the trap of extreme individualism.

Calvin was a pragmatist in all these matters. What he sought was the rule of love in human affairs. Laws and political restrictions are a legitimate and necessary means to curb the abuses of human selfishness. Humans will never live in a perfected society with completely unselfish people before the coming Kingdom of God. But human affairs can be arranged to curb selfishness, encourage human solidarity, and develop compassionate relations in the remaining hierarchies of wealth and power. Government interference is legitimate insofar as it promotes the general good and happiness of people in society. So the state serves to guard against business interests milking the populace. Yet the state itself cannot become an economic liability to its citizens either. Neither business nor government has unlimited rights to secure for itself the wealth created in society. Nor does the private individual have unlimited rights in property to hoard goods or to live a wastrel life of conspicuous consumption while other people starve.

In contrast with most thinkers of his day (including Luther), Calvin approved commerce as natural to the ways in which humans relate to each other. Exchanging goods is how God's provisions for human needs get distributed throughout society. For Calvin, no human activities are free from the corruption of evil (including farming, theologizing, pastoring, and politicking). Commerce is not in a different moral universe from "spiritual activities." Commerce is as good a form of work as any other human activity. And work is a necessary part of people's God-given task in society.

In spite of the curse pronounced by God on human labor, people are given the gift of work by God. To be sure, work is a fallen good. Yet each person must make a choice of occupation. Any occupation is relatively good, provided it is not banned or condemned by the Word of God. The goodness of any occupation or work is measured by the degree to which it serves the common good. Work is to benefit the whole Church and the larger global human community. When people do not work, they disobey God. Work does not mean a salaried job but activity that creates goods or performs services vital for other people's well-being. Whatever denies work to human beings corrupts the very structure of their existence and must be resisted. Work must, thus, be undertaken in conditions that are safe and not oppressive. God's will does not allow abusing the work of others.

So far as wages are concerned, no one deserves what he or she gets, whether as employer or employee. What one gets comes through the goodness and grace of God. Nonetheless, those who hire others for their labor are responsible for paying a just wage. A just wage is not based on the legal minimum that one can get away with when compensating a worker. It must be based on the norm of equity, rooted in the command, "Do unto others as you would have them do unto you." The employer must put himself or herself in the place of the worker and seriously consider what he or she would want to receive in order to be supported in a life of dignity. Because the ultimate wages come from God, what the employer actually is doing is paying out God's wages to God's servants. Not to pay proper wages is to defraud and embezzle from God.

Self-interest in matters of wealth is so powerful that something more than good religious ideas about working conditions and wages is needed. Employers (and employees) are often blinded by their own selfishness. Thus, binding contracts expressing agreements are necessary. So are laws dealing with general wage structures. Both of these measures are useful for defending against common inequities and injustices. The rule of love is the basic norm for Christians in civil life as in churchly affairs. Laws regulate human arrangements and ensure a measure of genuine justice in the context of human selfishness. However, Christians cannot take what is legal as the measure or standard of their own conduct. What is legal may be prohibited to the Christian because it falls short of the law of love.

One implication of these ideas is that pastors and Christian leaders should seek to speak to and influence every realm of human life. There is no part of the world that does not belong to God and is not subject to his Lordship, even in its rebellion. While Calvin and his followers accept the distinction between church and state, they refuse the false line between the sacred and the secular. Calvin's vision was ahead of his own time, however much some of his ideas are now behind the present times. Fred Graham is correct when he says:[3]

[Calvin's] ability to distinguish the spiritual and the temporal was uncommon for his day; his refusal to allow the spiritual to be subject to the temporal was uncommon to Protestantism in his day; his ability to suffuse the temporal with the values of the spiritual without robbing the former of its identity is instructive for our day.

Calvin was thoroughgoing in his concern for all affairs of human life, including government. He understood the gospel as something irrevocably concerned with the world in all its affairs. The Church is involved with and concerned for the full range of affairs over which the Lordship of Christ extends. Calvinism through the centuries shows a persistent tendency to involve its followers in the political order, for better or worse.

A Contemporary Expression of Calvin's Social Doctrine

By many accounts, the greatest Protestant theologian in the twentieth century is the Swiss Reformed thinker, Karl Barth (1886–1968). Some of his ideas are controversial and clearly contestable. There are places where evangelicals disagree most sharply with him. But his resistance to the Nazis in Germany gave him a distinct view on the relationship between the Church and the contemporary state. In 1935, while a professor at the university in Bonn, Germany, he refused to take the required oath of loyalty to Adolf Hitler. He was removed from his government teaching post. From Switzerland, he maintained close relations with the Christian resistance, the Confessing Church of Germany, which he helped bring into being. Over the years he wrote extensively about the Christian's responsibility for the state and civil society.

Barth was a Reformed theologian who followed many of Calvin's basic ideas. He agreed with Calvin that Christians cannot leave the larger social order alone. Christ claims all of one's life, not just one's heart. Spelling out what this means is a complicated, prayerful responsibility of the total Christian community. Furthermore, it can be done properly only when Christians place themselves in solidarity with the poor and the weak. Only then do they place themselves in solidarity with Christ, who himself was poor and weak.

The foundation for any sort of Christian ethics, according to Barth, is theological. To discern the political responsibility of the

Church, Christians must have a theological understanding of the state and politics. Only then can they spell out how to act Christianly in the political arena.[4]

For Barth, the primary understanding of the Kingdom of God (the heavens) is as a transcendent, future reality. This being the case, no this-worldly sociopolitical reality can be identified as God's Kingdom. The discontinuity between God and the world means that faith can identify *no* principle, program, party, or structure directly with God's action. God's action is *God's* action. The actions and principles of this world are *of this world*. The Kingdom of God does not come through the activity of human beings. Nor is the Church to be considered that Kingdom, as advocates of Christendom or a Christian civilization often do.

Nonetheless, the distance between God and the world is overcome by Jesus Christ. It is he who stands at the center not only of the Church but of the world.[5] There is no limit or boundary to the Kingdom of God. It has invaded this age and made its presence known in Jesus Christ. The fact that the Church is peculiarly commissioned to announce the objective facts of Christ's reconciliation in the world is a sign that there is a preliminary sanctification of this world. Both the Church and the state are "orders of reconciliation," established by God's grace in the time that stands between the resurrection of Christ and his coming again.

Reconciliation is in fact the central sociopolitical event of world history. It objectively grounds the Church as the realm of those who have obediently heard the Word of God. And reconciliation establishes the state as the realm that provides an external, relative degree of justice, freedom, and peace within which the Word can be proclaimed. Both church and state have tasks given them by God to accomplish for the good of all human beings.

In Barth's thought, the two realms of the Christian community and the civil community can be distinguished, even if both are rooted in the reality of the Kingdom of God. They each have a distinct commission to fulfill. The Church is the gathered community of people who come together by virtue of their common, conscious knowledge of Jesus Christ. The Church's commission is the direct service of the Word of God, the dissemination of a message that it alone is given and knows.[6] So the Church is always preeminently concerned with the study, purity, and proclamation of God's Word to all the world.

The state is commissioned also for the service of God but not for the direct or conscious service of the Word of God. Its service is to provide a social order of outward justice, peace, and freedom. These are not the justice, peace, and freedom of the Kingdom of God. Rather, they are the *promise* of these things in the midst of the chaos of the kingdom of the world.[7] The state accomplishes this commission only by recourse to physical force or to the threat of such force. This is what is learned, not only from direct experience, but from Romans 13. The state bears the sword and exercises power, not just authority. The essence of the state, however, is not power. Its essence is justice. But justice only occurs in a sinful world by the state resorting to power.[8]

The Church claims the state for this service of God by prayer, by vocal advocacy, by refusing to obey the state when it is disobedient to God, and by sending its members into the highest offices of the state. Yet in claiming the state for the service of God, it does not seek to turn the state into the Church.[9] Nor is the state to seek to turn itself into the Church. The Church cannot take the Kingdom of God into the state or expect the state to become the Kingdom of God. What it seeks from the state is that the state fulfill its divine purpose and destiny. It must be committed to justice *in principle* (a "justice state") and must provide a relative degree of *actual justice* in its day-to-day functioning (a "just state").[10] It is to be the servant of God that Paul pictures in Romans 13:1–7, limiting and punishing the evil while encouraging and rewarding the good. It is to be a *parable* or *promise* of the Kingdom of God by reflecting on a human scale and in a limited way the qualities of God's Kingdom. In its limited, flawed, even fallen way, the state can to some degree function in ways that will remind people of what the Kingdom of God is like.

Barth claims that what Christians need to do is actively engage themselves at every level of civic and political life. They alone consciously know the divine commission and task of the state. The modern state is secular and does not openly acknowledge the Word of God as its rule and guide. So Christians must be thoughtfully present in the civic arena, pressing for and advocating policies and decisions in line with justice, peace, and freedom. Part of this presence will be as elected or appointed officials.

For Barth, this does not mean that there ought to be a Christian political party or a Christian platform. In the civic arena, Christians seek the priorities and principles of the Kingdom of God. They wish the state to mirror in limited ways what the Kingdom of God is like. But that happens only through the regular course of debate and legislation where the ideas of Christians must compete with and succeed over many other ideas. The Christian is present in the civic arena *as a citizen*. There the discourse is not about the Bible and the Word of God. It is about what will further the common good of all citizens.

So Christians, having discovered principles of justice, peace, and freedom from their own deep study of Scripture and society, enter the civic arena "anonymously." They come to speak as citizens with no special privileges or even special insight other than the general knowledge of the state's divine commission. God does not give Christians detailed blueprints for political and social action. They will not quote Scripture as authoritative in this realm, for it does not have that status in the civic arena. Nonetheless, Christians will seek valid arguments, persuasive in a secularized civic arena, for social changes that will enhance and encourage the rule of human solidarity and love.

The reality of sin in this age means that the state, no less than the Church, can be subverted and that it will not function to fulfill its divine commission. The state can become an antistate, a state of chaos rather than order (just as the Church can become an antichurch that proclaims the word of the human instead of the Word of God). Because of the objective fact of Christ's reconciliation and triumph over the principalities and powers, however, this age will not see either the full face of the state as the Beast (Revelation 13) or the Church as the Antichrist. The powerful triumph of Christ on the cross objectively limits the ability of church and state to be subverted from their God-given tasks.

For these reasons, any particular, empirical state functions somewhere between the New Jerusalem (the Kingdom of God) and Babylon (the state as the Beast). One must always exercise discernment and wisdom in determining whether the actual government one faces has enough justice in it to legitimate its continued existence. If it is committed *in principle* to justice and struggles *in practice* to deliver justice to its citizens, Christians will seek to reform and correct it by all peaceful means. If a state *in principle* is no longer committed to justice (as happened in Nazi Germany) and even acts to punish the good and reward the evil *in practice*, then the Christian may revolt against it even by violent means. It no longer is a state but has become an antistate, a government of disorder and injustice in principle and in practice.

So the Christian and the community of Christians carry the responsibility of seeking the transformation and reformation of the larger civic community, including the state. Christians cannot be unconcerned and uninvolved in a realm where God is concerned and involved. If Christians are citizens of the Kingdom of God, they will also become motivated, compassionate, courageous change agents in the kingdoms of this world. If their hearts are transformed and obedient, their hands and feet will move to care for the hurt and impoverished in their societies.[11] But how? Is there a Christian or biblical philosophy of change?

Christian Approaches to Social Change

The Anabaptists typically see the transformationist approach to society as prone to fall into the arrogance of attempting to manage history and into the folly of using sinful means (coercion) to do so. The Calvinists, they say, have a history of failure because they overestimate the degree to which the state and the larger civic community can be transformed this side of the coming Kingdom of God. The transformationists normally reply that the Anabaptist approach borders on a counsel of despair. Much more can and has been modified by Christians' active political involvement in social change than the Anabaptists recognize. Even if the effort at transformation fails, it must be made in obedience to and solidarity with the universal Lordship of Christ. But their debate will probably not be settled in this lifetime.

Whatever one's conviction about the appropriate biblical approach to social involvement, it is clear that all Christians need great wisdom and understanding. The Bible stresses wisdom and discernment in human affairs because these affairs are so complicated that simple formulas cannot handle them. Besides, the human beings who occupy positions within social structures are of infinite value and often fragile creatures. They need to be handled with care. This takes change agents of maturity, love, and discernment. Unfortunately, people don't become such agents by learning a dash of management theory, a trace of sociology, a pinch of change agentry, and a bushel of political policies. It happens through one's concrete immersion in the lives of real people who are struggling to survive in the immensely varied worlds of wealth and poverty, power and oppression, sophistication and illiteracy.

The disagreements and strategies of social change can be categorized roughly by a few key distinctions and questions. Virtually all Christians believe that they can do *something* about the world they live in. They can certainly intercede for its hurts and pray for its compassionate healing. They can pray for God's forgiveness on those who do evil to them and bless those who persecute them.

But many feel that there is much more that Christians can do to live out their faith as whole people. They do not exist simply as devout Christians cordoned off in holy huddles. They are also parents, teachers, social workers, health care professionals, truck drivers, secretaries, executives, politicians, sales clerks, poets, musicians, and athletes. They are most definitely *in the world*. Many of the deficiencies of the Christian movement are not due to the Church not being fully Christian. Many are due to the fact that Christians are not thinking and living Christianly *in the world*.

When humans confront the awesome and frightening disintegration of the social fabric of modern industrial orders, they must do so as Christians possessing a variety of options for social change and transformation. The following chart summarizes the major options in terms of two major distinctions: who is to bring Christian influence to bear (the agent of change) and what sorts of actions will be used to effect change.[12]

The agents of change may be individual Christians, seeking through personal action to bring about greater justice, peace, and freedom in their own small circles of life. Some Christians argue that this is the only legitimate way in which the Church should be involved in the world. It ought to equip individual Christians with motives and insight and send them forth to live as Christians in the world. But the Church has no further responsibility or duty toward the larger social order.

Others consider the local church congregation as an important agent of social action. Thus, they see ministry radiating from the congregation into the world, setting up soup kitchens and food distribution centers, sponsoring refugee families, hosting clothes closets for the poor, lobbying against social evils. Others move a step further and see the denomination or even transdenominational organizational structures as appropriate actors for social change.

Then there is the spectrum of possible actions that can be taken to produce changes in the social world. Evangelism seeks to bring the Kingdom of God to the hearts of people. It invites intimate, personal changes in a person's life. Conversion of the heart serves as the basis for conversion of life, thought, and habit. Most Christians would also argue that the action of direct relief of those suffering is mandated by Matthew 25. Extending the cup of cold water, clothing the naked, feeding the hungry and housing the

Action for Social Change

AGENT	STRATEGY				
	EVANGELISM	MEETING PHYSICAL NEEDS	SPEAKING OUT	FILLING KEY SOCIETY POSITIONS	SOCIAL ACTION AIMED AT CHANGE
Individual Christians	Personal evangelism	Neighborliness	Statements by individual on needed changes	Training for and seeking key decision-making positions	Social action by the individual
Local Church or Christian Community	Evangelistic meetings or Bible studies	Programs put on by local group to meet needs of the congregation or its immediate community	Statements by the local group on social issues	Affirmation of this-worldly vocations as Christian ministry and encouragement/ support of "secular" callings by the local church	Social action by the local church or Christian community
Suprachurch Structure— Denominations, Parachurch Groups, International Movements	Evangelism through cooperative efforts, mass media	Christian social welfare, community development, hunger relief, refugee resettlement	Statements and policy papers by denominational and inter-denominational agencies or international movements	Support of Christians in high positions, use of such Christians and decision makers in planning and carrying out change in society	Social action led by denominational and other supra-congregational agencies

homeless, visiting the prisoner and caring for the sick—these are all appropriate actions Christians can take in this world.

More controversial are the last three sorts of action listed in the chart: speaking out and making pronouncements on social arrangements, seeking to place Christians in pivotal positions of power, and taking direct, confrontational social action. Pronouncements, especially those made by denominational or trans-denominational agencies, always provoke the ire of Christians who do not agree with them. Some churches reject the idea that one can be a *Christian* military general, police commissioner, or even president. Others see direct (even nonviolent) protest or action as beyond the boundaries of Christ's commission.

We are not attempting here to prescribe the correct answer so much as to display the range of options used by Christians of different stripes in the some two-hundred-odd countries where they reside. For the Reformed Christian, all of these options are legitimate tools in fulfilling the secular duty of the Church and seeking social transformation. The critical question is what each of these agents and actions can accomplish in moving the world toward higher levels of justice, peace, and freedom.

As in the case of the Anabaptist and Lutheran traditions, the sociological vocation is an important and valued one among Reformed Christians. Sociology serves to clarify the changing structures of societal life to which Reformed Christians seek to apply the law of love and justice. Sociology is a modern-day extension of the sort of social analysis that Calvin himself conducted as part of advocating a civic order that served the common good. It is another opportunity for the transformationist impulse to be put into practice. In this case, the transformationists seek a sociology integrally related to glorifying God by thinking Christianly. To think and live Christianly here is to relate Christ's Lordship to social reality. For Christians, this is a calling worthy of our lives.

But how can Christians take what they know of Christ's Lordship and of societal structures and bring about authentically Christian social analysis? That is the topic of the last chapter.

NOTES

1. William J. Bouwsma, *John Calvin: A Sixteenth-Century Portrait* (New York: Oxford University Press, 1988); W. Fred Graham, *The Constructive Revolutionary: John Calvin and His Socioeconomic Impact* (Atlanta, GA: John Knox, 1971); Alexandre Ganoczy, *The Young Calvin* (Philadelphia, PA: Westminster Press, 1987); John T. McNeill, *The History and Character of Calvinism* (New York: Oxford University Press, 1954).
2. The following section is heavily indebted to Graham, *The Constructive Revolutionary*.
3. Graham, *The Constructive Revolutionary*, p. 158.
4. Karl Barth's *Knowledge of God and the Service of God* (London: Hodder and Stoughton, 1938), pp. 219–239, and *Against the Stream* (New York: Philosophical Library, 1954), "The Christian Community and the Civil Community," are excellent, succinct statements of his theology of the state and the church.
5. Barth, *Knowledge of God*, p. 221.
6. Barth, *Against the Stream*, pp. 15, 22–23.
7. Barth, *Knowledge of God*, p. 221.
8. John D. Godsey, ed., *Karl Barth's Table Talk* (London: Oliver and Boyd, 1963), p. 75.
9. Barth, *Against the Stream*, p. 30.
10. John Howard Yoder, in *Karl Barth and the Problem of War* (Nashville, TN: Abingdon Press, 1970), pp. 50, 125, notes the important distinction in Barth between the *gerechte Staat* ("just state") and the *Rechtstaat* ("justice state").
11. Nicholas Wolterstorff's *Until Justice and Peace Embrace* (Grand Rapids, MI: Eerdmans, 1983) offers a fine example of a Reformed theology blended with sociological world systems analysis to suggest priorities for Christian transformational action.
12. This chart is based on Jack Balswick and J. K. Morland, *Social Problems*, p. 314. What this chart adds is the action of seeking occupational positions that provide societal leverage for effecting certain sorts of social change.

Chapter 17

BLENDING SOCIOLOGY AND FAITH

Most people have heard the old question: How do porcupines mate? Answer: very carefully. How does one get two feisty fields of intellectual practice and moral commitment like sociology and Christian faith together? Very carefully.

The first part of this book described some of the touchy relationships between sociology and faith. Nonetheless, using sociology and its careful distinctions showed why that tension is high and what it means. This relationship, however, can be far more positive than is often thought possible. But how? What possibilities and models exist for bringing the two more closely together?

Faith Made Cozy with Sociology

Pulling off a relationship between sociology and Christian faith is like planning an intercultural, interreligious wedding. The two families involved bring very different ideas about what to do. They are likely to disagree over where to hold the service and even its content. What to do about the reception, who's to pay, what sort of music and decorations—even what dances or whether to dance at all—may be up for grabs.

Strategies to set up an ongoing interrelationship between Christian faith and sociology are not uniform. Some even say that such a relationship should never occur. The following sections review a few of the major designs for faith snuggling up to sociology—or not, as the case may be.

King of the Mountain

There are some who see this matter as beyond reasonable hope. The differences are so great and the issues so important that all there can be is total warfare between "science and faith." This is the king-of-the-mountain game plan.

The attitude is simple. Each side says, "The only truth that exists belongs to me. All others must submit to me." This makes the quest for social knowledge like a gladiatorial contest where only one wins. We think it can be more like a white-water rafting adventure. In that experience, success means that everyone survives the dangerous waters and reaches safety together.

Some professional sociologists with strong value commitments to modernity see the issue in terms of intellectual warfare. Readers may even meet some of them in the classroom. We have. They use their professional authority to put faith down and to ridicule it. This book has stated our reasons for concluding that such an attitude is beyond the competence of sociology as a *science*. Such hostility comes from strongly felt, deeply rooted boundary mechanisms of modern sociology when allied with the symbolic universe of modernity. This attitude is not intrinsic to the discipline. Healthy sociology can thrive with robust faith as it has in the past and continues to do so in the present.

Readers must not let such sociologists intimidate them. Christian faith has too much to offer.

Some well-meaning but ill-informed Christians see the matter in a similar way, though they seek the defeat of sociology. The quicker people rid themselves of sociology, the better off all will be in the modern world. Sociology is nothing but pure secular humanism and that's that. When C. Wright Mills was a student at the University of Texas in Austin, a story circulated of a wealthy lady. She said, "I can't stand the University of Texas. It's full of sociology and sodobottomy."[1] She felt that sociology had so many false premises that nothing good could come of it. The choice must be faith or sociology.

Readers must not let such Christians intimidate them. Sociology has too much to offer.

This attitude perpetuates a false image of the possibilities for positive relationships between truths present in both sociology and Christian faith. Modern humans are in a small raft hurtling through rough rapids. They need the strength, insight, and gifts of both faith and science. How else are they to navigate their way to a new century more humane and equitable than the one that is shortly to end? Social orders are splitting at the seams. The track record so far shows how the modern world is incapable of constructing a just and peaceful international order.

Both faith and sociology say that they are after truth and justice in this world. Until one has clear and compelling evidence to the contrary, one ought to credit both with their stated intentions. Then one ought to get on with seeing what is true in each. There are more fruitful ways of developing their relationship than turning them into sweaty behemoths, breathing out death for the other, fighting to the bitter end.

The Freezer Treatment

Merely affirming the prospect of a positive relationship does not create one. For that to happen, people have to see how, where, and why sociology and faith offer benefit to each other.

When one first begins thinking about these issues, he or she often finds many puzzles and uncertainties. Rather than prematurely pasting the two together, one reasonable strategy is to suspend the process of interrelation. We call this the freezer treatment. This means that these matters are stored in an intellectual refrigerator until a recipe can be found for incorporating them into one's overall thinking. People do this because they believe the two ought to be blended but they need time to find the right recipe for doing so.

This is what humans often do when they begin a journey into any new arena of knowledge. They focus on making sure that they understand the knowledge claims made in the field. They need to know how strong the field's conclusions are. What sorts of evidence support these conclusions? What holes can various critics poke in the considered judgments of its scholarship? Until one understands the area's claims, it is difficult to say how they relate to similar claims made by other disciplines and approaches. So, temporarily, one does not let the issues heat up.

Furthermore, all Christians and sociologists have matters that remain puzzles, even after much research and thought. They do not fully understand the relevance or significance of certain Christian formulations for sociology. Or how particular findings and assumptions in sociology bear on Christian thought and practice. So for the present they hold these ideas in temporary suspension, outside a well-considered integration or network of concepts that incorporates these formulations and findings coherently.

However, at some point, connections must be made and the relationship negotiated. Intellectual schizophrenia is not very comfortable for thoughtful people. Christian sociologists must follow some strategy of bringing sociological and faith elements into a single whole. At times what may hold them together is a set of principles that actually keep them apart in a particular way. We now turn to some of the patterns that Christian scholars use.

The Tossed-Salad Approach

Once in a while, a work that strives to relate faith and learning does not manifest a coherent, consistent, or clear pattern of relationship. Such books illustrate a procedure that is very much like making a tossed salad. What's crucial is the quality of the ingredients and the brilliance of the chef doing the mixing.

Several ingredients are pulled out of the intellectual refrigerator. These are clearly distinct and separate ingredients from sociology and faith. All the ingredients are important to the finished product. A little of each ingredient is chopped and mixed with the others according to the taste of the particular chef. The recipe varies from occasion to occasion.

Some make a virtue of this way of handling faith-learning integration. They agree with T. S. Eliot that the only real method in science is that of being very intelligent. They make paramount the existential reality of the scientist doing science. They say that the various models of the scientific method are con games played by scientific professions to impress the naive and uninitiated. Actually, science is a mysterious, personal reality that moves forward more through nonrational, creative explosions of insight than on the basis of carefully patterned models. The real keys are human genius and creativity, not some formula or canned procedure and method.

While there is truth in this, it is not very satisfactory as an account of science. Although genius and creativity definitely can make a contribution, to emphasize them exclusively overstates the importance of the scientist in science and in relating science and faith. Instead, methods and strategies for relating differing elements of thought do play a significant role. This is especially true in validating and justifying the creative insights of genius, whether from the science or faith side of matters. Models that suggest patterned ways of relating faith and science help spell out possible ways of linking various intellectual components.

The specific mixtures of faith and learning displayed in "tossed salads" pay dividends if reflected on, especially when the mixture is particularly well made. Others wishing to relate their faith and learning will want to know how to create such a mixture. There are a number of systematic recipes developed and used by Christian thinkers for relating faith and learning. These strategies may even suggest ways to relate Christian faith specifically to the sociological imagination.

The Horse-and-Carriage Model

The first of these strategies sees faith and sociology as complementary yet clearly distinct matters. What's important is not confusing or confounding the one with the other. Otherwise, there will be many days on which the intellectual journey gets nowhere because the cart is put before the horse. Sociology and theology simply accomplish different intellectual goals. There are at least two versions of why this strategy is important.

By one account, sociology and theology differ because their objects of study are different. Sociology studies human beings. Theology studies God. Sociology deals with something purely empirical and public. Theology deals with the transcendent, with revelation and information knowable only within a relationship of trust with God.

An alternative account says that sociology and theology offer completely different angles of vision on the same object of study. Sociology looks at society from a scientific, factual, empirical angle. Theology looks at it from a metaphysical, value-oriented, normative angle. Their differences have to do with the typical things that each can and cannot say about the same object—in this case, social worlds. Sociology describes the way that they *are*; theology describes the way that they *ought to be*. Sociology provides a human view of social arrangements. Theology provides a divine view.

What is important to realize, says this strategy, is that this is not an either-or but a both-and situation. Faith and learning do not genuinely conflict any more than a horse and carriage do. What is needed is to hitch the horse properly to the carriage. The two together will carry humans and their baggage to destinations they could not easily reach on foot. Each accomplishes a different yet valid task. Too often people consider difference to be deficiency. Once differences are recognized as enhancing each other, then the question boils down to how the two can properly be connected.

The simplest linkage is through a *division of labor*. Sociology provides a description of social processes and problems—their nature, frequency, social and psychological consequences. Theology provides a framework of ideals and values in terms of which one can construct a Christian response to these social processes. Sociology offers "facts," and theology offers the "values" for deciding whether to affirm a set of social arrangements or fight for a different set.

This is a very common design for interrelating sociology and faith.[2] The problems with this strategy are the same as those found in the traditional gulf created by the Enlightenment between "facts" and "values." It is painfully evident now that "facts" and "values" have many more important and valid connections in human thinking than is represented by a clear division of labor. Science entails certain values and does not operate without faith assumptions. Conversely, biblical materials provide more than "values." They provide some critical facts that shape the way in which Christians think about social realities. This strategy is too simplistic to handle the full job of relating faith and learning. But there are alternatives to this pattern for harnessing the horse of theology to the carriage of sociology.

Some link them on the basis of *levels of analysis*. Any reality can be described exhaustively from several "levels"—the atomic, the molecular, the biological, the psychological, the sociological, the cultural, and the theological. A description at one level does not exclude description and analysis at another level. So the sociological occurs at one level (the scientific). The theological offers a different level of analysis (the religious). They neither exclude nor include each other. A full understanding requires various levels of analysis and description.

A common danger of this approach is reductionism. Durkheim was especially wary of this danger. Some call it, as noted in Chapter Ten, "nothing-buttery." Here a discipline enhances its contribution by saying, for example, "Mental functioning is *nothing but* the electrical activity of the brain." Or "The laws of social processes are *nothing but* the operation of psychological laws in millions of human relationships." This reduces one level of description and analysis to another, denying the validity and importance of (usually) the higher level.

Sociology's tendency is to say that religious phenomena are *nothing but* the operation of social and psychological principles in human affairs. Reductionism of this sort makes Christians wary of sociological analysis. Conversely, some Christians think that the supernatural activity of God precludes and excludes the operating of natural processes. So creation is nothing but the activity of God and excludes the millions and billions of years of change discussed in geology and physics. Or conversion is nothing but the action of the Holy Spirit. Such Christians exclude any valid analysis of the sociological or psychological influences used by the Spirit to bring a person to new life in Christ.

A third way of hitching them to each other is by *the dialectical pattern*. In this case, the relationship is paradoxical and multivalent (having many determinants). Linking the two together is not a simple or tensionless matter. Often the language of the two overlaps, but they may be saying very different things about the same realities. Both deal with the issues of human freedom and determinism, with relativism and absolutism, with the relationship of the individual to the community. Tying them together using a dialectical link means that both, even when paradoxical or apparently contradictory, are needed for the full understanding of reality. Jacques Ellul is the best-known proponent of this strategy.

The confrontation between the findings and conclusions of the two fields stimulates insights and intellectual currents that one could not have without both of them. But they can never be integrated, merged, or harmonized. They remain separate endeavors, dynamically confronting each other and setting off new explorations in their respective areas. It is foolish to think we can do without one or the other or can finally merge them together in an integrated, neat intellectual system.

The danger of the dialectical pattern is the tendency to keep the two separate instead of seeking appropriate ways of integrating and blending the two. Scripture portrays the human as intrinsically social, created in relationship with God, with fellow humans, and with the environment. Only in that set of relations is life full and rich. Sociology couldn't agree more. It spells out the ways in which the ensemble of social relationships helps create the human personality. So there are places where there is not dialectical paradox and confrontation but agreement. Dialectical linkage may work for some issues but not as a general rule of thumb.

The Somebody's-Got-to-Be-in-Charge Position

Some conclude that the relationship between faith and sociology cannot work unless one of the partners is in charge. How else, they say, can the apparent conflicts be resolved? Usually, down deep, there is more confidence in one intellectual discipline than the other. Proponents of this strategy don't want to risk in the relationship anything that they hold important.

Those more confident in sociology make it the central authority for social knowledge. Whatever faith says can be accepted so long as it agrees with sociology. For others, Christian faith is in the cockpit. They accept sociology only so far as it clearly reinforces and agrees with faith. Whichever field is the boss sets the terms of the relationship, including the grounds for admitting truth into the overall intellectual scheme. The controlling partner decides which elements are unchallengeable in the discussion between the two.

There is validity to this strategy. Both sociology and faith have strongly established centers that are widely shared in their respective arenas. It would take enormous intellectual work, evidence, and argumentation to convince a Christian that Jesus Christ is not the incarnate Son of God, the Lord of the universe and Savior of the world. The biblical data and two thousand years of theological debate and development make this the central conclusion of Christian faith.

Similarly, some elements in sociology are so firmly demonstrated and interwoven into every school of social thought that they are virtually nonnegotiable. That humans are cultural creatures capable of concocting an almost infinite number of cultural worlds is a truism to sociologists. The empirical evidence for this is overwhelming. It would require a monumental refutation to change sociological minds on this matter.

This is not to say in either case that these central convictions are not given different "spins" in the various paradigms of sociology and theology. Most certainly they are. Yet it must be recognized that both fields have centers and circumferences. The farther out one moves from the center, the more debatable and debated are the knowledge claims. One cannot expect disciplines to risk their centers in relating to other fields in the same way they risk perimeters that are already under dispute within the discipline.

Setting up a controlling or paramount partner facilitates several matters. It determines which partner carries the burden of proof. A burden of proof has to do with who is presumed correct when issues cannot be settled decisively in an authentic dispute between the partners. The process of reaching a verdict is very different in a legal system where the prisoner is considered *innocent until proven guilty* as contrasted with legal systems where a prisoner is considered *guilty until proven innocent*. By establishing a paramount partner, the system shifts the hard work of proving the case to the weaker partner. It settles in a one-sided fashion the question of who has to prove the case and by what criteria.

In some ways, integrating faith and learning cannot dispense with this tendency. There are matters on which the Christian sociologist is willing to give the benefit of the doubt to faith and other matters where this benefit goes to sociology. After all, the Gospels are first-century eyewitness accounts of the life, ministry, death, and resurrection of Jesus Christ. They are the best evidence that people have of what Jesus was like. Sociological speculations about him are not on the same level as the evidence of the contemporary testimony contained in the Gospels.

Similarly, sociology has a treasure house of information on industrial societies as well as on the processes and consequences of modernization. The Bible is silent about this particular form and period of social reality. It would simply be unreasonable to overturn sociology on those matters due to some particular interpretation of Christian faith.

The danger in this model is that of intellectual imperialism. This happens when the stronger partner arbitrarily vetoes or neglects authentic truth from the subordinate partner. The tendency of this sort of model, when taken by itself, is to neglect the other field as not significant *in practice*. After all, if faith describes everything that is really essential about society, why bother with sociology? Or if sociology provides the real story about society, why bother doing all the work necessary to tease social truth out of the Bible? Won't it just echo sociology? So even here there are problems in developing a recipe for mixing sociology and faith in all matters and settings.

A Partnership for Truth

A final strategy thinks of the two as dialogue partners in a long-term conversation whose goal is to express the truth about social reality. What each will say, how loudly, where each might probe and challenge the other—these things are not predictable. Not until the interaction occurs will it be clear what sorts of issues divide the two. Only then does one discover problems in translating terminology between the two. Only then does one see styles of thinking that must be reconciled for good communication. Moreover, one cannot forecast what the two will come up with as a fuller expression of the truth that both seek.

The partnership model considers the linking to be complex without one discipline (in principle and in all arenas) being superior to the other. The relationship is more like a dialogue between equal partners in which one may be more competent to speak on a specific issue than the other. Yet both continue to test and extend their own insights. They mutually correct each other. The burden of proof rests equally with both except where a clear, special competence is involved.

In cases of conflict, the options for settling disputes are multiple and not predetermined by a prior relational rule. The interpretations of either science or faith may be wrong. Both may be wrong, or both may be partly right. There is no automatic conclusion that conflict is to be resolved in favor of one or the other. Neither science nor given accounts of Christian faith are taken as absolute. Both are interpretative narratives that are not comprehensive or complete within their own disciplines.

The working hypothesis of partnership is that continued discourse will clarify how the two knowledge projects together can build a more complete picture than either does alone. The major premise is that God's truth in the Bible and the truth of social realities are compatible, even when that compatibility is not always immediately obvious. The partners must *work out* how what the Bible says about humans and their societies relates to what is developed empirically and theoretically in sociology. They must *spell out* how what sociology says relates to biblical truth.

The authors of this book engage sociology as Christians in terms of this last model. We believe that Christian faith and sociology make good partners, in spite of the arguments and differences that pop up between them. We like the advantage of disciplined eclecticism that the partnership model allows. This keeps the conversation going while both partners get on with extending and clarifying their respective bodies of knowledge.

Sometimes we put a question (and suggested answers to it) into our intellectual refrigerators until more work and evidence accumulate. Sometimes we link the descriptive treasures of sociology to the evaluative wisdom of faith, as though they were horse and carriage. Occasionally, we discover a brilliantly stimulating analysis in which there is no clear recipe other than the penetrating insight of the author-chef. Then we work away to figure out why this is such a valuable piece of work and how we might incorporate it into our own thinking and methods.

In this model, the partners, without being empty-headed or uncommitted, are willing to live with the messiness of a continuing, open-ended conversation. This strategy allows sociology and faith to continue to relate without having all the terms of the relationship settled up front. This is also one of its weaknesses. It permits and tolerates more confusion and less settling of accounts than is often warranted. So it feels like it is always on the way to truth without ever arriving.

In sum, there are a variety of ways to connect sociology with faith. We do not believe that mortal conflict is the real story of this relationship. Nor do we need to settle for an idiosyncratic product based on the taste of particular authors. There are good recipes for blending the two. We commend and enjoy the flexibility of the partnership model. Its disciplined eclecticism means that we can include and use several of the other strategies in the service of an overall search for social truth. We believe that we must acknowledge the centers of both fields in this conversation. Each ought to feel secure enough in its more settled and well-established truths that it doesn't have to prejudge the correctness of the other field of knowledge.

Besides, the point of all this is not the settling of the absolute truth for all time about social affairs. The point is to blend as much as one knows well in sociology with as much as one knows well in Christian faith. This is a lifelong task, especially since one must also embody what is true in the way humans live.

We are not alone in thinking this a worthy and important partnership. The excitement and challenge of linking Christian faith and sociology appear in the lives of a number of great sociologists. The next section introduces a few of them. Sometime we hope you will get a chance to learn from them by reading their writings or even hearing them speak.

Faith Active in Sociology Through Love

Chapter Seven quoted Charles Beard as saying that, as complex as physics might be, sociology is even more complex. This is because sociology includes the physicist as well as physics and all the other things that humans have thought and done. Yet there is something more complex than sociology. It is thinking Christianly about sociology, because this includes not only all that sociology encompasses but all that Christian faith entails as well.

From the very beginning, modern social science has had out-standing scholars who have found ways to do sociology while living out their Christian faith. Some are historically important figures such as Giambattista Vico and Frédéric Le Play. Others are contemporaries whose writings and activity are at the forefront in modern sociology. They too identify themselves as Christians. Some of them work within a school of Christian theological commitment that is different from our own evangelical tradition. Not all of them link their Christian faith and sociology in the way that we do. Nor do we always agree with their own assessments of where their linkage succeeds. Nevertheless, they have much to teach about the difficulties and the value of seeking to be whole persons as Christians who practice sociology.

Frédéric Le Play (1806–1882) was a staunch Roman Catholic, royalist, and conservative in nineteenth-century France.[3] A first-rate mind, he was head of the government committee on mining statistics in 1835 and professor of metallurgy and subdirector of the École des Mines in 1840. He even ran mines in Russia with forty-five thousand employees.

Yet he is best known as author of the first major empirical sociological work, a monstrous six-volume work called *The European Workers* (1855). The Académie des Sciences of France celebrated his work. A professional association was formed to continue his empirical study of families and occupation. The monographic case study method that he developed continues, with some refinements, to be widely used for understanding families and social problems.

Albion Small (1854–1926), a lifelong Baptist, grew up in Maine. His undergraduate education followed in the footsteps of his Baptist minister father. He took degrees from Colby College and Newton Theological Seminary. He did graduate work in Germany at Berlin and Leipzig. Between 1880 and 1881, Small studied at the British Museum before returning to the United States in 1882.

Small played a major role in the training of a whole genera-tion of sociologists. He is best known for his pivotal role in institutionalizing sociology in American university life. He headed the first graduate department of sociology in the world, located at the University of Chicago. It developed the most influential early paradigm in American sociology. In 1895 he founded the *American Journal of Sociology* and edited it for the next thirty years. It was the only U.S. journal in the field until 1921. In 1894, with George E. Vincent, he published the first systematic textbook in sociology. Small also helped found the American Sociological Society in 1905 and served as its president in 1912–1913. He was the first to translate the works of Georg Simmel, a German sociologist, into English. At Small's initiative, Max Weber took his one and only trip to America.[4]

Not all Christians who helped originate modern sociology are as well known as Le Play and Small. Norwegians consider Eilert Sundt (1817–1875) to be their first sociologist.[5] He graduated in theology from King Fredericks University (now the University of Oslo). Ordained in the Norwegian State Lutheran Church in 1846, he did not serve a parish until the last five years of his life. His adult life focused on social research that sought to clarify the situation of the poor, both in the countryside and in the slums of Oslo. He was the first to receive research money in sociology in Norway. His Christian faith motivated his seeking knowledge essential for solving the persistent problems brought by modernization.

There are also some well-known contemporary Christian sociologists. One is the best-selling contemporary author, Robert N. Bellah (1927–).[6] He is Elliott Professor of Sociology at the University of California in Berkeley. He was raised, as he puts it, "among the fragments of a once-coherent, southern Protestant culture." Bellah was a regular attender of a conservative Presbyterian church as he grew up, but he drifted from faith until recently. During the last decade or so, Bellah has become active in the Episcopal church. He preaches occasionally and now sees his vocation as bringing his intellectual training into relationship with his faith in a way that can speak to other people.[7]

Bellah's writings are well known, having been at the center of several important debates in recent sociology. *Beyond Belief* received national recognition by the National Book Awards. Bellah's paper entitled "Civil Religion in America"generated a small industry of analysis of civil religion in America that continues unabated.[8] *Broken Covenant*, which also dealt with civil religion, was given the Sorokin Award of the American Sociological Association. *Habits of the Heart* is the best-selling book ever published by the University of California Press. It touched off a national debate over the nature of American values and public policy.

The Lutheran Peter Berger was born in Vienna in 1929, the son of a businessman.[9] His secondary education was completed in England. He emigrated to the United States in 1946, attending Wagner Memorial Lutheran College on Staten Island and completing a major in philosophy. At one time, his vocational plans were to be a Lutheran pastor. Instead, he entered the New School for Social Research in New York and became one of the best-known contemporary sociologists. He now occupies a chair of sociology at Boston University.

He describes himself as both a humanist and a Christian (albeit a "heretical" or liberal Christian sociologist). His specialties have been the sociology of knowledge and the study of modernity. He draws on phenomenological sociology to show how everyday life-world knowledge affects and is affected by the structures of the society in which people live. More than most sociologists until recently, his concern is to connect the microworld of the individual with the macroworlds of large-scale social realities. His writings on modernity, modern capitalism, and the ethics of development are widely read as an important voice in the debate over the nature of industrial order (or disorder).

Jacques Ellul (1912–) may be the best-known sociologist among American evangelicals. His long, distinguished career at the University of Bordeaux in France made him an internationally respected theorist on technology and technique as the central forces in modern life. His book, *The Technological Society* (1964), remains a classic extension of Max Weber's notion of rationalization. His key concept is *technique*, by which he means the totality of methods rationally arrived at and having absolute efficiency for a given stage of development. The book is an exhaustive litany of the nature of and ways in which technique forms the fabric and environment of the modern world.

His childhood poverty shaped his outlook and life choices. First Marx and then Christ provided him with the tools necessary to seize the puzzles of his world and make sense of them. He describes his lifework as one of counterpoint. His writing is a dialectic between an ever-deepening sociological awareness and an ever-expanding biblical and theological meditation on the fallen world that humans inhabit. Often he will write a sociological study and later match it with a theological or biblical partner. The one sets forth what is socially real; the other, the spiritual meaning and context of that human reality. Although he is now a retired professor, he continues to add to his forty books and more than one thousand articles.[10]

Onward, Christian Sociologists

This chapter notes common strategies for linking sociology and faith. It has also introduced a few Christian sociologists. There are many more: Robert Wuthnow of Princeton University, Richard Perkins of Houghton College, Margaret Paloma of the University of Akron, David O. Moberg of Marquette University, Russell Heddendorf of Covenant College, Michael Leming of Saint Olaf College, Andrew Greeley of the National Opinion Research Center and the University of Arizona, Zondra Lindblade and Alan Neives of Wheaton College, Thomas Hood of the University of Tennessee, Sister Marie Augusta Neal of Emmanuel College in Boston, Ronald J. Burwell of Messiah College, George Hillery, Jr., of Virginia Polytechnic Institute and State University, Ruth Wallace of George Washington University in Washington D.C.,

David Lyon of Queen's University, Kingston, Canada, and hundreds more.

Many Christian sociologists participate in associations seeking the interlinking of sociology and faith. The Christian Sociological Society includes hundreds of North American sociologists and exists "to give witness to Jesus Christ in sociological areas." The Association of Christians Teaching Sociology meets annually to discuss issues of faith-science integration. How much still needs careful thought and exploration! This is one of many places where the laborers are few while the task is both immense and important.

It is our sincere hope that some students of sociology, reading this text, will hear God calling them to the sociological profession. There is yet so much to learn and understand about society. So much cries out for intelligent, compassionate social change. So many people need to experience more of God's abundant life. Christians in sociology can help make these things happen.

NOTES

1. Irving L. Horowitz, *C. Wright Mills: An American Utopian* (New York: Free Press, 1983), p. 18.
2. Balswick and Morland, in *Social Problems: A Christian Understanding and Response*, use this approach.
3. Le Play, *The Organization of Labor* (Philadelphia, PA: Claxton, 1872); "Le Play" in Carl Zimmerman and Merle Frampton, *Family and Society* (Princeton, NJ: Van Nostrand, 1935); selections from *European Workers*, pp. 359–595; P. F. Lazarsfeld, "Notes in the History of Quantification in Sociology: Trends, Sources, and Problems," *ISIS* 52, no. 2 (1961): 277–333; Terry N. Clark, *Prophets and Patrons: The French University and the Emergence of the Social Sciences* (Cambridge, MA: Harvard University Press, 1973), pp. 104–116.
4. Small's major writings include *The Beginnings of American Nationality* (Baltimore: Johns Hopkins, 1890); *An Introduction to the Study of Society*, with George Vincent (New York: American Book Co., 1894); *Some Undeveloped Resources in Christian Revelation* (Chicago: University of Chicago Press, 1898); *General Sociology* (Chicago: University of Chicago Press, 1905); *The Cameralists* (Chicago: University of Chicago Press, 1909); *The Meaning of Social Science* (Chicago: University of Chicago Press, 1910); *Between Eras: From Capitalism to Democracy* (Kansas City, MO: Inter-Collegiate Press, 1913);

"Fifty Years of Sociology in the United States (1865–1915)," *American Journal of Sociology* 21 (1916): 721–864; *The Origin of Sociology* (Chicago: University of Chicago Press, 1924).

5. Priscilla Reinertsen, "Report of a Sociological Pioneer: Eilert Sundt," *Journal of the History of the Behavioral Sciences* 6 (October 1969): 360–364.

6. Bellah, *Tokugawa Religion: The Values of Preindustrial Japan* (New York: Free Press, 1957); "Research Chronicle: Tokugawa Religion," in Philip Hammond, ed., *Sociologists at Work* (New York: Basic Books, 1964); *Beyond Belief: Essays on Religion in a Posttraditional World* (New York: Harper & Row, 1970); *The Broken Covenant: American Civil Religion in a Time of War* (1975); *The New Religious Consciousness*, ed. with Charles Y. Glock (Berkeley: University of California Press, 1976); *Varieties of Civil Religion*, ed. with Philip Hammond (New York: Harper & Row, 1980); *Habits of the Heart: Individualism and Commitment in American Life*, with Richard Madsen, William M. Sullivan, Ann Swidler, and Steven M. Tipton (Berkeley: University of California Press, 1985); *Uncivil Religion: Interreligious Hostility in America*, ed. with Frederick E. Greenspahn (New York: Crossroad, 1987).

7. Bellah, "Christian Faithfulness in a Pluralist World," in Frederic B. Burnham, *Postmodern Theology: Christian Faith in a Pluralist World* (New York: Harper & Row, 1989), pp. 74–91.

8. *Daedalus*, 96 (1967): 1–21.

9. Berger, *The Noise of Solemn Assemblies* (New York: Doubleday, 1961); *The Precarious Vision* (New York: Doubleday, 1961); *Invitation to Sociology* (New York: Doubleday, 1963); *The Social Construction of Reality*, with Thomas Luckmann (New York: Doubleday, 1966); *The Sacred Canopy* (New York: Doubleday, 1967); *The Rumor of Angels: Modern Society and the Rediscovery of the Supernatural* (New York: Doubleday, 1969); *Sociology: A Biographical Approach*, with Brigitte Berger (New York: Basic Books, 1972); *The Homeless Mind*, with Brigitte Berger and Hansfried Kellner (New York: Vintage, 1973); *Pyramids of Sacrifice* (New York: Doubleday, 1974); *Facing Up to Modernity* (New York: Basic Books, 1977); *To Empower People: The Role of Mediating Structures in Public Policy*, with Richard John Neuhaus (New York: American Enterprise Institute, 1977); *The Heretical Imperative* (New York: Doubleday, 1979); ed., *The Other Side of God* (New York: Doubleday, 1980); *Sociology Reinterpreted*, with Hansfried Kellner (New York: Doubleday, 1981); *The Capitalist Revolution: Fifty Propositions About Prosperity, Equality, and Liberty* (New York: Basic Books, 1986).

10. To mention a few: *The Presence of the Kingdom* (New York: Seabury, 1951); *The Technological Society* (New York: Vintage, 1964); *The Political Illusion* (New York: Vintage, 1967); *Violence* (New York: Seabury, 1969); *Prayer and Modern Man* (New York: Seabury, 1970); *Propaganda* (New York: Knopf, 1971); *The Politics of God and the Politics of Man* (Grand Rapids, MI: Eerdmans, 1972); *The New Demons* (New York: Seabury, 1975); *The Ethics of Freedom* (Grand Rapids, MI: Eerdmans, 1976); *The Technological System* (New York: Continuum, 1980); *Perspectives on Our Age* (New York: Seabury, 1981); *Jesus and Marx* (Grand Rapids, MI: Eerdmans, 1988); *The Technological Bluff* (Grand Rapids, MI: Eerdmans, 1990); *Reason for Being: A Meditation on Ecclesiastes* (Grand Rapids, MI: Eerdmans, 1990).

SCRIPTURE INDEX

Genesis 67; **1:26–27,** 251; **1:28–30,** 252; **2,** 82; **2:25,** 259; **6:22,** 258; **10,** 204–6; **10:1–11:9,** 204–10; **11:1–9,** 82, 206–10; **12:1,** 194; **15:18,** 258; **17:7–9,** 258

Exodus **12,** 197; **19:5–6,** 195; **21:24,** 197

Leviticus **19:19,** 197; **24:20,** 197; **25:1–55,** 197

Deuteronomy **6:5,** 197; **7:6,** 194; **10:17–18,** 197; **15:1–18,** 197; **15:7–11,** 197; **31:10ff,** 197

Ruth, 180; **1:16–17,** 180

I Samuel **16:7,** 249

II Samuel **7,** 258

II Chronicles **16:9,** 249

Ezra, 181

Nehemiah, 181; **9:7,** 194

Psalms **19:5–7,** 67; **87,** 196; **103:19,** 264; **145:11,** 264

Proverbs **6:16–19,** 249

Isaiah **11:9–10,** 195; **44:1, 21,** 195; **45:21–24,** 195; **52:7,** 264; **65:17,** 183

Hosea **2:13,** 238; **7:1,** 238; **10:4,** 238; **12:1,** 238

Amos **2:6–7,** 238; **3:2,** 196; **4:4–5,** 238; **9:13–15,** 183

Jonah, 195–96

Micah **6:8,** 238

Matthew **4:8,** 185; **4:17,** 264; **6:24,** 188; **7:3–5,** 13; **12:28,** 249; **12:48–50,** 261; **19:1–12,** 203; **19:19,** 262; **22:23–32,** 203; **24:21,** 184; **25,** 286–88; **25:45,** 198

Mark **1:15,** 264; **10:30,** 183

Luke, 264; **4:43,** 264; **10:25–37,** 262; **11:20,** 249; **11:50,** 184; **12:11,** 187; **16:9, 11,** 188; **19:12,** 264; **22:29,** 264; **23:42,** 264

John **1:1,** 82; **3:36,** 183; **18:36,** 264

Acts **2,** 182, 209; **8:12,** 264; **15,** 179, 182, 198; **17:24,** 184; **28:23,** 264

Romans **1:20,** 184; **1:25,** 183; **8:18–25,** 186; **8:38,** 187; **9:5,** 194; **12:2,** 183; **13,** 188, 282; **13:1,** 187; **13:1–7,** 282; **14,** 182, 198

I Corinthians **2:6,** 183; **7:8–9,** 27, 29, 32–35, 204; **9,** 198

II Corinthians **4:4,** 183

Galatians, 198; **1:5,** 183; **2:22,** 186; **3:28–29,** 198; **6:10,** 261

Ephesians **2:1–2,** 185; **5:21–6:9,** 199–201; **6:12,** 187

Colossians **1:16,** 187; **1:20,** 187; **2:8,** 186; **2:14–15,** 187; **2:15,** 183; **2:20,** 186; **3:18–4:1,** 199

I Timothy **1:17,** 183; **5:3,** 261

Titus **2:12,** 183; **3:3,** 187

Hebrews **4:3,** 184; **5:12,** 186

I Peter **1:20,** 184; **2:13–3:7,** 199; **3:22,** 187

II Peter **3:10–13,** 186

I John **2:15–17,** 185

Jude, **25,** 183

Revelation **7:9–10,** 210; **13,** 188, 284; **15:3,** 183; **17:12,** 264; **21–22,** 257; **21:24, 26,** 210

NAME INDEX

Abbot, Andrew, 48, 61n
Adler, Mortimer, 236–37
Althaus, Paul, 235n
Anselm, 5
Arendt, Hannah, 62, 78n
Aristotle, 53, 78n, 105
Augustine, 10n, 226

Bacon, Francis, 3–5
Bahr, Howard M., 20
Balswick, Jack and Judith, 257–63, 269n, 289n
Bannister, Roger, xxiin
Barrett, David, 75, 190n
Barth, Karl, 280–84, 289n
Barth, Markus, 211n
Baumer, Franklin L., xxiin
Beard, Charles, 109, 302
Bellah, Robert N., 44n, 61n, 304–5, 308n
Berger, Peter, 32–33, 39, 44n, 61n, 86, 100n, 305, 307n
Berger, Brigitte, 44n, 61n
Boas, Franz, 123, 125–26, 129, 134, 136
Bonald, Louis de, 192
Bright, John, 211n, 269n
Brueggemann, Walter, 209, 211n
Bruner, F. Dale, 265–67, 269n

Calvin, John, 78n, 150–51, 271–80, 288
Campanella, Tommaso, 193
Caplow, Theodore, 20, 137n

Chadwick, Bruce A., 20
Chesterton, G. K., 255
Cohn, Ronald, 83–84
Coleman, James S., 100n
Comte, Auguste, 16–17, 18, 23, 41, 46, 140–41, 161
Confucius, 61n
Constantine, 231
Cooper, John W., 246–48, 254n
Cox, Harvey, 41–42, 44n

Davenport, Charles, 127
Dayton, Donald W., 211n
Degler, Carl N., 137n
Descartes, René, 63
Douglas, Mary, 1, 10n
Durkheim, Émile, 18, 111–13, 124, 132, 138, 145–48, 151, 162, 296

Elias, Norbert, 44n
Eliot, T. S., 294
Ellingsen, Mark, 100n
Ellul, Jacques, 297, 305–6, 308n

Fee, Gordon D., 211n
Finley, M. I., 177, 190n
Flew, Anthony, 137n
Frazer, Sir James, 124
Freeman, Derek, 125–34, 137n

Gaede, Stan D., 239–41, 253n
Galbraith, John Kenneth, 100n
Galileo, xviii, 19, 62, 65, 66

Gallup, George, Jr., 25n
Gans, Herbert, 25n
Gandhi, 223–24
Göhre, Paul, 22
Gottwald, Norman, 211n
Goudzwaard, Bob, 241–45, 253n
Gouldner, Alvin, 61n
Graham, W. Fred, 271, 279, 289n
Grant, Madison, 127

Hall, Douglas, 250–52, 254n
Hall, G. Stanley, 125–26, 129
Hammond, Jeffrey, 100n
Hegel, G. F., 113
Helmreich, William, 26n
Heraclitus, xx
Herskovits, Melville, 130
Hobbes, Thomas, 111
Holmes, Lowell D., 130–32, 137n
Howard, Jane, 136n
Hunt, Morton, 25n

Johnson, Phillip E., 78n
Jones, Sarah, 25n

Kant, Immanuel, 63, 116
Kellner, Hansfried, 44n, 61n
King, Martin Luther, Jr., 223, 233
Klaaren, Eugene M., xxiin
Knorr-Cetina, Karin, 74–75, 78n
Kuhn, Thomas, 105–9, 121n

Ladd, George, 185, 190n, 269n
Ladurie, Emmanuel Le Roy, 44n
Latour, Bruce, 78n
Lawrence, Bruce W., 121n
Le Play, Frédéric, 21, 303, 307n
Lewis, Oscar, 131, 137n
Linden, Eugene, 100n
Lovejoy, Arthur, xxiin
Luckmann, Thomas, 86, 100n
Luther, Martin, 150–51, 226–30, 275, 278
Lynd, Robert S., 137n
Lynd, Helen M., 137n

Machiavelli, 113
MacIntyre, Alasdair, 78n
Malina, Bruce, 248–50, 254n
Martindale, Don, 121n
Marx, Karl, 18, 41, 55, 113–15, 124, 132, 138, 141–45, 148, 153n, 161–62, 214–15
Mazlish, Bruce, xxiin
Mead, George Herbert, 116
Mead, Margaret, 122–37
Merton, Robert K., xxiin, 78n, 95, 100n, 271–72
Michels, Robert, 73, 78n
Mills, C. Wright, 291
Mol, Hans, 25n
Morgan, Gareth, 121n
Morgan, I. Graham, 26n
Morgan, Lewis Henry, 124
Morland, J. Kenneth, 263, 269n, 289n

Müntzer, Thomas, 193
Myrdal, Gunnar, 131

Newbigin, Lesslie, 69, 78n
Newton, Sir Isaac, xvii, 53–54, 107
Niebuhr, H. Richard, 218–22, 230, 235n
Niebuhr, Reinhold, 223
Nietzsche, Friedrich, 116, 237
Nisbet, Robert, 153n

Oberschall, Anthony, 26n

Patterson, Francine, 83–84, 100n
Perdue, William D., 121n
Perkins, Richard, 26n, 306
Peshkin, Alan, 26n
Plato, 111
Polybius, 113

Rauschenbusch, Walter, 223
Redfield, Robert, 131, 137n
Reed, Myer Stratton, Jr., 100n
Reinertsen, Priscilla, 26n
Reinhold, Gottfried, xviii
Ritzer, George, 121n
Ross, Allen P., 211n
Rousseau, Jean-Jacques, 191–92
Runcimann, W. G., 78n, 155–63, 168n, 190n

Schutz, Alfred, 116
Scriven, Charles, 232–34, 235n
Shakespeare, xxiin
Simmel, Georg, 36, 304

Sire, James W., 100n
Small, Albion, 21, 303–4, 307n
Smith, Adam, 55
Spencer, Herbert, 46, 124
Stuart, Douglas, 211n
Sundt, Eilert, 21–22, 304
Swartley, Willard M., 211n

Terrace, Herbert, 84
Tocqueville, Alexis de, 112, 132, 139–40, 159, 161
Tönnies, Ferdinand, 144–47, 161
Toffler, Alvin, 31, 44n
Troeltsch, Ernst, 214–22
Tuiteleleapaga, Napoleone, 126, 130, 135, 137n
Turner, Jonathan, 121n

Van Till, Howard J., 78n
Vico, Giambattista, 17–18, 23, 53, 303

Walter, J. Anthony, 44n, 253n
Weber, Max, 18, 22, 116–18, 132, 138, 148–52, 162, 215, 217, 271, 276, 304, 306
Wenham, Gordon, 211n
Wesley, John, 151
Wesley, Charles, 151
Westermann, Claus, 211n
Whitehead, Alfred North, 62
Wilson, E. O., 67
Wolf, Eric, 211n
Wolfe, Alan, 61n

Wolterstorff, Nicholas, xi–xii, 289n
Wright, Robert, 78n
Wuthnow, Robert, 26n, 96, 100n

Yoder, John Howard, 225, 235n, 289n

Zuckerman, Harriet, 95

SUBJECT INDEX

Aion (The Age to Come), 183–84, 189
Alienation, 37–38, 115, 143–44, 155, 161, 189, 239, 244, 252, 261
American Sociological Association, 304
American Sociological Society, 21
Amish, 216, 224–25, 229, 270
Anabaptist theology of society, 216, 224, 225, 227, 230–34, 270, 274, 284–85, 288
Animals, 82–83, 210, 212n
Anomie, 147–48, 162, 242
Anthropology, 9, 52, 56, 123–36
Archai (Principalities), 187–89, 283–84
Association of Christians Teaching Sociology (ACTS), 307

Bias, 3–6, 16, 60–61, 64–65, 72, 134–35
Bible, 9, 19, 24, 58, 66–67, 163–64, 171–90, 192, 215, 300, 301
Bourgeoisie, 29, 54–55, 105, 142, 242
Bureaucracy, xix, 36, 50, 139–40, 149, 150–51, 162

Calvinist view of society. *See* Reformed theology of society
Capitalism, xviii, 54–55, 115, 141–43, 217, 234, 305
Change: social, xix, 6–8, 16, 27–28, 31, 37, 47, 50, 113, 114, 120, 138–52, 139–40, 154, 284; strategies for, 192–93, 222–25, 228–29, 232–34, 263, 267–68, 283, 284–88
Charismatic movement, 217–18
Christ and culture, 79–80
Christian Sociological Society, The, 307
Church, 20–21, 23, 27–43, 57, 68, 216, 222, 227, 232, 273–75, 280, 281, 287
Church, New Testament, 179, 189, 198–201, 203, 209, 213, 260–62
Church-Type movement, 215–18, 219, 222, 224
City, the, 32, 34, 42, 50, 142, 144, 145, 149, 154, 174, 207, 208, 257

Class, social, 32, 46, 55, 114, 117, 139, 141, 142–43, 145, 146–47, 149–50, 161–62
Clergy, 19, 28, 39, 46, 47, 49, 50, 51–52, 143, 195
Codification of disciplines, 95–96, 109–10
Communication pools, 79–93, 95–96, 125, 134, 171, 172, 174, 178, 188, 203, 208
Confucianism, 214
Consumerism, 239–41, 252
Contextualization, 80, 201–3, 250
Covenant as a norm, 257–60, 263
Crime. *See* Deviance
Culture, 79, 84–90, 123–36, 156–57, 164, 165, 172, 175–77, 179–80, 182, 186–87, 189–90, 193, 195, 199, 201, 203, 204–10, 213–35, 240–41, 298; objective, 36–37, 41; subjective, 37
Culture regulation, 196–98, 198–201, 211n, 228–29, 232–33, 256

Deviance, 118, 147–48, 150, 197, 252, 261

Ecology. *See* Nature
Economics, 9, 18, 29, 52, 55–56, 58, 88–89, 91, 93, 125, 177, 188
Education, 19, 21–23, 40, 51–52, 57, 69–70, 151, 228, 230, 233, 268, 304
Enlightenment, the, xiv, xviii, 16, 41, 42, 167, 296
Ethnicity. *See* Race
Evangelicalism, 97–98
Everyday life-world, 86–90, 96, 106, 118, 181, 183, 189, 305
Evil. *See* Sin
Evolution, social, 123–24, 192–93, 243
Exousia (Powers), 187–89

Facts: defined, 70–71, 76, 78n, 39–40, 56, 64, 70–73, 74–77, 99, 110, 111, 113, 155–57, 158, 160, 162, 163, 168; and sociology, 39, 43, 68–70, 99, 295–96

Family, Christian views of, 258–60, 261, 262
Family, the, 22, 31–32, 35, 49, 50, 57, 66, 91, 128–29, 144, 146, 149, 188, 192, 196, 197, 199–201, 203–4, 212n, 215, 226, 227, 230, 244, 249, 256
Feudalism, xviii, 30, 54, 115, 142
French Revolution, xvii–xix, 142, 159
Fundamentalism, 24, 97–98, 224

Gallup polls, 20, 25n
Gender, 32–33, 35, 46, 50, 126–27, 133, 139–40, 197, 199–201, 247, 251–52, 263, 273
Great Chain of Being, xv–xvii

Hinduism, 214
Human, as image of God, xvi, 5, 84, 91, 164, 167, 245–53, 258
Human, three-zone model of, 248–50
Humanities, 23, 58, 94–96, 117
Human nature, xv–xvi, 63, 111, 119, 125–26, 128, 135–36, 137n, 143–44, 148, 162, 181, 191, 236, 245–52, 297; and biology, 84–86; in the order paradigm, 112, 148; in the conflict paradigm, 114, 115, 143–44; in the pluralist paradigm, 116–17
Hutterites, 224–25, 229, 270

Idolatry, 164, 180–81, 186, 194, 196, 206–8, 238–45, 253, 256, 267, 276–77
Image of God. See Human, as image of God
Individualism, 36–37, 58–60, 105, 146, 154, 217, 236, 256, 277; defined, 58–59
Individualization, 38–39, 55
Industrial revolution, xvii–xix, 27, 54, 132, 178
Inequality. See Stratification
Injustice, 65, 91, 115, 119, 142, 162, 164, 180, 181, 186, 188, 194, 196, 198, 219, 225, 234, 238, 239, 241, 247–48, 252, 253, 256, 262, 267, 276, 278
Intermediate structures, 140, 147–47, 148, 260–63

Invisible complexity, problem of, 36–37
Islam, 208, 214
Israel, ancient, 177, 179–81, 194–98, 204–6, 207, 211n, 212n
Judaism, 181–82, 203

Kingdom of God, xiv, xx, xxi, 91, 183–84, 187, 189, 193, 201, 202, 203, 206, 209–10, 226–29, 231, 237, 247, 264–69, 272, 273, 277, 281, 282–84, 286; defined, 264–67
Knowledge, sociology of, 4, 14, 24, 74, 76, 94–98
Koinonia as a norm, 257, 260–62, 263
Kosmos (World), 184–86, 188–89

Labelling, 14
Language, 4, 37, 38, 81–84, 85, 87–88, 93, 111–12, 125, 136, 172, 177, 182, 194, 196, 204–10, 230, 248–49, 250–51, 297
Liberalism, 97–98
Liberation theology, 264, 266
Lutheran theology of society, 222–23, 226–29, 230, 270–71, 274, 288

Magic, 28
Markets, 30, 57–58, 91, 142, 150, 178, 241, 243, 262
Mennonites, 225, 229
Methodists, 151
Methodology, 53, 64, 69–70, 111, 117, 119, 123, 130, 155–63, 176, 245–46
Middletown, 20, 131
Minority groups, 28, 60, 114, 180
Missionary calling, 195, 201–2
Modern world, the, 138–52; according to Comte, 140–41, 161; Durkheim, 145–48, 161; Marx, 141–44, 161–62; Tocqueville, 139–40, 161; Tönnies, 144–45, 161; Weber, 149–52, 162
Modernity, xv, xix, xx, xxi, 8, 18, 29–30, 43, 49, 52, 57, 90, 97, 98, 99, 104, 110, 118, 121, 149, 154, 161, 167, 172, 173, 218, 242, 252, 261, 291, 305
Modernization, xv, 8, 27–43, 54, 58, 89, 132–33, 155, 241–44, 271, 299; defined, 30

Money, 139, 145, 188, 241, 276–77
Moral ideals, 16, 38, 39, 88, 90, 91, 99, 145, 147, 162, 186, 243, 256, 280
Mysticism, 216–18

Nationalism, 118, 204–6, 231–32, 263
Natural law, 220
Natural sciences. *See* Physical sciences
Nature, 239–41, 242, 250, 252, 257
Neighborliness as a norm, 257, 262–63
New Age religion, 218

Occam's Razor, 165–67
Oppression. *See* Injustice

Paradigms, 6, 73, 93, 95–96, 105–10, 119–21, 127, 129, 131, 133–34, 135, 166, 171, 172, 234–35, 299; defined, 106–7
Paradigms, theological, 173, 175, 189–90, 211, 213, 221–35, 237, 270, 299
Paradigms, sociological, 110–11, 235, 299, 304; order paradigm, 111–13; conflict paradigm, 113–15, 214; pluralist paradigm, 115–18
Philosophy, xv, xx, 3, 36, 53–54, 62, 63–64, 73–74, 80, 110
Physical sciences, xiii, xv, xviii, xix, 7, 8, 17–18, 20, 23–24, 53–54, 58, 60, 64, 66, 67–68, 71, 74–76, 94–96, 107, 108, 117, 165–66
Plausibility structures, 81, 91–92, 94–97, 99, 109, 202; defined, 91
Pluralism, xix, 42, 68–69, 72, 77, 91, 98, 146, 179, 181–82, 198, 204
Pluralization, 30–34, 41, 49, 68–69, 97, 209–10; defined, 31
Political science, 9, 29, 52, 55–56, 58, 91
Positivism, 16–17, 71–72, 77, 91, 140–41
Postindustrialism, 242
Postpositivism, 72
Poverty. *See* Stratification
Presentation of self, 34–35
Presuppositions, 72, 89
Primary groups, 256, 260–62
Private-public split, 34–40, 69, 72

Privatization, 34–41, 43, 98, 99; defined, 35
Professions, 45–48, 55, 91, 92–93, 294; psychology as, 48–52; sociology as, 52–61, 68, 90–92, 98, 99
Progress, xvi, xix, xx, 17, 42, 54, 105, 155, 161, 241–45, 263
Protestant Ethic, 150–51, 217, 271
Psychology, 9, 23n, 39, 48–52, 56, 93, 125, 126, 165–66, 171–72, 248
Public arena, the. *See* Private-public split
Public opinion, 139–40, 186
Puritans, 216, 228, 271–72
Purpose, 17–18, 63–65, 78n, 80

Race, 32–33, 35, 60, 68, 124, 125, 131, 133, 136, 139–40, 149, 180, 194, 195, 198, 203, 204–10, 247, 263
Racism, 14, 60–61, 114–15, 123–24, 127, 129, 134, 143, 159, 253, 261
Rationality traditions, 73, 77, 103, 171, 175, 192, 220
Rationalization, 148–51, 154, 162, 305–6
Reductionism, 165–67, 296–97
Reflexivity, 13–15, 25n
Reform, social, 21, 56–57, 60
Reformation, Protestant, 33, 150–51, 265
Reformed theology of society, 223–24, 225, 270–84, 285, 288
Relativism, xix, 25, 99, 297
Religion, sociology of, 94
Religion, 28, 31–34, 88, 91, 94–97, 140, 174–75, 196, 214–15; according to Comte, 141; Durkheim, 147; Marx, 143–44; Tocqueville, 140; Tönnies, 145; Weber, 150–52
Religious orders, 40, 216, 227
Research, 20, 56, 64, 74–76, 118, 125, 129, 130–35, 155–63
Roles, 35, 49, 113, 116, 156, 199–201, 203, 223, 225, 232, 233, 258
Roman Catholic, 21, 215–16, 220, 227, 243, 303
Roman Empire, 177, 181–82, 199–201, 203

Science vs. faith, 15, 18–24, 44n, 58, 67–68, 77, 79–80, 94–98
Science, sociology of, 74–76, 95–97

Science, philosophy of, 3, 16–18, 63–64, 73–74, 76
Scientism, 91, 110
Secondary groups, 260–62
Sect-Type movement, 151, 216–18, 219, 222
Secularism. *See* Secularization
Secularization, xiv, 18–21, 40–43, 98, 137n, 141, 143, 145, 151, 162, 192, 226, 283; defined, 18–19
Sexism, 14–15, 114, 115, 143, 253
Shalom as a norm, 257, 263, 268
Sin, 5, 164, 168, 181, 185–86, 187, 191, 209, 216, 219, 221–22, 228, 232–33, 239, 252
Slavery, 159, 196–98, 200, 202, 211n, 248, 268
Social construction, 74–75, 103, 117–18
Social gospel, 223, 266, 268
Social issues vs. individual troubles, 59–60
Social mobility, 34, 38, 50, 128, 139
Social work, 56
Socialization, 47, 59, 83–84, 92–93, 116, 122–36, 241, 246; in professions, 47–48, 51–52, 69–70
Society, traditional, xxi, 28, 31–34, 42, 56, 90, 177–78, 192, 197
Society: evaluation of, 160–63, 167–68, 192–94, 210, 221–25, 237–53, 255, 256, 263, 266–67, 268; explanation of, 157–58, 162, 163, 165–67, 255
Society, the Good, 162, 176, 191, 193, 252
Sociobiology, 136
Sociolinguistics, 208
Sociological realism, 59
Sociologists, Christian backgrounds, 21–22, 122–23, 303–7
Sociology: Christian, xiv, 2, 5, 9, 122–23, 229, 233–34, 288, 290–307; history of, xiii, 2, 15–18, 21–23, 52–60, 303–4; interpretive, 17, 117, 134–35, 155–63; and modernity, xxi, 8, 54, 55, 90–91, 98; as a moral code, 91; as fact-based objective culture, 39, 43; secularized version, xiv, 15–24, 42, 69–70, 77, 97, 98, 149, 167

State, the, xix, 33, 35, 50, 54, 56–58, 89, 91, 120, 133, 140, 142, 144–45, 146, 187, 188, 201, 223–24, 226, 231–32, 233, 234, 271, 274–76, 277, 281–84
State of Nature, 191–92
Status, 14, 46, 47, 114, 139, 149
Status groups, 149–50, 201
Stoicheion (Principles), 186–87, 189
Stratification, social, xvi, 112–13, 114, 119, 139–40, 142–43, 147, 154–55, 161, 253, 272, 273, 274, 277, 285
Symbolic universe, 77, 81, 88–93, 98, 99, 109, 118, 121, 167, 175, 181, 188, 199, 202, 207, 291; defined, 89

Theology, 8, 18, 20, 22, 28–29, 41–42, 51, 80, 92, 164, 167, 168, 235, 295–96, 298
Theories, 73, 88–89, 90–92, 95–96, 97, 111, 118, 158, 162, 163, 174, 179; defined, 158
Three-Zone model of Human. *See* Human, Three-Zone model
Tower of Babel, 206–9
Two-Kingdom doctrine. *See* Lutheran theology of society

Underclass, 50, 141–43, 197, 228, 241, 242, 262, 263, 272, 275–77, 280, 285
University of Chicago, 21, 303–4

Value freedom ideal, 64, 90, 160–62, 163
Values and religion, 39, 43
Values, 39–40, 56, 64, 68–70, 71, 74, 76, 85, 90, 96, 99, 105, 112, 113, 114, 116, 117, 119, 132, 148, 151, 220, 244, 295–96; of science, 72
Verstehen. See Sociology, interpretive
Voluntary associations, 57, 91
Work, 21–22, 34–35, 46, 49, 52, 59, 143–44, 145, 149, 243–44, 278–79, 303
World System, 55, 243, 263, 292
Worldview, 28, 67, 76–77, 88, 89, 99, 105, 112, 114, 141, 163, 171, 175, 250; defined, 100n; secular, 16, 40, 67–68, 99; traditional, xvi